Entrepreneurship and Business Start-Ups in Ireland

Volume 2: Cases

Thomas N. Garavan
Barra Ó Cinnéide
Mary Garavan
Briga Hynes
Fergus Walsh
with
Anne Ledwith
Ambrose Downey
Carole Hogan
Fergal O'Brien
Anne Morgan
Anna Cunningham

Oak Tree Press
Dublin

Oak Tree Press
Merrion Building
Lower Merrion Street
Dublin 2, Ireland

© 1997 Individual contributors

A catalogue record of this book is
available from the British Library.

ISBN 1-86076-049-X

Printed in Ireland by Colour Books Ltd.

Contents

About the Contributors vii
Preface xi

PART 1
SMALL BUSINESS START-UPS

Overview 1

1. **Ballyneety Business Ventures** 4
   Barra Ó Cinnéide

2. **Monaghan Mushrooms** 22
   Barra Ó Cinnéide

3. **The Independent Radio Sector in Ireland** 46
   Thomas N. Garavan and Carole Hogan

4. **Riverdance** 55
   Barra Ó Cinnéide

5. **Irish Breeze** 73
   Barra Ó Cinnéide and Ambrose Downey

6. **Kingspan Group plc** 82
   Thomas N. Garavan, Fergus Walsh and Mary Garavan

7. **The Irish National Lottery** 95
   Thomas N. Garavan and Anna Cunningham

8. **The LEADER Programme and Rural Enterprise
   Development** 105
   Thomas N. Garavan and Mary Garavan

PART 2
IRISH ENTREPRENEURS

Overview 114

9. **Ballygowan Spring Water** 116
   Barra Ó Cinnéide

10. **Noel C. Duggan — The Best is Yet to Come?** 131
    Barra Ó Cinnéide

11. **Woodlands House Hotel**..145
Anna Cunningham

12. **Supermac's**...151
Thomas N. Garavan and Mary Garavan

PART 3
**ENTREPRENEURSHIP AND FIRM GROWTH:
MANAGEMENT ISSUES**

Overview...157

13. **Four Entrepreneurial Start-Ups**....................................159
Briga Hynes

14. **The Small Business Exporting Decision: Seven Case
Situations** 176
Briga Hynes and Thomas N. Garavan

15. **Irish High-Technology Companies: New Product
Development**..187
Anne Ledwith

16. **Finance & the Small Business: Three Case
Studies**...206
Briga Hynes and Thomas N. Garavan

PART 4
SMALL BUSINESS MATURITY AND DECLINE

Overview...215

17. **Blarney Woollen Mills**...217
Barra Ó Cinnéide, Thomas N. Garavan and Fergus Walsh

18. **The Irish Credit Union Movement** 226
Thomas N. Garavan and Mary Garavan

19. **Foxford Woollen Mills**...236
Barra Ó Cinnéide and Fergus Walsh

20. **Leadmore Ice Cream**..244
Thomas N. Garavan and Mary Garavan

Bibliography...251

About the Contributors

THOMAS N. GARAVAN is a lecturer in human resource development at the University of Limerick. He is also editor of the Journal of European Industrial Training, an international human resource development journal published by MCB University Press in the UK. His research interests include the analysis of how companies structure and deliver training functions, continuing professional development and the effectiveness of company graduate training and development programmes. He is a Fellow of the Irish Institute of Training and Development, a member of the American Society of Training and Development and co-author of *Training and Development in Ireland: Context, Policy and Practice* and *Cases in Irish Business Strategy & Policy,* a leading training and development textbook, published by Oak Tree Press.

BARRA Ó CINNÉIDE is Professor of Entrepreneurship and Course Leader of the Agribusiness Programme at the University of Limerick. His research interests include analysis of Irish sectoral development, including the effects on agriculture and tourism following Ireland's membership of the EC, and emergent indigenous enterprises — the subject of over 80 case studies since 1979.

MARY GARAVAN lectures in human resource management at HSI College in Limerick. Her research interests include the analysis of trainer competencies, the roles of training and development specialists and health and safety law and practice.

BRIGA HYNES is a Lecturer in Entrepreneurship in the Department of Management and Marketing at the University of Limerick. In this role, Briga is responsible for the design, delivery and evaluation of entrepreneurship modules to undergraduate, graduate and postgraduate students. Before joining the Department, she was Manager of the Marketing Centre for Small Business at the University. Her main research interests and published works concentrate on entrepreneurship education, management practices and decision-making in the small firm, the role of training and development in the small firm and its impact on employment and growth of the firm.

FERGUS WALSH is a Researcher at the Centre for Employment Studies, University of Limerick. He also lectures on personnel management and has carried out a range of consultancy projects for the Marketing Centre for Small Business at the University of Limerick. His research interests are primarily associated with organisational change and innovation.

AMBROSE DOWNEY lectures in human resource management at the Mid-West Business Institute, Limerick. His research interests include organisational culture and the relationship between total quality management and the labour process debate.

CAROLE HOGAN is a training and development consultant who has carried out research and consultancy assignments with a range of small, medium and large companies. She is a graduate of the Training and Development programme at the University of Sheffield, and specialises in interpersonal skills training, management development and organisational reviews.

FERGAL O'BRIEN is an MBS research student at the Graduate Centre of Business at the University of Limerick. He teaches on Accounting and Finance undergraduate courses within and outside the university. His current research interests lie in the area of option pricing, with particular reference to estimating and modelling the variance parameter in option pricing formulas.

ANNE MORGAN is a Business Studies graduate from the University of Limerick. She specialised in marketing with a minor in human resource management. Her research interests include organisation culture, marketing and the small firm and customer service.

ANNA CUNNINGHAM lectures in strategic management and marketing at the Shannon College of Hotel Management. She also lectures in tourism marketing at the University of Limerick. Her research interests include hospitality marketing, services marketing and management development in the hospitality industry.

ANNE LEDWITH lectures in Entrepreneurship at the University of Limerick. She has a primary degree in Electronic Engineering and has worked for over twelve years as a Product Development Engineer and as a Manager of Product Development in small high-technology firms. She has recently completed an MBA. Her research interests include R&D management, new product development, management of technology, innovation management and the management of small firms.

Preface

The case method is now well established in the teaching of entrepreneurship and business studies. The aim of this volume is to provide suitable material which explores issues relating to entrepreneurship and small business start-ups and is intended to support Volume 1 which deals with concepts and issues relating to entrepreneurship and small business formation.

The process of entrepreneurship and small business start-ups and the set of decisions which these areas entail is a theme reflected throughout the cases presented in this volume. The body of knowledge offered by entrepreneurship can be explained in the analysis of the cases. Few of the cases deal with a single issue and individual cases follow a common structure commencing with background information to set the context for what happened. This is followed by facts relevant to the decisions made, the behaviour of particular individuals and the outcomes to date.

The main objective behind the cases is the application of theoretical knowledge to practical situations. They are designed to enable students to demonstrate analytical ability, logical thinking, judgement, creative skills and the ability to apply concepts and models. They can also act as a vehicle to reinforce basic concepts and skills and can be used for individual or group assessments. The Harvard Business School approach to case analysis advocates the use of open discussion amongst group members. However, it may also be possible to give consideration to formal presentations and role plays by students. It should be recognised that students often find difficulty in defining problems and dealing with ambiguous problems, particularly where there is no right answer. However, the true benefit of cases is to provide students with a vehicle for developing skills which are essential to entrepreneurs and eventual managers of ventures, and it allows experimentation in the learning process.

The authors wish to thank all those organisations who provided information and granted interviews. The authors, however, accept responsibility for any errors of fact which appear in the book and will seek to correct them in later editions.

A large number of people provided support and direct assistance during the production of this book. Specifically, the authors would like to thank the following at the University of Limerick for their encouragement: Professor Noel Whelan, Dean, College of Business; Joseph Wallace, Head, Department of Personnel and Employment Relations; Jim Dalton, Head, Department of Management and Marketing; Professor Donal Dineen, Associate Dean, College of Business; and Professor Paddy Gunnigle. We would also like to thank Mr Philip Smyth, Director, Shannon College of Hotel Management; and Michael McNamara, Director, HSI College Limerick.

Other individuals who provided support include Dr. David McKevitt, Michael Morley, Noreen Heraty, Sarah Moore, Patricia Fleming, Gerard Fitzgerald, Colette Noonan, Helena Lenihan, Paul Sweeney, Sarah McCurtin, Catherine Horgan, Rita Garavan, Anne Morgan, Ricky Cullen, Juliet McMahon, Fergal O'Brien, Bernard Delaney, Fergus Walsh, Joseph McDonnell, Derry McMahon, Margaret Kinsella and Stephanie Coughlan of the Irish League of Credit Unions, and others too numerous to mention.

It is customary to give thanks to the person who helped type the manuscript, but rarely can so much be owed to one person. Our heartfelt thanks go to Kim O'Neill, University of Limerick, whose skill helped to create graphics and keep track of the numerous changes made to the cases as the material took shape. We would have been lost without her.

To our families, our thanks for being so understanding about and supportive of this project that took away much of our time with them.

Finally, it should be pointed out that the views expressed in this book belong solely to the authors of each chapter and in no way reflect those of the other contributors.

PART 1

SMALL BUSINESS START-UPS

Overview

The last ten years have witnessed a notable increase in interest in the small firm sector of the Irish economy. The Task Force on Small Business Report (1994) asserts that Ireland is a nation of small business. Some 98 per cent of Ireland's estimated 160,000 non-farm businesses are small within its definition (under 50 employees and under £3 million in turnover):

> Indeed, Ireland is a nation of micro business, because more than 90 per cent of enterprises employ fewer than 10 people. In total, small business accounts for around half of all employment in the private sector (p. 2).

The Task Force's estimate is that almost half of indigenous companies employ between 1 and 5 people. Over 70 per cent of enterprises with employees have fewer than 4 employees. Around 85 per cent have fewer than 10 employees and approximately 97 per cent have fewer than 50 employees.

Employers with 50 or more employees consequently account for approximately 3 per cent of the total number of enterprises, but employ about 40 per cent of the total number of employees. If enterprises which only employ the owner are included, enterprises with fewer than 10 persons rises to over 90 per cent of the total, and if we include those with under 50 employees it increases to around 98 per cent of the total. Enterprises with fewer than 10 persons employed account for roughly 30 per cent of the total private sector labour force.

Small firms are not "scaled down" versions of large firms. Wynarczyk et al. (1993) argue that small firms differ from large firms in three important respects which they identify as uncertainty, innovation and evolution. Factors which lead to uncertainty include their small share of the market place and the fact that they must be price takers, unless they operate in a special niche market where they offer a differentiated product or service.

[1]

There is a much greater diversity of aims and objectives between the owners of small firms and those of big firms, therefore greater internal uncertainty. An owner/manager may just wish for a comfortable living from the business whereas another may wish to grow it to its full potential. While the "internal conflict" which management control can generate is absent in the large firm, in the small firm the attitude of the owner/manager is crucial and so must contribute in the broader sense to uncertainty.

> The central distinction between large and small firms, then, is the greater external uncertainty of the environment with the greater internal consistency of its motivations and actions (Storey, 1994:11).

When considering the reasons for business failure, Kuratko and Hodgetts (1992) argue that the basic causes of small business failure are managerial incompetence or inexperience, neglect, weak control systems and under-capitalisation. In terms of managerial problems they list hiring and promotions on the basis of nepotism, rather than qualifications, as one of the major reasons for business failure. In terms of human resource problems, they list inflated owner ego, employee relations concerns and control factors as being instrumental in new venture failure. They also mention "unclear business definition" as being a cause of failure, i.e. "uncertainty about the 'exact' business they were in caused some firms to undergo constant change and to lack stabilisation".

Many owners tend to be whimsical or inconsistent in their behaviour, because after all, they are not as accountable to higher authority as are paid managers. Atkinson and Meager (1994) point out that when a firm has grown to between 10 and 20 employees non-owner managers are appointed. It is at this point that the greater consistency occurs in the management of small firms.

Small firms are more likely to introduce fundamentally new innovations than larger firms. Many small firms are set up because their founder has discovered a new way to produce some product or deliver a service. The general research suggests that small firms are more likely to be innovative because they are less committed to existing products within their industry.

In referring to the evolution and the growth ambitions and growth potential of small firms (Cross, 1983:109) refers to the fallacy that all firms want to grow into medium or large firms as "patently absurd". Many owners prefer to maintain a "lifestyle"-type business and prefer to stay small.

> Most small businesses are born to die or stagnate. In Britain almost one third of all new businesses cease trading within the first

three years of their life; of those that go beyond this stage most will never grow to any size but will plateau out to provide the owner/manager with an acceptable living (Burns and Dewhurst, 1991:4).

The cases presented in Part 1 deal with new business start-ups in a range of business sectors. In almost all of the cases the first stage involved the identification of a new business concept on which to establish a firm. This "new" business concept may not be entirely new but instead was a modification of existing products available in the market. Few of the new businesses started out with a completely original concept. They predominantly used existing ideas or modifications and relied on superior execution and energy to get them going. Riverdance is perhaps the exception in this respect. This case demonstrates the role of creativity needed to arrive at a new product concept and the need for the founders to be totally absorbed and committed to its execution.

A number of cases, particularly Monaghan Mushrooms and Ballyneety Business Ventures, demonstrate effectively the start-up stage of the business. While creativity may be a critical success factor at the idea stage in order for the firm to develop, the founder(s) must provide leadership and tackle head-on important management issues. This is particularly difficult for founders who enjoy the initial creative phase with its informality and lack of structure. The cases presented here demonstrate that in order to get the business up and running, two important considerations are the identification of the venture's competitive advantage and the location of sources of finance. A potential stress factor is the possibility of the venture being undercapitalised. Many of the ventures had to ensure careful financial planning because, as Dodge and Poblins (1992) illustrate, financial issues are most common at the start-up stage.

Cases in later sections of the book illustrate some of the problems associated with existence/survival and growth of the venture.

1

Ballyneety Business Ventures

Barra Ó Cinnéide

Introduction

Over nearly two decades, Liam Ryan and his business colleagues have established and developed a series of business initiatives that currently employ over 60 people, with the potential for significant additional job creation if current plans come to fruition. Although originally established with the domestic Irish market in mind, the Limerick-based enterprises incorporated in the Ryan group have concentrated in recent years on export growth. This has been achieved through a phased approach to corporate development, which includes upgrading of workforce skills and management expertise.

The company developed from humble beginnings in the small rural Irish village of Ballyneety, near Limerick, Ireland's third largest city. Originally it operated as a trading company but, through acquisitions and new enterprise developments, it has become a "mini-conglomerate" (for which this case-writer has coined the name, "Ballyneety Business Ventures") with interests ranging from manufacturing, through tourism and leisure activities, to retail sales.

From its initial objective of fulfilling local industrial needs related to Limerick city and its hinterland, the current organisation, although modest in size by international standards, is attempting to become a world-leader in its field with a new technology product, an electronic torque wrench, and, in its efforts to do so, it has been establishing strategic international alliances.

BBV's Evolution

Liam Ryan left school in 1966 and completed a training programme offered by AnCo (the Industrial Training Authority), now FÁS, which qualified him as a machinist/lathe operator. He was employed by a large engineering supply company, first as a store-man and then as a sales representative. Although he never practised his trade as a machinist, the technical background has been of constant benefit to him,

[4]

as it helped him to understand the technical details of the products he was selling and removed the "fear of production". He still happily takes things apart to see how they work and how they could be manufactured. After four years, he became distribution manager of engineering products with his original employer. By the time he left to set up his own company with the help of his wife Norah, Liam Ryan had completed various management courses in accounting, general management, purchasing and marketing.

Norah Ryan was to play an important role in setting up and assisting in the management of the new company. Her work experience included employment in the accounts department of a large industrial firm and, by the time of their marriage, she had experience in work study, personnel management and wages.

Liam's industrial background, coupled with the experience gained from attendance on training programmes concerned with engineering, electronics and automation, provided him with an important basis from which to develop his career. As part of his managerial functions, he had continuous direct and indirect contact with a broad customer base. From this exposure, Liam identified a number of potentially viable market opportunities — in particular, service elements which offered attractive business options. At this stage, he was becoming dissatisfied with his work situation and aspects of the corporate culture of his employer's firm. The inflexible policies and procedures that he experienced became a "push factor" in the process of establishing his own business. His opportunistic and positive attitudes facilitated the ultimate decision to start up on his own.

In 1973, Euro Equipment Ltd. was set up by Liam and Norah. The company was founded with capital of less than £1,000 and was located in the founders' private house in Caherconlish, a small village in Co. Limerick. The primary aim of the firm was to provide a range of general engineering products, such as precision tools, hand tools, balancing spools, bearing and small electrical equipment tools. Despite competing in the same market as his previous employer, Ryan managed to leave on good terms. By building up good relations with customers and suppliers, the business prospered and grew steadily.

In response to identified industrial market demand, Liam developed a broad range of products to suit the requirements of a diverse customer-base. Euro Equipment did not get involved in manufacturing products, but became expert in trading operations. As the business expanded, it became apparent that the firm was suffering from an inconvenient location, and so it was decided to move to an alternative centre — Ballyneety, a village less than 10 kilometres from Limerick city. The company at this stage was employing four people on a full-time basis. Euro Equipment progressed well and provided Liam Ryan with a base for further enterprise development.

As a result of visiting a major industrial exhibition in Frankfurt, Liam Ryan saw opportunities for expansion of his operations, and established a new venture in 1977. Originally named Gen Weld Services, but now abbreviated to GWS, this firm employs 15 people, with an annual turnover of £3 million in 1995. It is involved in the manufacture and sale of safety items — the products sold include protective gloves and clothing and safety equipment.

GWS was developed on a partnership basis. In 1979, it was set up with 70 per cent owned by Liam Ryan and the remaining 30 per cent owned by Bert Gleeson, who was appointed GWS managing director, with total responsibility for development. This provided an opportunity for establishing a good "team management" culture, and, perhaps more importantly, it allowed Liam Ryan the time to develop other unrelated business interests. This company sells on the domestic Irish market only. GWS sales progressed along with those of Euro Equipment, since they were selling compatible product ranges to the same, or similar, customers.

In keeping with his opportunistic outlook, Liam Ryan saw a market niche in Limerick city, the capital of the Shannon region, and he decided to open a retail unit there. Euro Tools was established in 1980, with the acquisition of a suitable premises, comprising 115 square metres. Initially, the product was similar to that sold at Ballyneety. However, Ryan quickly began to respond to market demand for a broad range of sometimes unrelated product lines. The retail outlet now (1995) employs four people, including the manager who is given authority and responsibility to manage the organisation. At the initial stages, Liam Ryan maintained close control over the management of the business, as is typical with most entrepreneurs. However, as other aspects of Liam Ryan's business interests became time-consuming, he realised the importance of delegation. The manager of the retail outlet now has full responsibility for the day-to-day management and meets once a week with Ryan to discuss the week's activities.

The primary thrust or mission associated with the outlet is to be market-driven, alert to customer requirements and providing products and services to meet these demands. This is effectively undertaken by organising the products around a "seasonal chart". This chart highlights the various products and services in the hardware area required in the various seasons, and it is management's responsibility to ensure that these products are available when required by the customer. Euro Tools has also introduced a "maximum discount card" for all customers of the Liam Ryan group of enterprises. This incentive has proven very positive. The "maximum discount card" implies that cardholders are allowed to purchase products at wholesale prices. Subsequently, this maximum discount policy was extended to those who are employed in the group.

Background to BMS Ireland

BMS Ireland (originally Ballyneety Manufacturing Services Ltd.) is the manufacturing arm of Liam Ryan's group of companies. The group has achieved significant growth and diversity since its formation in 1973 with equity capital of £650. Originally, BMS concentrated on serving the engineering sector with equipment, tools and supplies. The growth in sales has mainly been a result of manufacturing operations rather than trading operations.

This increase in manufacturing output was accomplished by a production strategy not often employed by Irish manufacturers, but one that could be particularly suited to Irish conditions — that of entering into licensing agreements with foreign companies to produce goods in Ireland. The main advantages claimed for licensed manufacturing include:

- Its relatively low price in terms of transferring technology

- The build-up of native production skills

- Enhanced prospects for export and import substitution products.

Trigger for Licence Search

Liam Ryan says that he always had an urge to invent or manufacture something, but a combination of circumstances was needed to give him the final push into manufacturing. As sales of equipment continued to grow, he saw that there were savings to be made by carrying out semi-assembly operations. For instance, the company sold bandsaw blades in a number of different lengths. They were cheaper to buy and stock if the blade material was purchased in 100-metre quantities, cut to size and welded seamlessly in the warehouse premises. As sales increased, strong pressure grew to provide further products and services. The need to reduce the cost of an ever-expanding range of items by semi-assembly, and to provide an adequate service base for the firm's existing and future customers, made the acquisition of more factory space imperative.

Liam Ryan approached his bank for funding. The manager was "cautious" about such a venture, and the loan was refused. Lack of bank support was to be a continuing problem for the developing enterprise. Because of the difficulty in obtaining finance by other means, he approached Shannon Development, the State agency for development of the Mid-West region of Ireland, for grant aid or loan guarantees. The initial answer was negative. Shannon Development did not grant aid service industries, but if Ryan were to manufacture, it could probably help him.

Thus Liam Ryan went into the warehouse and started looking for something in his product range that he could manufacture. On examining the products and agencies in their tools/equipment trading operations, it was possible to spot niche markets in Ireland and abroad for a certain size range of compressors and generators. BMS was able to benefit from technology transfer through two licensing agreements — first with an Italian supplier of compressors, and later with an American generator manufacturer.

The First Licensing Venture: SIP

SIP was an Italian company, well established in the European market as a supplier of compressors, with which Liam Ryan had had contacts over the years. SIP personnel had visited Ireland on several occasions, and Ryan's firm was one of the regular customers. Ryan's orders were filled from Leicester in England, which was SIP's first overseas base. Ryan decided that if, through SIP, he could gain access to suppliers of certain vital components, the manufacture of compression in Ballyneety would be technically feasible. Confident that he could actually produce the equipment, Ryan began to negotiate simultaneously with SIP for a licensing agreement to produce its compressors, and with Shannon Development for grant aid. He recounts the events and his philosophy:

> The negotiations were concurrent — I knew what Shannon Development wanted and I knew what I wanted, and I had a good idea of what SIP wanted, so I went ahead.

In 1980, Liam Ryan successfully negotiated a licensing agreement with SIP. BMS contracted to manufacture compressors, to SIP's specifications, for sale in Ireland through the latter's agent. In addition, the company was to act as a back-up supplier for SIP on the UK market. Furthermore, BMS manufactured and marketed its "own brand" compressors, being careful to avoid conflicts with SIP's sales territories and the Italian firm's marketing efforts.

Liam Ryan was pleased with the agreement:

> It worked out well for us this way. If we had geared up to produce for the UK market we'd have had to effect redundancies as the falling world demand was reflected in sales there . . . whereas we know our Irish market well and we were able to achieve good growth during this period.

BMS did well out of the arrangement — a major advantage was the ability to start up a manufacturing facility with the security of an assured market. The company was able to avoid the research and development (R&D) and marketing costs normally associated with bringing out a new product, it gained enough production experience with the generic product/market to be independent of SIP should a disagreement arise, and it also obtained a foothold in export markets. A key clause in the agreement obliged SIP to provide the key components for a fixed percentage of its own catalogue price, which meant that BMS margins could not be squeezed by price increases.

Shannon Development played an important role in bringing the venture to life — and not just through technical advice and grant aiding. The technical help given was largely in the area of standards specification and guarantees. Shannon Development also advised on the negotiations and checked the final sub-contracting document. The grant aid was significant — 40 per cent of building and equipment costs and, in addition, valuable training grants from FÁS. Ryan now feels that the help that Shannon Development gave in forcing him to adopt systematic accounting and management procedures was even more useful for long-term growth than was the grant aid itself.

Onward to Fresh Fields: Search for New Ventures

Obliged by the terms of the Shannon agreement to maintain much more detailed management accounts, Ryan was made aware of the importance of cash flow and of obtaining maximum usage of the factory premises and workforce.

The first compressors were produced in May 1980, about six months after negotiations with SIP had begun, and by early 1981 the venture was successful enough for Ryan to begin seriously considering further licensing agreements in order to increase the manufactured product range.

The search for another licensing partner was carried out more systematically. Ryan had a close relationship with Shannon Development and also with the Innovation Centre located at the National Technological Park, Limerick, incorporating the University of Limerick campus and, in an attempt to develop his business further, he turned to both these agencies for help.

In 1982, Ryan initiated a licensing agreement with a US firm, Agtronic Inc. based in Nebraska, specialising in generators. With two weeks' notice, Ryan, helped by the Innovation Centre, was able to undertake some preliminary market research and to contact several of Agtronic's customers.

> We knew quite a lot more about them by the time we met. A small company was ideally suited to their needs, so there was a lot in common from the beginning.

All that was left was for Ryan to see the American operation. The Agtronic management team was holding a sales seminar a month or so later, and it was decided that Ryan's visit could be made much more effective if it were scheduled to enable him to attend this. In late May 1982, Ryan went to Nebraska with his production manager, who would spend his time with the Agtronic production people.

> We left Ireland on Saturday, and I attended the sales seminar on Monday just as if I were one of their staff. It was very well-organised and covered a great deal, from the technical side, right through to the marketing programme — the whole lot. On Wednesday evening, we sat down with the president and the marketing vice-president, and we concluded the deal. The first shipment of components was ordered and was ready for dispatch before we left on Friday.

By June 1982, the generators were in production at the Ballyneety plant. There was no single detailed licensing agreement document. On the one hand, there was a verbal agreement between the president of Agtronic and Liam Ryan; on the other hand, a series of confirmatory and explanatory letters had been exchanged regarding the details of what each party would do. Ryan confirms how the relationship developed:

> We took each other at face value, having had some exchange of trade and banking references. No lawyers were involved, but Shannon Development checked out the legal aspects for us. Agtronic had experience in negotiating licensing arrangements and they knew that written contracts were very expensive and hard to enforce internationally. Therefore, they go for an assessment of the people concerned and what is said about them.

Marketing Arrangements with Agtronic

Agtronic was already supplying customers in Europe, but liked to ship only full container loads — part loads were very expensive. The recession meant that the company had smaller order quantities and was beginning to need some sort of manufacturing facility in Europe. Agtronic's customers were mainly in the UK, France, Germany and Belgium, with no sales in Ireland. The US firm was not interested in the Irish market, which was subsequently developed under the BMS brand name. Agtronic's main concern was to ensure that its mainland European customers were adequately and efficiently serviced.

The agreement guaranteed that Agtronic would pass on successive stages of production. This was achieved according to schedule. As BMS gradually built up production output, and Agtronic was satisfied with the quality of the Irish output for servicing, the US firm handed over its customer process to BMS, and sales grew steadily. Credit terms — 120 days — were more generous than the industry norm. The deal allowed BMS to go into competition with Agtronic, which had concluded a similar arrangement with another American company selling a "green generator" — Agtronic components assembled and painted green. This arrangement ensured a larger share of the specialist components market for Agtronic, either directly or indirectly. However, BMS had not really begun to sell to other European customers, though the company fortuitously picked up one or two customers not previously handled by Agtronic.

The marketing effort as far as BMS was concerned was still very much concentrated in Ireland. The main customers were equipment hire firms and contract builders, but a vigorous attempt was made to penetrate and develop the market for stand-by electrical generators. BMS explored with Agtronic the possibility of producing gas-powered generators that might be more suitable to European needs, and which could overcome some of the fuel-storage dangers inherent in using petrol and diesel as fuel.

The contribution of BMS to the Ryan group of companies, which were previously confined to the trading area, is evidenced in the sales data. Manufacturing turnover accounted for:

- 1.5 per cent of turnover in 1980

- 6.0 per cent of turnover in 1981

- 13.4 per cent of turnover in 1982

- 31.9 per cent of turnover in 1983.

This was against a compounded growth of over 12 per cent in non-manufacturing sales for the group in the same period. Over this "learning curve" and growth phase, everybody was happy with the situation. The licensers permitted BMS to sell own-brand replicas of its own products, so BMS was able to pick up business in its own name, as well as producing for the branded suppliers. Most importantly, the Ryan group's sales (and profits) showed a healthy upward surge.

However, despite good products, a firm grip on the production technology, and a market that was receptive, 1984 issued in a period of "Orwellian gloom" for BMS. There began a worldwide recession which badly affected the building and machine trades that were the main users of compressors and generators. Industry retrenched, in line with its customers. By the end of 1986, manufacturing profits were down to 3 per cent, sales growth had stopped and reversed, and prospects for these two product lines had effectively declined beyond the point of no return.

Chronology of Development at BMS, 1986–90

In 1985, Moore and Wright, a UK manufacturer of measuring instruments, introduced a new electronic micrometer capable of measurements within the range 0–25mm. Liam Ryan, through Euro Equipment, became the first person to offer the product for sale in Ireland. In spite of its relatively high retail price (£400), several prestigious Irish-based manufacturing operations, like those of De Beers and General Electric, purchased the product. This led Liam Ryan to consider the particular benefits that the Moore and Wright innovation offered, including those of reading and manipulation of the new instrument compared with conventional products.

This experience provoked Liam Ryan to scan through the entire range of products offered by Euro Equipment to consider items in which it might be possible to replace mechanical components with digital readouts. As a result of iterative screenings, the following product categories were considered for detailed analysis: measuring tapes, measuring levels, temperature gauges, pressure gauges and torque wrenches.

A ranked list of options was devised, leading to the decision to initiate more detailed analysis on an electronic torque wrench. Although this was the product selected for priority commitment of resources, the other potential ideas were not discarded, with items such as levels and bathroom scales being put on hold, but kept under constant review.

In October 1986, the company initiated a feasibility study on a range of electronic torque tools, and throughout 1987, a large-scale R&D programme was undertaken on a range of such tools, complete with data-logging facilities. BMS discontinued manufacture of compressors and generators because of the economic recession and the introduction in the marketplace of a range of Taiwanese and Spanish products that were directly competitive.

Superabrasives

Late in 1987, Ryan learned that a small Irish enterprise, Scorpio Diamond Tools, based at Thomondgate, Limerick city, had gone into liquidation. Scorpio manufactured a range of superabrasive products, resin bond, diamond and CBN wheels, dressers, PCD and PCB tooling. It took Liam two days to assess the company, and the following week, in mid-December 1987, he bought it. All six members of the Scorpio staff and one of the partners, who became production manager, joined the company, and the product range was reintroduced under the BMS label.

Superabrasives are a relatively new range of products now being used in many industries to machine a wide variety of products, such as ferrous and non-ferrous metals, plastics, ceramics, glass, crystal, stone, concrete, marble and wood. The market growth for these products is increasing rapidly with the trend towards the use of more exotic materials by modern industry.

Conveniently, BMS is located close to De Beers Industrial Diamonds, Shannon, which acts as supplier of raw materials for superabrasive products. A second source of supply, General Electric Superabrasives, is located in Dublin. These two companies are the largest manufacturers worldwide of synthetic diamond. BMS has access to their R&D departments in Shannon, Dublin and Frankfurt. The market segments with which BMS Ireland are primarily concerned are diamond-based metal bond grinding and resin bond grinding.

Marketing Support for Superabrasive Products

BMS has produced a range of short-form catalogues, product overviews and specification sheets, in both English and German. Technical and marketing seminars have been held at BMS and in agents' premises, and trade-fair promotions will continue to be part of the BMS marketing strategy.

Technical support is available from the manufacturing base. The R&D team, which includes a materials science engineer, continue to upgrade the product range and provide technical back-up to the BMS marketing team.

In 1988, Ballyneety Manufacturing Services Ltd. and Euro Equipment Ltd. were amalgamated. They now manufacture and market under the trade name BMS Ireland. Gen Weld Safety, GWS, trades under its own name.

In September, in tandem with the development of the electronic torque tools, a permanent design consultation centre was established. BMS Ireland was now in a position to quote for R&D projects, and was successful in acquiring contracts from firms such as Krups, Aughinish Alumina and Erin Peat. In December, an agent was appointed in southern Germany to market the superabrasive products range.

In March 1989, a major disaster occurred when the BMS premises at Ballyneety, its stock and most of the machinery were destroyed by fire. This happened at a time when superabrasives were gaining a stronghold in the marketplace, and when BMS was close to finalisation of the torque tool project. However, within two days, BMS was back in business in temporary premises — the nearby "Stroller Inn", owned by Liam and Norah Ryan. At the end of June, new premises were purchased and production was commenced in Raheen, Limerick city, on 20 July. In September, 1989 an agent was appointed in northern Germany to market the superabrasive products, and in November additional agents were employed to cover Britain and Northern Ireland, separately.

At the beginning of 1990, Liam Ryan philosophised about developments that had occurred over time:

> We have a management structure which can implement multimillion pound sales and now it is a question of holding things there with the intention of increasing gradually again from a solid base, rather than very rapid growth. We have to watch profit margins very closely. We have a good financial controller, now, who is looking at this. At the beginning we wanted a certain level of profit, and we needed to develop our products enough and we want to hold, or better still, improve our margins. Now the company is no longer so dependent on me. People in the functional areas have responsibilities and make the decisions . . . .

The installation of a functional management structure has changed the nature of Liam Ryan's job. Fourteen-hour working days full of operational decisions have been replaced by a normal working week and a more strategic viewpoint:

> The management structure frees me to think and to make better decisions. Now I have time for new ideas, new products, new development. I have time to meet our customers, suppliers and outside agencies like the University of Limerick and Shannon Development. I keep a closer eye on costs and prices, and longer-term projects . . . and I'm constantly asking: "What business should we be in, five to ten years from now?" There must be something more we could do with the skills and facilities we've got . . .

Ryan has redefined his job as continuously checking to see that the company is in the right business, a job that all management textbooks would agree is vital and, at the same time, a duty neglected by most managers. The search for new products has become more systematic — technical journals are circulated for comment, while product-identification services provided by Forbairt, An Bord Tráchtála (the Irish Trade Board) and the Innovation Centre are regularly checked. Observation and comments by all employees are strongly encouraged. To date these activities have resulted in some small but profitable extensions of the product range — for instance, soldering irons for a State agency, Telecom Éireann, and warning lights required by local authorities. Additions to the product line included a range of gaskets for industrial use. The original intention was to buy for resale, but Ryan decided to semi-manufacture, by making dies to cut the gaskets. This decision was prompted by the discovery that a local cardboard manufacturer was using such dies, which it agreed to purchase from BMS.

These search procedures will be continued, and Liam Ryan is sure that, with its experience of licensing ventures, and the R&D expertise it has developed, BMS will be able to exploit new product opportunities. He is also convinced that attractive licensing deals are readily available to other Irish companies:

> It was pointed out to me by the US Small Business Association that most American businesses have never supplied as much as a button outside the US. Ireland is a very attractive location to many of those thinking of a first venture — we speak their language and they feel they understand us. For many such companies licensing is a relatively safe and inexpensive way of exporting. Deals similar to my own are very widely available to Irish companies if only they could learn to take advantage of them.

The Principle of Torque

Torque, by definition, is the result of a force applied to an object through a lever arm, thus tending to rotate the object.

$T = F \times L$, where

T = Torque

F = Applied force

L = Lever length measured from the centre of rotation to, and at 90 degrees to, the direction of force.

Force and length can be expressed in several units of measurement. However, the most common units used in measuring torque are: inch-pound (in-lb or lb-in), foot-pound (ft-lb or lb-ft), metre-kilo (mkg) and Newton-metre (N-m).

When torque is applied to a threaded fastener, it produces a clamping force that holds the components together. Too much force, and the fastener will break; not enough, and the assembly will not stay together. By controlling the amount of torque, the clamping or holding force is controlled.

When undertaking the initial feasibility studies on electronic tools, referred to earlier, Liam Ryan discovered that electronic wrenches had been introduced on to the international market around 1985, ranging in price from £850 to £4,000. Mechanical torque tools had been available for many years, in the price bracket £90–£120.

BMS designed and developed a range of electronic torque tools using the latest technology in mechanical and electronic design. Ease of assembly and manufacturing cost were given serious consideration at the design stage. The Limerick company successfully launched its range of torque wrenches, with on-board memory, in 1990.

Figure 1.1: Importance of Torque

Safety	Bolts or nuts which are not tightened enough may vibrate and become loose while over-tightened ones may break.
Economy	Improperly tightened components may cause damage or accelerated wear. "Blown out" gaskets and broken head bolts are typical examples of such costly errors.
Performance	Today's equipment is made of many precision parts which need to be assembled precisely, to achieve maximum efficiency and performance. Improperly tightened head bolts may result in poor compression or problems with overtight bearings can lead to serious mechanical failure.

BMS claims to have produced the most accurate, least expensive, slimline, precision hand-measuring tool on the market. The products, which can be used with either imperial or metric measures, constitute a customised electronic system complete with memory capacity of 300 measurements, with RS232 serial link to a data logger or computer, and interchangeable heads. The BMS range was rapidly developed to incorporate six tools produced from the one standard body, cut to the required size.

BMS originally forecast sales of 6,000–8,000 units per annum, within two or three years of full production, to cater for the industrial, aerospace and electronics sectors, since there has been positive reaction from potential customers. The Limerick product is considered superior to any other known hand-held digital torque wrench, and prices are not perceived as prohibitive.

Market Developments

Belzer is a large German manufacturer of high-quality band tools. Belzer manufactured and distributed torque tools from the company's inception. In 1986, the German firm introduced an expensive electronic tool which, in 1992, it decided to replace with the BMS product. Belzer successfully market-tested the BMS torque tools over a three-month period and, as a result, Limerick-produced wrenches were introduced to the European market, under the brand names "Belzer" and "Bahco". One of Sweden's largest corporations, Sandvik, acquired Belzer and Bahco in 1990, and, in late 1992, it contracted with BMS Ireland to develop all the electronic products with the Belzer and Bahco ranges.

BMS identified an apparently attractive market in the United States — the automotive sector, including the after-market and professional mechanic segments. This is traditionally a high-volume/low-price market. BMS has chosen a higher price level to keep volumes in this market segment at moderate levels. Based on the present price structure, the survey forecasts 3,000–5,000 units per annum for the standard wrench. Within the US, the BMS electronic tool range is distributed through the Triangle Tool group, while negotiations were concluded with the Stanley corporation in North America for distribution worldwide.

Industrial Trends and Market Demands

With the use of aluminium, light gauge materials, ceramics and performance-related equipment, the demand for torque control and quality control is becoming more important. The fact that their tools incorporate memory capacity to store information and to produce statistical analysis is a decided product plus, in BMS's estimation. Features such as these are becoming increasingly necessary in the following industries: automotive manufacturing and after-market, aerospace and aircraft, chemical and military and naval sectors.

Prior to the entry of BMS Ireland into the electronic torque wrench market, the prevailing price was three or four times the Irish product's current level — £300 (DM800). Liam Ryan's objective now is to reduce the price further to around £100–£120 retail value to compete with top-of-the-range mechanical wrenches. If desired cost reductions can be achieved through simplification of the existing product, especially in terms of the wrench's body, transducer design, the number of electronic components and ease of assembly, it is confidently expected that sales of 100,000 units per annum can be achieved.

BMS Ireland negotiated an assistance package with Shannon Development, for industrial grants and a long-term loan facility, to enable the enterprise to implement an R&D/Technology enhancement programme costing £300,000. Financing of the venture was further strengthened by the raising of over £400,000 equity finance through a Dublin-based finance firm, Riada, under the Business Expansion Scheme.

Back to Ballyneety Roots

Even though transfer of the BMS manufacture activities from Bally-neety to Raheen Industrial Estate has brought significant benefits such as higher visibility to suppliers and customers, better access to shipping agents, mailing and delivery services, etc., Liam Ryan has never lost his enthusiasm for attempting to generate as much economic activity as possible in his home location, Ballyneety. Several years ago, he established "The Good Company Inn Ltd." as a separate trading operation to acquire and manage a long-established pub, "The Stroller", which had been the village tavern since 1860.

In 1991, in association with two other Limerick businessmen, Ryan developed the concept of establishing a new tourism/recreation facility at Ballyneety — the Limerick County Golf and Country Club. Through personal contacts and close relationships with the local community, he arranged for the successful purchase of 120 hectares in the immediate vicinity of Ballyneety (70 hectares for development of the golf course and leisure facilities, and 50 hectares for development of up-market accommodation including 24–30 holiday villas). The project has been financed by nine directors, each with a significant equity stake in the venture. It is estimated that the proceeds of the sales to professional property developers of land zoned for 60 exclusive residences will generate much of the remaining funding required. In addition, the project has attracted financial support from the EU Structural Fund, in recognition of its potential contribution to tourism.

Over time, it is envisaged that corporate and industrial membership fees will contribute significant further finance and it is planned that with income from green fees, the clubhouse catering and bar, and the holiday villas, the Limerick County venture should achieve a break-even position within the next three years.

Limerick city already has two long-established golf courses — Castletroy Golf Club (beside the University) and Limerick Golf Club, Ballyclough. In addition, Adare, although about 16 kilometres from the city, provides another option for Limerick golfers. Each of the three existing golf clubs has approximately 600 members with a significant waiting list. Liam Ryan and his business-venture colleagues believe that as Limerick and its environs has a population of 100,000, there is a substantial target market for new golfing amenities, particularly as the sport has shown dramatic increases in recent years.

Apart from local demand, there is constant pressure to allow tourists access to golf courses, particularly at weekends. The concept of a combined holiday village/recreation facility is an attempt to respond to these needs. Ballyneety is favourably situated, being only 8 km from Limerick city, and strategically placed between the Cas-

tletroy and Limerick clubs. The gently sloping and open site provides
what is considered to be one of the best soil conditions for golf-course
construction yet encountered in Ireland. The site's high gravel content and gradients gives the land its dry and free-draining qualities,
ensuring excellent all-year-round playing conditions. Des Smyth and
Associates designed an attractive and challenging 18-hole course
which was built to US golfing association standards. The large and
well-equipped driving range, measuring over 300 metres in length
was opened in October 1992; the clubhouse was completed in December 1993, and the course itself was opened in Summer 1994. During
the construction phase full-time employment was created for up to 40
workers, and when fully operational, the Limerick County Club will
employ 20 people.

BBV's Corporate Culture

Every organisation, whether it is aware of it or not, develops a core
set of beliefs and assumptions — a culture specific to itself. As might
be expected, a significant part of the culture that predominates at the
Ryan group of companies can be attributed to its founder. His particular traits and attitudes to developing various ventures have given rise
to a special management climate in the Ryan group. This culture has
evolved and changed over time with the founder's experience, personal development and business growth, as Liam Ryan has attempted
to control a number of apparently diverse enterprises.

Management / Leadership Style

Liam Ryan has evolved from the typical genre of "entrepreneurial"
manager, who retains rigid control over his business and is reluctant
to delegate, to the more "charismatic" style, which inspires colleagues
by behaviour and leadership abilities. The change has been reflected
positively in the organisation, which encourages an "open door" management policy in relation to all staff. This facilitates effective communication with willingness of management to listen to employees.
Liam Ryan has adopted the contingency approach to management
practices. His approach has evolved because of changes and developments in both the internal and external environments. This contingency approach has had a significant impact on the development of
BBV's corporate culture.

Organisational Structure and Control

The BBV organisation is structured on a flat matrix basis. The flat
structure is particularly conducive to the development of closer links
between management and staff, encouraging the "open door" approach mentioned above.

Liam Ryan maintains final control over all his business ventures. As in the case of his management style, his system and means of control have changed over time. As is typical with the normative entrepreneur, the founder was concerned, initially, with the detail of the day-to-day running of each new venture. However, because of the founder's nature, and his desire to diversify into other business areas, the need to relinquish control soon became apparent.

The decision to delegate emerged at the early stages when establishing the structures of GWS and Euro Tools. In the latter case, the responsibility and authority for management of the operation were handed over to the most senior member of the existing staff at the retail outlet. A similar pattern followed with his other businesses when he appointed an existing staff member, or an outsider with experience in the relevant sector, to management positions.

All managers are accountable, finally, to Liam Ryan. Meetings, both formal and informal, are held on a regular basis to review progress and discuss any problems or queries. This system of control, Liam Ryan feels, has allowed him to develop and diversify away from his core business, while facilitating management of the component elements of the group.

Staff Development

Liam Ryan believes that his staff are the critical ingredient of his organisation. The group experiences very low staff turnover. Ryan encourages his employees to develop and advance within the firm. Opportunities for self-development are provided for all staff through participation in various training and educational programmes. Many, including Ryan himself, are pursuing academic programmes at the University of Limerick — several for a masters degree, and one at doctoral level.

Management of the Enterprises

As indicated above, Liam Ryan has established a whole range of enterprises over the past decade-and-a-half. BMS Ireland, with 41 employees and estimated current annual turnover of £2.8 million, claims a major part of his attention — while GWS with 15 employees and sales of £2.5 million also commands a fair amount of his time. It is of interest that, as part of Liam Ryan's principle for delegation, BMS contracts out most of the torque wrench manufacture. Up to 90 per cent of components are produced by outside contractors — BMS tries to confine its manufacturing-process activities to final assembly and collaboration.

In addition to direct employment for over 60 employees in Liam Ryan's enterprises (excluding the Limerick County venture), includ-

ing four staff in the BMS retail store in Lim
Stroller pub in Ballyneety, it is estimate
agreements provide an additional 10 full-time

When queried on the rationale for such a s
Ryan justifies his actions in terms of both se
being able and willing to react to business opp
tous), as they arise. He is a firm believer in ke
with the market so that needs, and in particul
can be identified. Perhaps the most critical question is how does he
manage such a diverse portfolio of activities? He believes in keeping a
flexible approach to management of his enterprises and he is convinced of the need for delegation (and the giving of commensurate
authority). He tries to emphasise the personal approach, having confidence in people's abilities and, in turn, gaining their confidence.

Above all, he is an avid practitioner of time management. His approach might be seen, on the one hand, to be at variance with the old
Irish saying, "When God made time, he made plenty of it". On the
other hand, if you wish to live life to the full, like Liam Ryan, you will
welcome this providential gift of time.

Sources: Interviews with Liam Ryan.

2

Monaghan Mushrooms

Barra Ó Cinnéide

Introduction

Monaghan, situated in the north-east of the Republic of Ireland, is one of the country's smallest counties in terms of size and population. It borders on Northern Ireland and retains many features of the traditional culture/lifestyle of the historic province of Ulster, of which it is a constituent part. The agricultural holdings, averaging 15–20 hectares, are well below the EU average and the whole of Co. Monaghan has been classified as "disadvantaged" in EU terms, therefore entitling farmers to maximum support funding for agricultural and regional development. The principal source of income is agriculture — the mainstays of the local economy are dairying and beef production but, traditionally, the county has been a prime contributor also to white-meat (pig and poultry) production in Ireland. In recent decades, however, the north-east of Ireland has become a significant base for horticulture, gearing most of its output to export markets, particularly the United Kingdom. One firm in particular, Monaghan Mushrooms, located at Tyholland, five kilometres from Monaghan town, has been influential in developing this sector of agribusiness activity.

In the early 1980s, against the background of small-sized, marginal farms, a young VEC (Vocational Educational Committee) school teacher, Ronnie Wilson, explored the potential for developing alternative indigenous enterprises. One of his initial interests concerned the prospects for profitable use of agricultural or horticultural expertise, and he decided to establish a new venture in Tyholland, Co. Monaghan, that would help to encourage neighbouring farmers to participate in a new initiative. This initiative, run as a private enterprise subsidiary of the Pleroma group, is now one of the leading mushroom companies in the UK/Ireland. In 1995, the enterprise could claim to have created employment for over 1,100 people, on either a full-time of part-time basis. Figure 2.1 presents a breakdown of employment.

Figure 2.1: "On-Farm" Employment (combined full-time and part-time) Monaghan Mushrooms, 1994

Location	Employers	No. of Employees
Republic of Ireland	Independent growers	945
Northern Ireland	Kernans (MM) subsidiary	135
Scotland	Monaghan Mushrooms (MM) Fenton Barnes — Scotland	*65
Total		**1,145**

* Mostly full-time (contract employees of Monaghan Mushrooms).

Note: A member of Monaghan Mushrooms' staff estimates that "on-farm" employment can be apportioned 15 per cent full-time and 85 per cent part-time approximately).

Excluding its growing operations, Monaghan Mushrooms maintains a payroll for more than 300 employees, including over 100 dedicated to collection/distribution, 65 in composting operations, more than 50 within the fresh division and on-processing activities, 10 specialist advisors to growers, and up to 90 involved in marketing, administration and management. Figure 2.2 presents the organisation structure within Monaghan Mushrooms at year-end 1993.

The Irish Mushroom Sector

Pre-1980, the Irish mushroom sector consisted mainly of a few large production units. Their operations were based on the traditional British system of growing in large wooden trays, stacked four or five high in the cropping houses. The farms were fully self-contained in that, in addition to growing mushrooms, they produced their own compost and each company undertook the task of marketing its own output. These companies were remarkably innovative and enterprising for their time, but they suffered from several serious drawbacks. These included high capital investment and the difficulty of achieving a sufficient quantity of high-quality product, together with attendant management problems because of the large-sized units and high labour costs. In addition, the concept of individual marketing made it difficult to penetrate the upper end of the market where quality and continuity of supply are necessities. These farms were thus in a weak position to compete successfully on the British market, while the home market had proven to be too small to warrant significant further expansion. However, integrated corporate groups, like Monaghan Mushrooms, emerged and began to apply the benefits of research and development (R&D) and "best practice" promoted by Teagasc (the Agriculture and Food Development Authority), while adopting new strategic business approaches.

Figure 2.2: Monaghan Mushrooms — Organisational Structure

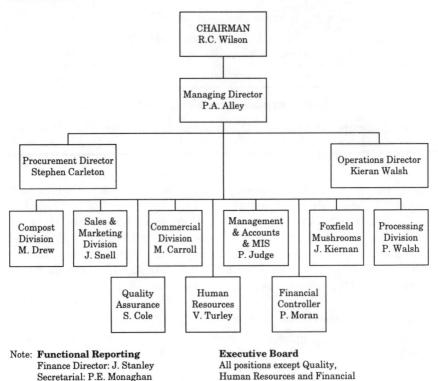

Note: **Functional Reporting**   **Executive Board**
Finance Director: J. Stanley   All positions except Quality,
Secretarial: P.E. Monaghan   Human Resources and Financial

The Role of Research and Development

During the 1970s, research workers at the Kinsealy Research Centre of Teagasc examined alternative systems of mushroom production. These included the use of plastic bags placed on the floor of insulated plastic tunnels. Every aspect of the system was investigated, including type of compost, size of bags, and general crop management. The result was the prototyping and development of a new system of mushroom production suited to Irish circumstances. One of its main features was the low capital cost. This new system proved to be attractive commercially, in that it allowed people with little capital to develop a small mushroom enterprise. From such research activities and subsequent exploitation, this particular aspect of Irish horticulture has literally "mushroomed"!

The R&D undertaken at Teagasc gave rise to the concept of specialist central compost facilities supplying spawned compost to many small "satellite" growing units. Additionally, in order to ensure that the new system would function effectively and efficiently, an integrated organisational structure was proposed as the "model", with central marketing of the mushrooms as a critical core activity. The researchers mainly responsible for this innovative thinking at the time were Cathal MacCanna and Jim Flanagan at Kinsealy. The "Kinsealy model" was successfully commercialised, with the adoption of the system described above, by a number of entrepreneurs such as Ronnie Wilson of Tyholland, Co. Monaghan, and Pat Walsh of Gorey, Co. Wexford. They set about constructing compost facilities to the required high standards, arranging networks of small growing units and establishing appropriate marketing systems. This was done with considerable back-up from the research and advisory personnel of the relevant State bodies.

Origins of Monaghan Mushrooms

In 1981, Monaghan Mushrooms set up its franchised network of mushroom growers — a group of enterprising small farmers dedicated to production of quality mushrooms. By establishing its satellite system of mushroom production, the Tyholland firm encouraged the participation of neighbouring farmers in a new initiative which, although run on a private enterprise basis, would rely on community effort. The system that evolved fitted very well into the socioeconomic structure of Irish agriculture, which is mainly based on small farms. Many of these farms, being on marginal land, were looking for a means of supplementing family farm income, and the Kinsealy model provided such an opportunity, with its relatively low cost of establishing viable small mushroom units. Training in mushroom-growing was provided by the advisory services and, within a short time, most of the new growers became technically proficient, while quickly developing their business expertise "on-the-job". The company's control systems were designed to align as effectively as possible with the growers' commitment to grow and hand-pick mushrooms, in order to keep pace with market requirements. Monaghan Mushrooms now comprises a wide range of activities.

Compost Manufacture and the Growing Process

All the main players within the Irish mushroom sector have a strong commitment to investment in purpose-built facilities, including coldstores, work areas that are environmentally controlled, packing and labelling machinery, and transportation systems. For instance, in production of one of the basic inputs, compost, advanced technology is employed. Today's composters have developed reliable systems of re-producing compost to the quality level needed for yielding firm white mushrooms with high dry-matter content. As all the inputs of mush-room compost are natural materials — mainly straw and animal ma-nure — there can be significant variations in their nutrient proper-ties. The composters have imposed stringent monitoring of raw ma-terials to ensure that the production process gives a consistent for-mula and, consequently, reliable results at the individual farm level.

Monaghan Mushrooms claim that its grower franchise network, using the bag-growing system, offers many advantages, as it has been designed to ensure:

- The supply of firm white mushrooms with a high dry-matter con-tent and long shelf-life.

- The dedication of specific growers to harvest mushrooms selec-tively for individual customers to their specifications and packag-ing requirements.

- The curtailment of the spread of disease, by virtue of the segre-gated grower network.

- The individual quality of product, with the features of a "cottage industry" environment (Mushrooms are picked when ready, im-mediately placed in the grower's cold-store, the first link in the "cool chain" distribution system).

- The flexibility to increase mushroom production as market condi-tions dictate.

Range of Monaghan Mushrooms' Operations

The Tyholland plant is the focus for "adding value" either through the "Fresh Division" or within processing operations (canning). Mona-ghan Mushroom's operations now include:

- Mushroom compost production

- Supply and erection of growing facilities to mushroom farms

- Mushroom-growing

- Organising/controlling a franchised growing network

- Servicing the UK retail and food-processing markets with quality fresh mushrooms

- Processing mushrooms in cans and jars for the European market.

Fresh Mushrooms

Monaghan Mushrooms has an impressive portfolio of customers for its fresh products, including all the major multiple retailers. It supplies mostly on a non-exclusive basis to the "Big Five" chains in Britain: Sainsbury, Tesco, Safeway, ASDA and Somerfield, formerly Gateway (see Exhibit 1, Retail Mushroom Market, in the Appendix). The company offers an extensive range of fresh mushrooms, sized and graded to customer requirements. Monaghan Mushrooms has its own specialist transport fleet to collect the output from contracted growers, concentrating its operations at five depots. In addition to its operations at Tyholland, where indigenous production is aggregated, Monaghan Mushrooms has 30 large growing units — that is "houses" — in the UK at Fenton Barnes, where the Irish group has an integrated centre combining production, collection, packaging, sales and distribution in Scotland. Figure 2.3 presents a breakdown of production. The Monaghan plant remains the focus for adding value, either through the fresh division or within processing operations (mixed delivery system — 50:50 company-owned/contract hauliers) to its customers, the UK multiple retailers.

Figure 2.3: Monaghan Mushrooms Depots/Growers (houses)

Depot	No. of Growers	Houses
Tyholland, Co. Monaghan	132	(590)
Glenveagh, Co. Donegal	29	(118)
Foxfield, Kilnaleck, Co. Cavan	49	(218)
Benburb, Co. Tyrone, N. Ireland	38	(166)
Fenton Barnes, Scotland — all large houses	3	(30)
Total	**275**	**(1,122)**

Processing Division

As well as being now one of the leading suppliers of quality fresh products to the UK market, Monaghan Mushrooms is also a strong force in the food-processing sector. In conjunction with its fresh division, the processing operation at Monaghan Mushrooms gives the company flexibility in the production and supply of quality mushrooms to many markets. Processing takes place within a "stainless steel environment" and, in line with its policy of continuously updating its plant, the company has recently installed modern profile-slicing and sterilisation equipment, undertaking laboratory testing and analysis throughout the process. The product range of whole and profile-sliced mushrooms is packed in a comprehensive range of sizes (cans and glass jars) for the retail, catering and food-processing markets. Fresh sliced and semi-processed products are now supplied in large packs to food processors.

Maintaining Standards/Competitiveness

New "satellite" growers are selected following interview by the management of the contracting "central organisation" — Monaghan Mushrooms. When selected, growers are supplied with a total mushroom-growing package, incorporating a well-defined code of practice for producing and harvesting the product. The growers are supported by professional advisory staff and quality assurance personnel who monitor and audit their performance. Incentive and award schemes motivate the growers to produce mushrooms to the required quality and hygiene standards. A stringent quality-assurance programme has been adopted, with control systems operating throughout the chain — from the growers through to customer delivery. Only the highest-quality mushrooms are delivered to meet the demands of "today's consumer, today". Mechanical harvesting of the mushrooms is avoided in order to ensure a standard high-quality end product.

The increasing popularity of mushrooms in today's fresh product market is the result of changing consumer attitudes towards healthier eating lifestyles. Mushrooms are supplied to specification, in a comprehensive range of sizes in both metric and imperial weights. Monaghan's product range covers the whole spectrum of customer requirements and currently includes baby buttons, buttons, closed cups, open cups and flats in white and brown varieties, as well as canned products. Monaghan Mushrooms operates a just-in-time (JIT) system of deliveries, with "window-slot" timing at multiple retail depots. The temperature-controlled transport fleets, cushioned with air suspension, collect the mushrooms from the growers and, after sorting, packing and cooling, the mushrooms are delivered daily to customers throughout the UK (see Figure 2.4).

Advantages of the Irish System

In recent years, the performance of the mushroom sector in competing successfully on export markets indicates that the Irish system has a number of advantages, including the following:

- The central composter, by specialising, can supply a compost material of the highest quality.

- The grower, with a relatively small unit and personal incentives, can give great attention to detail.

- The system of production in plastic bags on one level with a large air-to-bed ratio facilitates production of very high-quality mushrooms with reasonable capital outlay.

- The central marketing system guarantees a continuity of supply of high-quality product and access to major customers.

As indicated above, one of the main benefits has undoubtedly been the central marketing system developed by enterprises such as Monaghan Mushrooms.

It is noteworthy that Monaghan is so oriented to international marketing that it has consistently refrained from supplying the domestic Irish market.

Figure 2.4: Monaghan Mushrooms: Production and Distribution

Attempts to Stay at the Forefront

Through attention to quality, customer service, investment in technology and R&D, Monaghan Mushrooms has attempted to become a trendsetter for the industry (see Exhibits 2 and 3 in the Appendix) through:

- Investing in technology and enhancing the quality of its product/service to customers

- Promoting mushroom as a health food

- Maintaining its leading position within the European mushroom sector through development, acquisitions and diversification.

A breakdown of Monaghan's projected sales is given in Figure 2.5 while the latest data on European production is contained in Figure 2.6. Details of recent acquisitions and corporate development at Monaghan Mushrooms are contained in Exhibit 4 in the Appendix.

Figure 2.5: Projected Sales, Monaghan Mushrooms, 1994

Division	Projected Sales
Fresh Division	IR£36.5 million
Processed Products	IR£6.5 million
Total	**IR£43.0 million**

Figure 2.6: EU Mushroom Production, 1992

Country	(000 tonnes)
France	220
Netherlands	190
UK	118
Italy	115
Germany	60
Ireland	41
Belgium	31*
Denmark	n/a
Spain	n/a
Luxembourg	n/a
Portugal	n/a
Greece	n/a
Total	**780****

* = 1991 figure, ** = Estimated global production for the EU.
Source: *Mushroom News*, 1993; 1994: 2(3).

Co-ordination/Organisational Development

The Irish Mushroom Growers Association (IMGA), an umbrella body representing composting/marketing companies, growers, and associated firms — such as spawn suppliers — was established several years ago and includes most of the "major players" such as: Monaghan Mushrooms, Tyholland, Co. Monaghan; Carbury Mushrooms, Co. Kildare; Connaught Mushrooms, Galway; Greenhill Compost, Carnagh, Kilogy, Co. Longford; Marley Compost, Crush, Carrickroe, Co. Monaghan; and Walsh Mushrooms, Wexford. In addition, regional groups representing individual mushroom growers have IMGA membership. The industry, through IMGA, has devised a voluntary levy scheme on the basis of IR£0.5 contribution per tonne of compost. Approximately 10 per cent of this levy is devoted to IMGA's administration, and the remainder to funding R&D projects. Basic and applied research is carried out for the industry, on an on-going basis, by Teagasc, both through its horticultural division at Kinsealy Research Centre and through its food research centre in Dunsinea, Co. Dublin. There is also a Mushroom Research Group at the National Agricultural and Veterinary Biotechnology Centre, University College Dublin.

In addition to the advisory services provided by the industry's major firms, short intensive courses, both for new mushroom-growers and to assist the transfer of technology to existing farm enterprises, are organised under the aegis of Teagasc. An Bord Glas operates a National Auditing Programme, and in 1993 instituted its National Hygiene Awards for the mushroom industry. It recently announced incorporation of its award scheme, (organised on a regional basis) within the auditing programme, (see An Bord Glas Hygiene Awards in Exhibit 5 of the Appendix).

Irish Mushrooms: Performance/Prospective Future

It has been acknowledged generally that the mushroom sector has been the main success story of Irish horticulture (see Figure 2.7). The sector doubled full-time jobs to 1,400 and increased part-time employment to 4,000 in the period 1988/1992. Its sales, the majority in the UK, have doubled to IR£54 million in the past seven years (Murphy, 1994).

A potential for controlled, market-led expansion in the mushroom industry, leading to additional employment of 3,000 (880 full-time and 2,200 part time) is forecast by Teagasc (1994). Significantly, the mushroom industry was targeted as the main plank in a new five-year plan (Central Bank of Ireland, 1993) presented to the government in June 1994 by An Bord Glas (the Horticultural Development Board). Brendan O'Donnell, chief executive of An Bord Glas, believes that:

. . . the UK market provides the main opportunity — a study of the German market, the largest in Europe, has shown it is not commercially viable to export fresh horticultural products to it.

Figure 2.7: Ireland, Mushroom Production, 1980–93 (000 Tonnes)

Year	"Fresh" Home Market	"Fresh" UK Exports	"Processed" Exports	Total Production
1980	1.8	5.0	—	6.8
1981	1.7	5.4	0.6	7.7
1982	2.4	5.2	1.8	9.4
1983	3.2	5.4	2.5	11.1
1984	4.6	6.0	3.3	13.9
1985	4.8	9.4	4.1	18.3
1986	6.2	8.5	3.4	18.1
1987	6.2	12.1	2.7	21.0
1988	7.0	13.1	2.2	22.4
1989	9.1	18.0	3.5	30.6
1990	7.6	26.2	3.0	36.8
1991	7.7	27.0	4.5	39.2
1992	8.7	29.1	3.2	41.0
1993	9.5	32.5	2.0	44.0

Note: While the average annual rate of growth of production within the EU was 5.5 per cent (compound), Irish producers achieved an average of 16.3 per cent per annum over this period.

Source: *Mushroom News* (1994): 2(1): 4.

The State board has been given comparatively extensive powers and funding to develop and promote the Irish horticultural sector, with statutory powers to impose levies within the horticultural industry. To date, however, it has preferred to encourage co-operative efforts in undertaking initiatives in training and R&D for the mushroom sector.

Apparent Dangers on the Horizon

In spite of optimistic projections of future growth, several potentially serious threats to the Irish mushroom sector have arisen.

The first five months of 1992 saw a period of relative exchange-rate stability, with reserves rising and interest-rate differential *vis-à-vis* other Exchange Rate Mechanism (ERM) countries narrowing to historically low levels. Conditions began to deteriorate in June, however, when the prospect of steady progress toward economic and Monetary Union (EMU) was questioned, following rejection of provisions of the Maastricht Treaty in the first Dutch referendum on further integration into the EU. The following statement describes the ensuing events, from the Irish perspective:

> Pressures intensified in September 1992, and remained for the rest of the year. Liquidity conditions deteriorated sharply and money market interest rates rose to unprecedented levels as the Central Bank utilised increases in its overnight support rate to defend the currency. Difficulties persisted in early 1993 and eventually the Irish pound's central rate was realigned with the ERM on January 1993. (Central Bank of Ireland, 1993)

After an expensive defence of the Irish currency over five months, in the latter half of 1992, and the beginning of 1993 (Leddin, 1992) the Irish pound was devalued in line with sterling, but later became one of the strongest currencies within the European Monetary System (EMS) "upper hand" (see Exhibit 6 in the Appendix and Figure 2.8 below), raising fears of a drastic decline in profit margins for Irish horticulture, and the mushroom industry in particular. Fluctuations in exchange rates, particularly pressures on the Irish pound, vis-à-vis UK sterling, pose major problems for the Irish mushroom industry. Currency instability on the money markets in late 1992 resulted in devaluation of most of the EU currencies, including UK sterling, to a more significant degree than initially occurred in the case of the Irish pound. Consequently, it was widely reported that many of the elements of the Irish economy, including the mushroom sector, suffered heavily in terms of export competitiveness.

Since the late 1950s, the Irish government has been anxious to provide as many incentives as possible to encourage development of the industrial sector — in particular, by attracting overseas firms to establish manufacturing facilities to serve European markets. Up to the 1980s, a benign fiscal system designated that all profits on exports were tax-free. However, on joining the European Community in 1973, Ireland was forced to eliminate any discrimination in its tax policy in relation to firms in domestic as opposed to export markets.

Derogation from the European regulations allowed the Irish government a lengthy period in which to develop an appropriate response strategy. Mushroom production was deemed to be "manufacturing" up to recently, and so, qualified for the preferential rate of 10 per cent corporate tax, which the Irish government had applied to the manufacturing sector of the economy. However, in 1993, following pressure from its own mushroom-growers, the British government submitted a formal complaint to the European Commission concerning the Irish preferential rate, claiming "unfair competition" — since a standard rate of corporate tax (27 per cent) was applied across the UK embracing all industries, the horticultural sector

Figure 2.8: Exchange Rates in Dublin Market, 1992-94: Period Averages, IR£

	v UK£		v UK£	v DM	v ECU	Effective Index
1992						
Jan	0.9323					
Feb	0.9275					
Mar	0.9312	Qtr. 1 1992	0.9304	2.6662	1.3053	67.98
Apr	0.9209					
May	0.9101					
Jun	0.9158	Qtr. 2 1992	0.9155	2.6692	1.3013	67.63
July	0.9320					
Aug	0.9434					
Sept	0.9861	Qtr. 3 1992	0.9538	2.6530	1.3087	69.81
Oct	1.0705					
Nov	1.0892					
Dec	1.0753	Qtr. 4 1992	1.0784	2.6363	1.3426	72.50
1993						
Jan	1.0673					
Feb	0.9622					
Mar	**	Qtr. 1 1993	1.0353	2.4995	1.2834	68.85
Apr	0.9677					
May	0.9882					
Jun	0.9800	Qtr. 2 1993	0.9817	2.4386	1.2486	66.40
July	0.9772					
Aug	0.9425					
Sept	0.9324	Qtr. 3 1993	0.9391	2.3676	1.2283	64.00
Oct	0.9421					
Nov	0.9542					
Dec	0.9491	Qtr. 4 1993	0.9516	2.3881	1.2442	64.72
	0.9516					
1994						
Jan	0.9597					
Feb	0.9603					
Mar	0.9619	Qtr. 1 1994	0.9607	2.4625	1.2706	

* Trade weighted exchange-rate index for the Irish pound (base 1971 = 100).

** Realignment of the EMS occurred on 20 January 1993, resulting in an effective 10 per cent devaluation of the Irish pound.

Source: Central Bank of Ireland, *Quarterly Report*.

included. The Dublin government was forced by Brussels to declassify mushroom production as "manufacturing" and, under the Finance Bill 1994, imposed the standard 40 per cent corporation profit tax on mushroom-producing companies, though composting companies retained their 10 per cent tax status.

Storm clouds for the industry are also visibly gathering as a result of a claimed increase in production capacity in Holland. Mushrooms are among the most important horticultural crops in the Netherlands, where 190,000 tonnes were harvested in 1993. Exports of fresh mushrooms have grown to 50,000 tonnes, with the UK being the second largest customer of Dutch fresh mushrooms in 1993. British sales represent 19 per cent (9,500 tonnes) of mushroom exports from the Netherlands.

In the UK, multiple supermarkets continue to predominate as the main channels for the household purchase of fresh produce. The multiples' share of the market is still growing, having control of in excess of 60 per cent of the retail market segment (in terms of volume). The major chains continually compete aggressively with each other to increase their individual market share. Currently, the multiple chains are involved in a price war — with fresh produce, including mushrooms, being a prime target. Loose mushrooms, which up to recently had achieved a selling price of £1.53 per pound, without having any apparent negative adverse effect on consumption, are now being sold below this price level. On the other hand, the consumer can purchase more mushrooms at a reduced cost by choosing from the "value-pack" ranges — for example, 750g retailing at £1.59, or 1 lb packs retailing at £0.89, etc. It is known that Irish mushroom producers are attempting to gauge the likely effects of these developments on the sector and to develop appropriate strategies to guard their respective market shares.

In the medium to long term, availability of straw could prove to be a critical factor. Increased "set-aside" provision under the Common Agricultural Policy (CAP) programme were set to release over 86,500 acres of land from cereal production in Ireland in the course of 1994. When the prospective effects of this EU measure are combined with the potentially increased demand for straw from the thriving Northern Ireland export market, there is the threat of a significant increase in the price of straw to Irish mushroom-growers, who may be forced to import straw from the UK. On the other hand, there could be an increase in the indigenous supply of this critical raw material because of production of longer straw, as a result of EU prohibition of growth regulations under the Rural Environment Protection Scheme (REPS).

Ireland is probably the only country where mushrooms are entirely hand-picked. The work is done mainly by women who work hours that suit their personal and domestic situation. The introduction of the new Workers Protection Act by the Irish government means that new rates of PRSI (Pay Related Social Insurance) now apply to casual workers. Some pickers are now saying that they will discontinue picking work because of the risk of losing social welfare benefits, since if the "margin" — part-time earnings from mushroom picking — is added to existing family income, workers and their families may lose some entitlements. It is feared that the mushroom sector will find it difficult to survive without a plentiful supply of casual labour, and a strong case has been made for the retention of the Farm Causal Scheme, allowing farmers to take on workers for purposes such as harvest cropping.

APPENDIX

Exhibit 1: UK Retail Mushroom Market (September 1993 – August 1994)

Value-Pack Culture: A Worrying Trend

The UK mushroom market can be divided into a number of segments: retail, catering and processing sectors. All these sectors are important outlets for Irish mushrooms, particularly the retail market which is responsible for just under half of the total fresh mushroom sales in the UK. Thus developments and trends in this sector are of critical importance to the Irish industry.

The retail sector is made up of multiple grocers, co-operatives stores, symbol and independent grocers, farm shops/stalls and other miscellaneous outlets. The multiple grocers have the major share of the retail mushroom market as they do with all fresh produce. The major multiple grocers include Sainsbury, Tesco, Safeway, Asda and Gateway.

A continuous market measurement of mushrooms in the UK retail market is carried out and for the purpose of this market research mushrooms are included as a salad vegetable (with cucumbers, celery, peppers, tomatoes and lettuce). In the year ending August 1994 expenditure on salad vegetables showed a 4 per cent increase (3 per cent by volume) on the previous year. The majority of the salad vegetables are sold through the multiple outlets with a 62 per cent share of the volume, an increase of 7 per cent on the previous year. Tesco and Sainsbury lead the way in terms of market share, having now achieved between them 34 per cent (volume) of the retail sales for salad vegetables.

Figure 2.9: UK Retail market — Outlet shares of Total Mushrooms

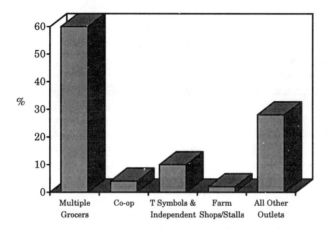

Looking at this more closely and keeping in mind that the overall retail market grew by 7 per cent annually to August '94, the percentage share of the total retail market held by loose mushrooms dropped by 3 per cent. Closed loose mushrooms have dropped 1 per cent and open loose mushrooms by 2 per cent in market share. In contrast the closed pre-pack and open pre-pack/value-pack segments have each increased their market share (volume) by 1.5 per cent. The "value-pack segment" is estimated to have an 8 per cent share of the total retail market. In summary, within the last year the consumer has purchased more pre-packed mushrooms than in the previous year with a resultant loss in market share by loose mushrooms. The repercussions of this trend will be discussed later.

The multiple supermarkets continue to dominate the retail market with 66 per cent of all expenditure on mushrooms taking place in these outlets. In volume terms this is equal to 61 per cent, an increase of 9 per cent on the previous year. This was achieved at the expense of the other varied outlets. This had led to gain in market share by all the major multiples. Sainsbury are currently recording the highest volume sales of mushrooms with 18 per cent (up 3 per cent), Tesco 15 per cent (up 3 per cent), Gateway 3.3 per cent (up 1 per cent), Safeway 8.2 per cent (up 1 per cent) and Asda 9 per cent (up 1 per cent). Thus because of the increasing power of the major multiples and the share of business the Irish mushroom industry has within the multiple sector, developments and trends which occur on the supermarket shelf will directly impinge on the Irish industry and how it develops in the future.

1994 UK Retail Market Data Observations
While the overall growth in the retail market is obviously a positive sign, a closer examination of the data throws up a worrying trend. In 1994 the major multiple supermarkets have been engaged in an ongoing promotional campaign to win market share from their competitors. Fresh produce including mushrooms have been a prime target. The promotions are leading to an overall downward pressure on the price of mushrooms on the supermarket shelf. The phenomenon of the "value-pack" has developed at an alarming rate and this development is not in the longer-term interest of the Irish industry. A "value-pack" is where a specified pre-packed quantity of mushrooms of a lower quality is sold at a lower price than loose produce. The data clearly shows that the retail market is being driven forward and that the "value-pack" content of the pre-pack sector is primarily responsible for this. Loose mushrooms as a share of the total retail market have lost share while the pre-pack sector (including value-packs) has gained.

One of the main strengths of the Irish industry to date has been its ability to produce uniform chips of prime quality, graded mushrooms. While loose mushrooms still hold the greater share of the market, present indications are that the "value-pack" line is beginning to eat into this share. The quality requirement of this line is not as high as the prime loose product and thus from a marketing point of view the major quality advantage that the Irish industry has had to date is now being eroded. Ireland's competitors in the market place will look on this as an indication that the production of this value-pack line is more suitable to their production system. The sales of the "value-packs" are resulting in an overall downward pressure on the retail price of mushrooms and at a time when input costs for producers are rising this is an unfavourable development as it makes the likelihood of recording a price increase in the market place more difficult. Over the coming months the retail market will be watched closely, particularly in relation to the development of the overall market but more especially in relation to the ongoing progress of the "value-pack" sector.

Figure 2.10: Type Shares of Total Mushrooms Based on Volume (000 lb)

Total Market 16,704

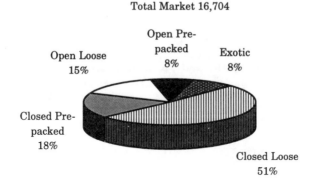

Open Loose
15%

Open Pre-packed
8%

Exotic
8%

Closed Pre-packed
18%

Closed Loose
51%

Figure 2.11: Type Shares of Defined Salad Vegetables Based on Expenditure (£000)

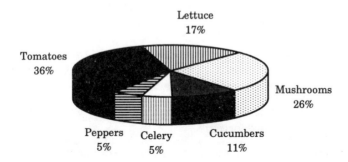

Lettuce
17%

Tomatoes
36%

Mushrooms
26%

Peppers
5%

Celery
5%

Cucumbers
11%

Wholesale Markets

The UK wholesale markets, despite going through a state of decline at the present time, are an important outlet for mushroom sales and have a major influence on the price of mushrooms in the overall market. The first quarter of 1994 evidenced a good supply/demand situation resulting in satisfactory returns. The second quarter saw a deterioration in the market with supply out-stripping demand for a number of weeks. The reasons for this included a drop in demand, increased producer yields, change in weather conditions (higher temperatures) bringing volumes of mushrooms on-stream and also extra produce from additional houses.

The summer months generally saw the markets in a state of over-supply. The normal dip in demand was further accelerated by very warm weather conditions experienced in the UK this summer. Recent reports from the wholesale markets are showing a reasonably tight supply/demand situation. Some of the reasons for this situation included an increased demand following the summer months and an overall reduction in producer yields (reportedly due to straw quality).

Predictions are that in the short-term this tight supply/demand situation will prevail.

Source: Derived from *Mushroom News*, 1994.

Exhibit 2: Kabeyun Ltd. — Compost Manufacture

Kabeyun Ltd., a wholly owned subsidiary of Pleroma, the holding company of the Monaghan Mushrooms group, is the largest producer of mushroom compost in Britain or Ireland. Using advanced technology, the company produces quality compost needed to yield firm white mushrooms with high dry-matter content. As all the inputs of mushroom compost are natural materials, mainly straw and animal manure, there are consequent variations in their nutrient properties. The company imposes stringent monitoring of raw materials to ensure that the production processes give a consistent formula.

The Kabeyun enterprise strives to achieve consistency by providing a wide range of expertise and back-up resources, such as:

- Sophisticated blending equipment which mixes the raw materials in their correct proportions

- Computerised environmental control throughout the sterilisation process

- Laboratory analysis of raw material and finished product

- Special facilities for filling and sealing the compost for the bag-growing system

- An efficient fleet of distribution vehicles equipped with forklift trucks, giving prompt delivery of the bagged compost to the growing units, with minimum exposure to the elements.

The group has compost-making facilities at four locations, including Scotland, and it has indicated that one of its prime missions is to be at the forefront of development in compost manufacture.

Exhibit 3: Clonkeen Mushroom Developments Ltd. — Mushroom Technology and Horticultural Equipment

The Pleroma group also owns Clonkeen Mushroom Developments Ltd. Founded to service the expanding mushroom industry with growing units, the company's product range has expanded significantly in recent years. The firm is now a major supplier of growing tunnels, control technology and ancillary supplies to the mushroom and horticultural sectors in Ireland. The company's R&D team is available to assist in the design and development of custom-designed facilities.

The current product range offered by Clonkeen Mushroom Developments includes the following facilities and equipment:

- Growing tunnels constructed from quality heavy-wall (2mm) steel tubing, which has been hot-dip galvanised for lasting protection against corrosion. Units are insulated with 120mm fibre-glass between two 1,000-gram polythene covers

- Twin-fan ventilation systems designed to give accurate and fully automatic environmental control in the growing tunnels

- Cooling systems with specially designed 6-row cooling coil

- Control equipment giving temperature and humidity readings on a digital display unit

- CO_2 meters complete with water separator, piping and filters

- Production supplies — thermometers, watering and harvesting equipment.

Exhibit 4: Profile — Ronnie Wilson

In October 1994, Monaghan Mushrooms purchased Britain's second-largest mushroom producer, Middlebrook Farms, for an undisclosed sum. The deal should increase Monaghan Mushroom's annual turnover, currently estimated at £50 million, by about 40 per cent, and its successful completion has transformed Ronnie Wilson into one of the major players in the £400 million British and Irish mushroom market. Most Irish companies would have made quite a hullabaloo about such a deal, but that is not Mr. Wilson's style. The negotiations and sale of Middlebrook, which has its headquarters at Avon, south of Bristol, were completed in secret and when news of the deal broke Mr Wilson declined to comment. Some Irish agriculture sources were surprised by the Middlebrook deal as the UK company is a direct employer, and operates large commercial farms. It would appear to be exactly the sort of operation that Mr. Wilson and Monaghan out-manoeuvred in the 1980s.

In stereotypical Ulsterman fashion Ronnie Wilson says very little and generally keeps himself to himself. He is reputed to be a straight talker and a shrewd but tough negotiator. According to colleagues, he is a workaholic who adopts a hands-on approach to everything,. One said that his only problem may be delegating responsibility, and letting go sufficiently to allow himself time to explore other directions. Until quite recently the soft-spoken Mr Wilson met his growers on a regular basis, but he has now handed over the day-to-day running of the mushroom business to his management team. While the humble mushroom has made him a great deal of money, the former school teacher has a lifestyle that belies his wealth. Ronnie Wilson is rarely interviewed, even more rarely photographed, and could conceivably be termed Ireland's most reclusive businessman. He still lives in Tyholland, Co. Monaghan, with the company's compost and processing facilities within sight of his front door.

During its 15 years in business, the turnover and profits of Monaghan Mushrooms have never been revealed. With annual sales of £50 million, market analysts believe that the company generates profits of about £3 million a year. The actual ownership of Pleroma, the holding company which owns Monaghan and Middlebrook, is also a matter of some conjecture. It is known that Mr Wilson, who is its chief executive, holds a majority stake in the company while a substantial minority stake, thought to be about 20 per cent, is held by Mercury Asset Management, the investment arm of the British merchant bank S.G. Warburg. The Scottish businessman Mr Joe Barber, who is the chairman of Pleroma, is also believed to have a stake in the company.

In the early 1990s Monaghan bought competitors Foxfield of Cavan and Kernans of Armagh, which had a combined turnover of £21 million. Ronnie Wilson entered the pig-processing market in February 1994 with the purchase of the troubled Uniport group and he now spends most of his time at its headquarters in Cookstown, Co. Tyrone. Mr Wilson has a strategic vision to expand Pleroma into a broad-based food company, and he is reported to be interested in purchasing the former Tunney Meats plant in Clones. He was also part of a consortium that made a failed bid for Leckpatrick Dairies which was bought by Golden Vale.

Source: Adapted from O'Kane, 1994.

Exhibit 5: An Bord Glas, Hygiene Awards

The National Auditing Programme and the Second National Hygiene Awards

Mushroom Unit Assessment
The following is the assessment checklist against which your mushroom unit will be assessed. No marking will occur until the third assessment visit. Marks will be allocated on the basis of standards achieved in each category (overall category marks indicated). A minimum mark will need to be achieved in each category before consideration can be given for inclusion in awards.

Cropping Tunnel Practices (30 per cent)
- Prefilling
- Filling
- Casting
- Pre-cropping
- Cropping/Picking
- Emptying
- Equipment.

Hygiene/Quality (45 per cent)
- Personnel
- Premises
- Picking/Packing Equipment
- Handling Produce
- General.

Records (10 per cent)

Crop Production (15 per cent)
- Uses and Practices

Exhibit 6: Irish Pound Performance on Financial Markets, 1992–93

EMS stability was dramatically shaken in September 1992 when sterling and the lira left the Exchange Rate Mechanism (ERM) and, along with the Spanish Peseta, were devalued. It is estimated that well over a billion pounds left Irish financial markets in a few days. The Central Bank's external reserves fell nearly £2 billion, from £3.05 billion at the end of August to £1.07 billion at the end of September.

There were four phases in the management of the Irish pound exchange rate during 1992 and early 1993. The first, from January to May, was a period of relative exchange-rate stability. During the second phase, from June to mid-September, tensions in the European Monetary System (EMS) resulted in sizeable negative foreign exchange interventions and higher interest rates in support of the Irish currency. The third phase was from mid-September to January 1993, during which time here was intermittent severe pressure on the Irish pound. Over this period, the external reserves were depleted, the EMS support system was extensively utilised and domestic liquidity conditions tightened significantly as pressures on the currency culminated in a realignment of the Irish pound with the ERM on 30 January 1993. The final phase — February to April 1993 — was marked by a significant improvement in sentiment in the foreign exchange and money markets. Before the end of March, interest rates were reduced below pre-crisis levels, outstanding debts for market support were repaid and the external reserves were rebuilt.

Sterling had always been the Achilles' heel of Ireland's EMS policy. The view of foreign investors was that the Irish pound was susceptible to devaluation during periods of sterling weakness — the devaluation of the Irish pound in 1983 and 1986 provided ample justification. Hence, when Sterling devalued in September 1992, foreign investors withdrew their funds from Ireland in order to avoid incurring a capital loss. However, contrary to the earlier episodes, the Central Bank decided in September 1992 not to devalue but, instead, to raise interest rates to defend the exchange rate.

Since a devaluation in 1986, the Irish government had pursued a policy of fixing the Irish pound in the EMS band in order to keep interest rates and inflation close to the German levels. The government was intent on sticking to this policy despite the sterling depreciation. There was a danger, of course, that the loss of competitiveness associated with the sterling devaluation would reduce Irish exports and increase imports.

In order to compensate for this, the government introduced a "market development fund" which paid IR£50 per job per week to firms affected by the devaluation of sterling. This fund was intended to be only a temporary measure as it was expected that sterling would appreciate in the near future and the trading difficulties facing Irish firms would disappear. In the event, the UK pound did not appreciate within the expected time-span, leading to the forecast by one commentator that the market development fund was designed to "prove unworkable and effective".

Source: Leddin, 1992.

References

Central Bank of Ireland (1993): *Annual Report 1992* (incorporating *Quarterly Bulletin*, Summer 1993), Dublin: Central Bank.

Leddin, Anthony, J. (1992): "Unemployment and EMS Membership", *Labour Market Review*, Winter, Dublin: Training and Employment Authority.

Murphy, Colm (1994): "Horticultural plan looks to UK market", *Sunday Tribune*, 5 June.

Mushroom News (1993): 1(3): Dublin: An Bord Glas.

Mushroom News (1994): 2(1), (2) and (3): Dublin: An Bord Glas.

O'Kane, Paul (1994): "Mushrooming Millions", (Profile/Ronnie Wilson), "Business This Week", *The Irish Times*, 14 October.

Teagasc (1994): *A Strategy for Horticultural Development*, Dublin: Teagasc.

3

The Independent Radio Sector in Ireland

Thomas N. Garavan and Carole Hogan

Origins of Radio in Ireland

Radio, as a mass medium, began in the USA in the 1920s. Thousands of American companies began broadcasting on the airwaves as no entry barriers, rules or regulations existed. Soon every frequency on the airwaves was occupied. Broadcasting in Europe subsequently developed differently as the American experience highlighted that this new form of mass media required some form of regulation. This was evidenced in the UK, where the British government decided that a broadcasting monopoly controlled by the State should be put into place. To this end, the British Broadcasting Corporation (BBC) was founded. Its monopoly of the airwaves remained in place until 1973, when independent radio was established under contract to the Independent Broadcasting Authority.

Even in the initial stages, the debate between public and private ownership dominated in Ireland. The government of the day wavered between inviting Irish companies to form an independent private Irish broadcasting company with commercial backing on the one hand, the other option being a model that would be owned by the government, modelled on the BBC. This centralised model viewed radio as being "a medium that would educate, inform and entertain". A special Committee of the Dáil desired State control of broadcasting and maintained that "broadcasting should be a State service purely, the installation and working of which was to be solely in the hands of the postal ministry". On the other hand, the Radio Association of Ireland believed that should broadcasting "get in the hands of government officials, it would eventually get wound up in red tape". However the government of the day opted for centralisation and so a broadcasting monopoly, which was to last for over 60 years, began on 1 January 1926. Its status was further confirmed by the passing of the Wireless Telegraph Act 1926.

The State service, 2RN, began broadcasting from Dublin. The Government was determined from the outset that the station should be self-financing, primarily through the sale of advertising space on the station. There were difficulties initially, due to the reluctance of advertisers to sponsor programmes that catered for minority interests only, such as classical music and Irish language programmes which, at the time, dominated 2RN. Advertisers looked instead to the more popular formula of jazz and swing music to sell their products.

The station subsequently changed its name to Radio Éireann and then to RTE Radio 1, after the introduction of Radio 2 in 1979. Radio 2 (called 2FM from 1989, when it was relaunched) was introduced by RTE to provide a change from the talk show format of Radio 1 and to provide a legal answer to the pirate radio stations that had mushroomed throughout Ireland in the early 1970s.

The early 2RN provided "listeners" with an almost undiluted diet of live music, with the remainder of programming consisting of foreign languages, gardening tips and just five minutes of news each morning. The formative 2RN was also very Dublin-based. However, with the appointment of the innovative Dr. T.J. Kiernan as director in 1935, this slowly changed. He foresaw that in order to win more listeners outside Dublin, the radio station would have to reflect the lives and views of people living in towns and villages throughout the country. Kiernan's "regional scheme", which saw him take to the country armed with a microphone, could be said to be the forerunner of community or local radio. The 1960s saw the introduction of mobile recording units which further improved the range and quality of regional broadcasting.

When the pirate radio stations began to emerge, Radio 1 was the only Irish radio station in existence and was incapable of catering for the diverse needs and interests of the nation at that time. The increasingly youthful market meant that, by the 1970s, Radio Éireann's programming was completely at odds with its audience. Pirate radio dominated the scene from 1977. In 1978 there were an estimated 25 pirate stations operating all over the country. When Radio 2 came on air in 1979, the pirates were well established and even Radio 2 could not compete with the superpirates — Nova and Sunshine.

The Introduction of Legislation

It soon became clear that a legal local alternative to RTE was needed. The 1980s saw various attempts by different governments to lay a foundation for the introduction of legal local radio. The 1981 Independent Local Radio Authority Bill and the 1985 Local Radio Bill were two such efforts.

Much of the debate in the run-up to the introduction of legal local radio centred on the public versus private debate. In a decade that witnessed many general elections, leanings towards either model changed with the government. Eventually the Fianna Fáil government decided the issue, stating that Ireland no longer needed the State to lay down in detail what the public could have in its radio broadcasting service.

In 1988, the Broadcasting and Wireless Telegraphy Act and the Sound Broadcasting Act provided for the establishment of national commercial radio and television stations and the franchising of sound broadcasting services at local level.

The Independent Radio and Television Commission (IRTC) was established to oversee independent broadcasting in Ireland. Twenty-five independent local radio stations and one national station were licensed to broadcast. Only 21 have survived to date and Century, the national commercial station, went into liquidation in 1991. The IRTC conducts spot-checks in order to assess standards and to ensure that the statutory provisions relating to advertising, news and current affairs are being observed. The independent stations are limited to a maximum of 10 minutes advertising per hour (as specified by Section 10 of the 1988 Broadcasting Act).

The Governing Bodies

The Independent Radio and Television Commission (IRTC) was established under the Radio and Television Act 1988. Its institutional importance was stressed by the appointment of a retired Supreme Court judge as the first Chairman. Other members were drawn from broadcasting, entertainment, business and trade union spheres. The IRTC applied primarily economic criteria in judging applicants for new licences — requiring applicants to produce a detailed two-year business plan when making submissions for licences. This plan had to include market analysis and outline the incomes and expenditures expected for the period of the plan. Candidates granted a licence must comply with detailed regulations. The most important of these is that 20 per cent of transmission time is allocated to news and current affairs.

Ownership of stations by other stations (cross-ownership) is limited to 25 per cent of voting shares. This restriction on cross-ownership applies to holdings by local and national newspapers, communications companies and political and religious groups. For the local radio stations this has proved to be a limiting factor due to the high fixed initial costs of starting a station (estimated at a minimum of £300,000).

Initially 26 licences were issued. The proverbial "settling-down period" led to the closing of three stations and the reluctant merger of two further stations. While the individual stations changed blueprints and adjusted their objectives, the IRTC refused to allow investment requirements to be met by other stations. Attempts in 1990 by Capital and 98FM in to invest in Century and Galway Bay FM respectively were blocked.

Listenership Levels of Independent Radio in Ireland

Listenership levels and a station's market share are very important. The full potential and power of radio in terms of advertising has yet to be explored in Ireland. FM104 has carried out research into the recall of slogans from advertisements and concluded that radio as an advertising medium is "very powerful". This is certainly accurate as Irish people, traditionally, listen to more radio than our UK counterparts.

In the UK, national radio has a weekly reach of 30–35 per cent of the adult population. RTE Radio 1 reaches 85 per cent of adults in Ireland. In terms of advertising, UK radio gets less than 2 per cent of the revenue cake; in Ireland a comparative figure is around 15 per cent.

How are listenership and market share measured? To enable each station gain some insight into its market share and listenership, the IRTC commissions the Market Research Bureau of Ireland (MRBI) to undertake six-monthly surveys, referred to as the Joint National Listenership Research (JNLR). These results are published in March and August annually and, at the end of every year, figures are compiled for that year. The figures are classified by age, sex, class, country, etc. for different times during the day and for weekends. Two important criteria reported are listenership (the percentage of people who confirm listening to a particular radio station the previous day) and market share (the percentage of the market that a particular radio station has in a certain region).

The August 1995 JNLR/MRBI Report provided some good news for the independent radio sector, indicating that over half of the adult population tune into a local radio station daily.

In terms of listenership, just under half of the independent stations included in the survey increased their audience in 1995. Nationally, the combined independent sector had a listenership of 51 per cent, compared to RTE Radio 1 at 37 per cent and 2FM at 28 per cent. In terms of market share, the independent sector has consistently increased its share to a level of 43 per cent in 1995, compared with RTE Radio 1 at 35 per cent and 2FM at 21 per cent. In 1995, 12 of the 20 independent stations included in the JNLR/MRBI survey increased their market share, and 13 showed the highest rating in their franchise area.

Stations on the western seaboard enjoy high listenership levels, largely because the national stations do not put much emphasis on this part of the country. Highland Radio in Donegal has the highest listenership levels in Ireland at 64 per cent and Kerry Radio the second highest at 59 per cent.

Local radio really comes into its own in the afternoons and especially after 7 pm. RTE's national market share falls considerably after 7 pm, when independent radio has 64 per cent combined market share, while RTE has approximately 36 per cent.

RTE still has the highest listenership throughout the country. In its literature RTE claims that Radio 1 is by far the most popular radio station in Ireland, with the most listened-to programmes being hosted by top name presenters (Gay Byrne, Marian Finucane). These programmes boast audience levels that are unmatched in almost every other European country. 2FM still maintains its position as Ireland's most listened-to music station. The pattern of presenter popularity experienced by Radio 1 is again evident with the big name presenters attracting the largest audiences.

Advertising in Independent Radio

Since its inception, independent radio has had a difficult task convincing national advertisers that it could command a comparable audience to RTE. This is one of the main reasons suggested for Century Radio's failure.

Century promised too much in the way of audience listenership and advertisers bought it — for a while. When Century came on air, it had only 15 per cent listenership compared to the 25–30 per cent promised. Advertisers' belief in independent radio was seriously undermined as a result.

Listener loyalty is reflected in advertising sales. Independent radio stations derive their income principally from advertising revenue, with sponsorship growing in importance. Some observers believe that the entire independent local radio sector currently earns between £11 and £12 million of national advertising on an annualised basis. There was an average growth of 9 per cent in the advertising and sponsorship income of independent radio stations during 1994. Total revenue for the year amounted to £19.7 million. Approximately 52 per cent of total revenue came from national/agency sales, with the balance made up of direct sales.

How is advertising on local radio managed? A percentage of advertising, which differs for each station, comes from advertising agencies and through Independent Radio Sales (IRS). The remainder, which is generally local, is produced in-house by the individual stations themselves.

In 1991, the IRTC sought submissions for the appointment of a single advertising sales company that would introduce a centralised direct sales bureau. AIRTIME was subsequently appointed and it set up "Independent Radio Sales" (IRS). IRS operates as follows: Advertising agencies give IRS details of their "spend" for a particular company's product/service and IRS advises the agency how to spend the money to achieve the maximum effect.

The managing director of IRS, Don Harris, estimates that over 50 per cent of independent radio advertising goes through IRS. He maintains that IRS has been important in establishing advertising success for local stations. He believes that collective action and networking is very important among local stations, to enable them compete successfully with the might of RTE.

What Is Local Radio?

What exactly is local radio? Is there a formula for success? According to a brochure for one of the stations, LMFM, "local radio is the most immediate source of information available for those interested in what is happening in their local area". Local radio is seen as an increasingly important means of communications. Therefore a key objective of local radio can be taken to be the provision of a good local news service and coverage of items and issues that are of local concern.

The Dublin-based perception is that rural independent local stations are "ear-to-ear" Country and Irish music and death notices. However, the daily recitation of death notices and other items of local interest make good business sense. Research shows that the death notices segment has very high listenership levels — because it provides what the listeners want.

The question of whether a local radio station can be made to work depends on its ability to attract an audience. Radio Kerry is a model local station in this regard, because it reflects the lives of its listeners, enables them to communicate, entertains and informs, and is thus successful in both broadcasting and commercial terms. The chief executive of Radio Kerry, Dan Collins, believes that the strength of local radio is the very fact that it is local — neighbour talking to neighbour.

What is clear is that there is no one formula for success. Des Whelan of Waterford's WLR attributes his station's success to a concentration on local news and speech. Michael Moriarty, chief executive of CKR (Carlow/Laois Local Radio, located in Kilkenny) attributes the success of his station to the fact that it is personality-led and not just a "talking clock".

However, just being a "talking clock" works for some stations like FM 104, where its mixture of brash news programmes and high music content has ensured the station's success by attracting big audiences. The same formula seems to be working for 98FM, which also has a high music content and a "fast food" news service.

However, Radio 3, a station based in the Offaly region, tried this formula initially but failed to make an impression. Michael O'Donnell, a consultant to local radio stations, attributes this failure to the fact that, by broadcasting continuous chart music to a rural audience, the station was not providing the listeners with what they wanted — thus ensuring failure. The station has subsequently been reformatted and now caters for local issues, news and for both middle-of-the-road and Irish music. As a result, more people are now tuning in.

The provision of the right mix of programming for the target audience seems to be the key to success for the local radio stations. There is no magic formula — ingredients for success vary from station to station. While 50 per cent news and current affairs content works well for Radio Kerry, for another station it may prove disastrous. In general, the music-led stations in Dublin, Cork and Galway are complemented by the more locally focused elements.

The end result is that all these various formats have given rise to a rich and varied mix of programme styles around the country, each designed to appeal to the different communities' special needs and, whatever the format, it seems that local radio is becoming part of the fabric of Irish country and city life.

Psuedo-local?

Local radio is also here to stay according to Michael O'Donnell, when he says of local radio: "People want it. A good local radio is as vital to the community of the nineties as good roads and telecommunications."

Just how local are the independent radio stations? Seamus White carried out a study estimating the degree to which local stations in Ireland can justifiably be titled "local". He took a sample of three stations — North West Radio (NWR), LMFM and 92FM Dublin — recording and analysing their output on a given day. In the absence of any criteria against which stations could be compared and justify being called local, White used the criteria set out in the 1988 Radio and Television Act. These criteria attempted to create a local radio system which would have a wide range and type of programme appealing to a large variety of tastes (including minority), and which would be "recognisably local and supported by the community".

White's findings led him conclude that programmes on NWR and LMFM, which did cater for tastes other than the target audience (minority interests), which supported Irish music, or which reflected particularly local concerns, were exceptions to the rule. In the case of 92FM, White critically announced their programming as consisting almost entirely of wall-to-wall music, "fast food" news, interspersed with meaningless continuity. He concluded that 92FM had nothing "local" about it and was critical of the fact that the IRTC has no regulations and rules regarding programming content.

He sees the local radio stations, instead of breaking RTE's monopoly, creating a monopoly themselves in their local areas. As such, he believes that they should be compelled by law to reflect the interests of, and provide programming for, all groups in their area to justify being called local.

Many commentators, in defence of the IRTC, point out that each station is different and that a single set of rules for all local stations would neither be practical nor in the best interests of local stations. The very essence of local radio is that it reflects the needs of its franchise area. Thus a rural population in Donegal would have different needs to a population with a high proportion of urban listeners. As such, the IRTC approves each station's programme schedule on an individual basis, looking for such items as the provision of local news, local issues and other matters of interest to that particular franchise area.

Local radio, unlike RTE, does not receive any State money or any slice of the licence fee. RTE, as the State-sponsored broadcasting organisation, is therefore clearly in a much better position to give the public a wide range of programming, and to cater for minority interests than the independent local stations. However, many commentators feel that local radio should provide much the same service as the public broadcaster.

The advent of Community Radio (there are currently 11 licences) may go some way towards alleviating some commentators' concern that local radio stations are not local enough in their orientation. The aim of community radio is specifically to be "radio by the community for the community". It will operate on a volunteer/part-time basis, will be non-profit making and take very little or no advertisement revenue.

At the end of the day, the question of whether/which local radio can be made to work depends on its ability to attract an audience. In turn, its ability to attract an audience depends on the needs and desires of a station's audience regarding programming and the fulfilment of those needs. Research appears to be the key. According to FM104's chief executive, FM104 is a very consumer-led business which spends an enormous amount on research in order to ascertain the exact needs of its audience. He says:

> For example, if research shows that an audience wants to hear four hours of Gregorian Chant, that's what the audience will be given. FM104's mixture of brash new programmes and music is reaching its biggest audience ever and is making money. After all, local radio stations are commercial in nature as well as being local.

Future Developments

There are many ongoing issues that will affect local radio and its development. One of the main factors is the Green Paper on Broadcasting, which indicates that it will provide for a viable future for the local independent stations.

The IRTC would like to see financial support for both the development of an independent national news service to supply the local stations and also to help stations in the West of Ireland which, because of their terrain, have higher transmission costs than stations situated in flatter areas.

The stations themselves would love to get a slice of the licence fee. Clare FM manager, John O'Flaherty, believes that this would put the local radio stations on a more "level playing field" with RTE and would go some way towards enabling local stations to improve programming content and competitiveness. For a sector that depends almost totally on advertising revenue for its income, these measures would be most welcome. If something is not done towards improving the financial position of local stations, the Clare FM manager believes there will be mergers among stations. Another possibility may be networking. This would involve stations sharing programmes as part of a cost-cutting exercise.

The future could also see the movement of radio into the satellite arena. Already, Radio Limerick has begun broadcasting on the Astra satellite, beaming its programmes into homes all over Europe. 98FM recently announced that it was to deliver its news service via Astra satellite.

Nonetheless most commentators agree that local radio is here to stay. Celine Craig of the IRTC is in no doubt on this issue. She maintains that, over the last five years, local radio has established and consolidated its position in the local community, providing an important service and, as such, will definitely remain. Craig believes that mergers will only occur only if commercial interests dictate, a point also expressed by the Clare FM manager. Craig is, however, more optimistic as regards the financial future of the stations, pointing out that at present up to 75 per cent of local stations are making profits. However, the question of whether local radio will survive will depend very much on its ability to serve and reflect the needs of its listeners in its programme content.

The most significant development in 1997 is undoubtedly the launch in March of Radio Ireland. Stepping into the gap left by the collapse of Century, Radio Ireland hopes to challenge RTE's domination at the national level. Despite its well-publicised teething problems (particularly the dismissal of chief executive Dan Collins a month before the launch), the station was launched on St. Patrick's Day. Its survival and success remains to be seen, but will certainly depend on the station management and programmers learning from the costly mistakes of Century.

4

Riverdance

Barra Ó Cinnéide

Introduction

The story behind this case study began with the hosting of the 39th annual Eurovision Song Contest at the Point Theatre in Dublin in 1994. A music/dance sequence of less than seven minutes' duration, *Riverdance*, which was specially commissioned by RTE as an interval presentation for the song contest, has become the most discussed artistic/cultural topic in Ireland since the production was networked on television screens worldwide in April 1994.

For instance, the lead dancers in the *Riverdance* performance, Jean Butler and Michael Flatley, received the Performance of the Year accolade at the National Entertainment Awards presented at the National Concert Hall, Dublin in December 1994. Interestingly, the panel of over 40 professional adjudicators, although making at least four nominations in each of the 10 other categories designated for awards in the performing arts, unanimously selected the Eurovision item as the outstanding Irish performance of 1994.

Riverdance, as one commentator (Courtney, 1994) rather irreverently reported, was:

> . . . originally meant to be a Eurovision space filler — an entertaining diversion while the judges made up their minds which piece of sub-pop drivel would be given the exaggerated title of best song.

Ironically, therefore, the Eurovision Song Contest, one of the main showpieces of pop music, has been responsible for the wide-ranging debate that ensued on whether a new cultural art form had been created or whether was it a mere "showbiz extravaganza". (Ireland had hosted the Eurovision Song Contest on three previous occasions — 1971, 1981 and 1993 — with Dublin as the venue for all but the last year, when Millstreet, Co. Cork became the first non-urban centre ever to stage the song contest. On that occasion, a local entrepreneur,

Noel C. Duggan, succeeded in attracting the event to his small rural village by offering RTE free use of his £4 million horse show arena (see Chapter 10). Subsequently *National Geographic* featured Noel C. in a leader article on Ireland, pointing out that his Green Glen arena was not exactly donated *gratis*, with confirmation, as it were, that "there's no business like (horse) show business".

> He made sure that participants from 25 nations would each begin with the same greeting "Good Evening Millstreet" — a promotional mantra going out from his backwater to 300 million television viewers world-wide (Conniff, 1994).)

Bill Whelan, Composer

In 1992, Ireland participated in the World Fair held in Seville, Spain. The Irish government was committed to presenting an appealing national image to the world, but more particularly to a Spanish audience. A programme of cultural events was staged at the Irish Pavilion, including a new musical piece, *Seville Suite*, from the Limerick-born composer, Bill Whelan. It is not surprising, perhaps, that Spanish strains were entwined in *Seville Suite*, and that the theatrical production became a fusion of Flamenco and Irish dance styles.

After initial consideration of the need to develop an imaginative sequence to serve as an attractive intermission feature for the 1994 Eurovision Song Contest, the RTE production group, under Moya Doherty, took a decision to contact Bill Whelan to discuss the possibility of composing an original musical piece which would illustrate Irish culture for an international audience, while ensuring a high entertainment value. It was hoped that, within the given brief, it would prove possible to capture an aquatic theme. It had been decided to interlace the three-hour-long Eurovision programme with many video inserts of riverside aspects of Ireland's capital city, bearing in mind the Point Theatre's location on the banks of the River Liffey, at Dublin port.

Bill Whelan wrote the musical score for *Riverdance*, which was performed by the RTE Concert Orchestra conducted by Noel Keleghan.

The *"Riverdance"*

Although the Eurovision feature item contained a troupe of 20 dancers, most attention has been directed at the performance of the lead duo, Jean Butler and Michael Flatley, as, for instance, in the following media comments:

> Combined with Bill Whelan's music, the machine-gun feet of Michael Flatley and Jean Butler conjured up visions of a mystic

and proud nationality, and re-awakened a Celtic revival, providing a fast, sexy link between our dissolving heritage and the genius of a pure pop moment. So *Riverdance* has taken its place in Irish folk history, with a rush of national pride — up there with U2 who conquered the globe in the eighties.

Besides the attractions of *Riverdance*'s supercharged dance routines and Whelan's twilight music, there is also the sexual chemistry on stage between Flatley and Butler. Back at Eurovision, their open interpretation of Irish dancing won acclaim, but the smouldering intensity of parts of the performance was also applauded. Flatley says:

"When Jean and I saw the piece, we started to realise that that energy was there and we tried to go ahead and develop it. It just seemed to happen. We didn't purposefully go out and say, let's look sexy; it came out a lot more sexy that night than we'd ever planned, that's for sure, and I think it will be developed to a further extent with the up-coming "*Riverdance* — The Show". I think people need that chemistry: they want to see a show that's exciting and entertaining, that has a little bit of sex, a little bit of lovingness and a little bit of everything. Most of all, they need to come away feeling they've been entertained and go home happy" (Corr, 1994).

Similarly, in an otherwise controversial piece in his "Second Opinion" column, *Irish Times* journalist Kevin Courtney extols the artistry of *Riverdance*:

The dancing is breathtaking, and from the moment that Jean Butler emerges in her sexy black number and makes those precisely-placed kicks, you're hooked. When Michael Flatley bounds on-stage like a dervish, playing the mischievous Pan, tempting the dancers out of their staid routines and into something altogether more devilish, you feel a mixture of fear and liberation. By the end of the dance, nothing less than wild abandon could be the appropriate response (Courtney, 1994).

Michael Flatley, described by the National Geographic Society, following his appearance in New York with The Chieftains, as "a living treasure", is a twice-world-champion Irish flute player, a Golden Gloves boxing champion, a master-level chess player and a member of Mensa (with an IQ of 170). A repertoire of Flatley's flute music was released on Son Records.

Although equal credit has been given to the lead dancers, media coverage has centred on the male partner, as in the following commentary (Corr, 1994):

Flatley clocks 28 taps a second and he's performed in Carnegie Hall, NY, the Moulin Rouge, Paris and the Hollywood Bowl, LA. Not bad for the boy who was sent home from his first dancing class at eleven years old because the teacher thought he was starting too late. He's a perfectionist; he likes to work for many hours until he finds it comfortable but still challenging. He is characteristically modest about his own combination of ballet, tap, Flamenco, and Irish. He says:

> "My dancing is a mixture of many different styles. I've incorporated some Flamenco, a little bit of tap, but more than anything, I guess I've accelerated a form of Irish tap dancing and a little ballet with arm work."

Anúna

For most viewers, perhaps, the orchestral music and the dance sequences overshadowed the performance of the other main artistic contributors to the Eurovision interlude, Anúna, the Celtic Chamber Choir based in Dublin. The group's name is derived from the Irish "An Uaithne" which has many interpretations — several of which seem appropriate: "joining together", "concordance in verse", and "green". Anúna has been dedicated to three ancient types of Irish music: "Suantraí" (lullaby), "Geantraí" (happy song) and "Goltraí" (lament) and has a commitment ". . . to raise interest in the vast quantity of Irish music which is ignored by the general listener" (Corr, 1994).

Although Eurovision provided an unexpected promotional breakthrough for the group, Anúna had already released two best-selling albums — *Anúna* and *Innovation*. At the National Entertainment Awards ceremony held in Dublin in December 1994, Anúna was adjudicated to be the top classical group for its performance during 1994, including its choral contribution to *Riverdance*. Several media commentators have referred to the fact that, generally, the euphoric analysis of the Eurovision intermission piece gave insufficient acknowledgement to Anúna's contribution — particularly the part played by the lead singer, Katie McMahon, who was given no credit whatsoever on the sleeve of the best-selling *Riverdance* audio and video. The following extracts from an article based on an interview with Michael McGlynn, Anúna's 30-year-old founder, composer and arranger, provides an opportunity to assess the group's contribution to the *Riverdance* "happening" and McGlynn's vision of the future:

> Now and then, amid the morass of mediocrity that these days passes for music, there surfaces a sound which is so sublime it immediately reminds one of poetry, purity and perfection. The voice of Katie McMahon could be thus described, particularly as

set against the accompanying voices of Anúna in the opening section of *Riverdance*, which itself was probably the musical highlight of 1994. However, as with the way in which *Riverdance* evolves, the relatively sparse vocal lines created by Anúna were undoubtedly overshadowed by the more sexy and spectacular talents of dancers Jean Butler and Michael Flatley. Happily, no such distraction exists on Anúna's latest album, *Innovation*, which is one of the most surprising musical highlights of the year (Jackson, 1994).

Michael McGlynn says:

> In order to do anything new, you have to have a certain fire burning in you and see the end product before you start. Therefore to try to develop something like Anúna so that it becomes commercially viable and artistically satisfying, you sometimes have to reach so far ahead of the people around you that it can appear arrogant (Courtney, 1994).

Does McGlynn ever feel that *Riverdance* has become a dead-weight around the neck of Anúna? This could be particularly so in their concerts, which probably peak for many people after that particular piece of music is performed.

> We don't perform the opening section in isolation very often, because people do tend to associate *Riverdance* with the actual studio recording and that sound is difficult to recreate in an acoustic space like a church. But in some respects, yes, people do think of Anúna only in terms of *Riverdance*. Yet when you're carried along on something as positive as that, you can't really complain, can you? I mean, let's face it, our work is highly specialised and compared with similar groups in other countries, we now are selling huge amounts of product, directly as a result of *Riverdance* (Jackson, 1994).

On the other hand, isn't there also the danger that Anúna will now yield to the commercial pressures that arise from shifting large amounts of product and sell out on their original aesthetic — especially as fashioned on their first album? On hearing his relatively esoteric collection of neglected choral works and originals, Elvis Costello reportedly said to McGlynn:

> Even though you mightn't sell as many records, don't change what you do. You've got a vision, don't compromise. (Jackson, 1994)

McGlynn replies:

No. Indeed, "Innovation" is an indication of how we are not going to compromise. I once played an original version of that album for record company people in America and they said, "You can't release that here, no one will buy it because there isn't anything to latch on to". I said: "So you think I should add what? Synthesisers and drums?" They replied: "No, melodic structure people can tune into. If you make yourself too distant from your audience you will alienate them." And they were right! (Jackson, 1994).

In line with the aquatic theme of the Eurovision piece, Michael McGlynn stated in the same *Irish Times* interview that he regarded his art as a river of sound flowing directly from God as a potential means of transcendence.

That is what Anúna is all about, absolutely. If I didn't feel we were creating something beyond what we are, then I wouldn't bother doing it at all (Jackson, 1994).

Post-Mortem on *Riverdance*

Post-Eurovision, most critiques, even including the irreverent "Second Opinion" piece referred to above (Courtney, 1994), were effusive in their praise of the actual *Riverdance* performance. For example:

This year, *Riverdance* came to represent all things to all Irishmen and Irishwomen. Could it be the unofficial national anthem? Well why not, considering some of the claims made on behalf of the piece's potency? It stemmed the Great Irish Diaspora, embracing our ethnic communities, worldwide, it has done more for national pride than a generation of political leaders; and it might even settle the national debt! (Corr, 1994).

Public acclaim of *Riverdance* was demonstrated by sales of audio and video recordings of the Eurovision performance. Immediately on its release, soon after Eurovision, *Riverdance* became the best-selling single in Ireland for 18 weeks and, by the year-end, it had been charted in the "Top 30" ratings continuously for 33 weeks. All proceeds from the video sales were donated to the Irish Rwanda Relief Fund.

Following the *Riverdance* presentation at the end of the year in London at the Royal Command Performance, it reached the number 17 position in the UK singles rankings at the beginning of 1995, having entered the charts a few weeks before Christmas. It was broadcast on *Top of the Pops* on BBC1 television on 12 January 1995.

Adverse Comments on *Riverdance*

However, not all responded enthusiastically to what seemed to be an emerging *Riverdance* cult. A controversial article — "Go Dance in the Lake, *Riverdance*" (Courtney, 1994) — provided an adversarial view of its long-term impact on the Irish arts/culture scene:

> I've had *Riverdance* up to my neck. It has opened the floodgates for a deluge of widely sycophantic articles discussing the possible ripple effects of *Riverdance* on Irish dancing, in particular, and Irish culture in general. If the papers, including *The Irish Times*, were to be believed, *Riverdance* had dragged a once-staid art form kicking and screaming into the modern world. Might I respectfully suggest that *Riverdance* has also shoved Irish dancing unceremoniously into the realm of showbiz?
>
> When *Riverdance* exploded on to the stage, it was a pleasant distraction, a late rally for a show which had sagged progressively after a promising opening sequence. Nobody could possibly have been thinking while watching the piece that they were witnessing a seismic event in Irish cultural history, could they? Nobody sat there dizzy from watching Michael Flatley's startling dance routine and shouted, "all is changed, changed utterly!". I suspect all that came later, when the scribes sat down and dampened their quills for the big cultural rewrite.
>
> Please don't get me wrong: *Riverdance* is an excellent piece which is well-written, well-choreographed and perfectly-paced, with a superbly-executed climax. It's a fine piece of popular entertainment, and certainly deserves its place in modern Irish culture. The music is haunting, evocative, with echoes of traditional, classical and new age, and reminiscent of the best Irish music from The Chieftains to Enya. It's certainly a lot better than "Rock 'n Roll Kids" [Eurovision winner].
>
> But let's get our feet back on the ground here. Just because something is well-performed — and *Riverdance* is among the best performances you'll see in any genre this year — doesn't mean we should adopt it as some national symbol of artistic freedom, a metaphor for a changing vision of Ireland at the millennium's close.
>
> It's Irish dancing with a dash of Broadway, and it's done as well as you would expect from two of the finest professionals in the business. Irish Americans Flatley and Butler have not returned to Ireland to find their roots, but to borrow a piece of national history and incorporate it into a clever dance routine.
>
> They haven't exactly plundered our heritage, but neither do they hold the key to it. They're like a Torvil and Dean of Irish dance, slick and professional, showy and hugely talented, but with a marked showbiz streak.

Gala Events as Springboards for Artistic/Cultural Promotion

In seeking some explanation for what transpired following the Point Theatre performance, it is interesting to note that, in recent times, at globally screened events such as the World Cup Finals ("Italia '90", for example) and the 1992 Barcelona Olympic Games, host nations have introduced indigenous forms of the performing arts that have tried to illustrate features of their country's culture — for example, the much-extolled performance by José Carreras, Placido Domingo and Luciano Pavarotti on 7 July 1990 to celebrate the World Cup Final event in Rome. This "musical intermission" spawned a series of highly successful operatic audio and video recordings. The audio recording of what has become known as "The Three Tenors in Concert" has popularised the talents of Carreras, Domingo and Pavarotti to an unprecedented level, with the Italia '90 performance becoming the world No. 1 classical best-seller, attaining sales of over 10 million with a highly successful follow-up "Three Tenors" album that, by the end of 1994, had sold 7 million copies.

Strategy literature indicates that two broad categories of stimulatory influences — "push" and "pull" factors — can be the inspiration for initiating ventures. Although there have been many instances of new ventures being developed from "push" influences, there is general agreement among the marketing fraternity that "pull" factors emanating from the marketplace are the most likely to lead to traditional business success. Responding to the "pull" factors of the market is the philosophy underlying one of marketing's basic tenets — the marketing concept — which extols customer orientation, as distinct from doing what is considered best from the producers' viewpoint.

Usually, however, the organisers of major events such as Italia '90 do not undertake market research to discover customer preferences and do not seem to have availed of opportunities to pre-test the prospective product with sample audiences. So it might be claimed, justifiably, that the "push" orientation predominates normally since little is really known about the "dark side" of performing arts — the "pull"/demand factors!

The difficulties of pre-testing gala performances, intended as one-off spectacular events, can be understood. However, in the case of traditional theatre, it is quite common for new productions to be tested, first in the provinces, or as our American colleagues might say "off Broadway", before bringing the final versions to the major venues, for example the West End.

With the television mega-events that have included specially commissioned items, the producers have usually been innovative with the particular theatrical pieces but have engaged "superstar" performers to ensure that there will be audience attention and acceptance of the novelty of the presentation. It could be said, perhaps, that in such instances the "halo effect" of television operates, whereby the medium is so powerful that audiences can come to accept that if a star performer is involved the artistic piece itself must be high calibre.

Riverdance's Compatibility with Traditional Irish Dancing

Post-*Riverdance*, a major controversy arose regarding the challenges it posed for traditional Irish dancing.

Towards the end of the last century, dancing had become an increasingly important component of Irish folk culture as a result of popularisation of nationalist traditions with the Gaelic revival, but this particular indigenous art form had been developed in an unorganised, non-regulated manner. In 1929, Conradh na Gaeilge (Gaelic League), which had been responsible for much of the earlier cultural renaissance, established Coimisiún le Rincí Gaelacha (Irish Dance Commission) to regulate the then lawless Irish dancing world. This organisation laid down strict rules in relation to teaching practices and standards, and is now the controlling body in regard to all official Irish dancing championships which, because of large-scale emigration patterns over generations, are major events among the global ethnic communities, or what has become known in the media as the Great Irish Diaspora embracing Britain, North America and Australia.

Although the Coimisiún is the only organisation controlling and promoting Irish dancing worldwide, Comhdháil Múinteoirí na Rincí Gaelacha (Association of Irish Dance Teachers) has existed since 1969 as a result of an acrimonious teacher-led rift within the Coimisiún. By comparison with the Coimisiún, the Comhdháil's membership is confined mostly to Ireland.

The following extracts from an *Irish Times* article (McNally, 1994) indicate that, amongst the Irish dancing fraternity, there was divided opinion on aspects of the staging of *Riverdance*, even if the artistry of the Eurovision spectacle seemed to be universally acclaimed. What did Conradh na Gaeilge think of *Riverdance*? Séamus MacConuladh, chief executive of the Coimisiún, answers:

> Fantastic. As far as I'm concerned it did a hell of a lot of good for Irish dancing. It has given it a profile where for so long it was a poor relation. I think it has provided a great platform, not for competition, but for one of the directions in which dance should be going. It was a piece of music with Irish dance steps, like drama with Irish dancing.

Others, Séamus MacConuladh accepts, were less sure of the event:

Some people, especially those who'd achieved success in competition, didn't like the fact that there was an outside choreographer involved, and I think there was a feeling that this might represent a bastardisation of Irish dancing. It's probably fair to say that there may have been an element of jealousy involved because, whereas Michael Flatley is a former world champion, Jean Butler was still involved in competition and finished fourth in this year's World Championships.

For their part, Comhdháil personnel felt that Irish dancers were unfairly eclipsed in the event.

The Coimisiún was involved in the *Riverdance* project almost from the very start. The body's vice-president, Séamus O Sé, and his wife, Anne, through the O Sé School of Dancing, provided 17 of the Eurovision troupe.

Grainne McCormack is assistant secretary of Comhdháil Múinteoirí na Rincí Gaelacha. She, and her husband Martin Fay of The Chieftains, are parents of two multiple All-Ireland champions, and they eventually withdrew their daughter from the *Riverdance* line-up because of misgivings. Grainne McCormack says:

> Personally, I thought that *Riverdance* was wonderful. You can ask any of the teachers, and they will tell you it was brilliant. But my argument is that they had to bring in outside dancers. Our All-Ireland championships were on that weekend and there were any number of accomplished dancers on display. Michael Flatley and Jean Butler are two very nice people, but we felt that, by comparison, the Irish dancers were being taken for granted. They were asked for 80 hours of rehearsal and they seemed to be expected to do it for nothing at first. I know they did eventually get a fee. It is not just people in dancing who feel this way. I've spoken to others who were surprised that Irish children didn't get a chance to show what they could do. At the very least, I think that backing dancers could have been given more to do.

Sexuality is unlikely to invade competitive dancing in the near future, according to Comhdháil secretary, Bernie Downey:

> We have contact dances of course, like the two-handed reel, but the dancers never look at each other. There's no strict rule on eye contact, but you have to bear in mind that 90 per cent of Irish dancing is done by children, so I don't think you could have that flirtation bit, seen in the interpretative section. It is not so long ago since all the senior girls had to wear black tights. If we'd done something like *Riverdance*, a few years ago, we'd have had the bishop after us.

Bernie Downey is annoyed that RTE's undoubted triumph on Eurovision night was tinged with some triumphalism. She says:

> A lot could be done if you had a budget like *Riverdance* had. We
> have never had the opportunity to do something like that. We've
> always felt that RTE looked down its nose at Irish dancing.
> Irish dancing is alive, today, because all of us ordinary teachers
> kept it alive, doing the classes in all areas and all weathers,
> every night of the week. I certainly object to the notion that this
> was the awakening of Irish dancing. If there was nothing there
> to begin with, you couldn't waken it.

So, although the advent of *Riverdance* provoked a vigorous discussion
on several issues, it was inevitable, perhaps, that the major debate
seemed to concern its implications for the strict application of traditional Irish dance conventions. In particular, the stiffness of the
dancers' arms, so conventionally ingrained in Irish dancing, and
flouted by Flatley and Butler, was the subject of much debate. With
the imposition of strict standards since 1929 by the Coimisiún, the
potential for personal interpretation and expression with a dance
routine was all but foregone.

In this context, it is ironic, perhaps, that in the January 1994 issue
of Coimisiún le Rincí Gaelacha's magazine, *Céim*, the cover photo-
graph showed a young girl dancing with hands on hips at a local Feis
in Co. Antrim in 1906. This, of course, was in the era preceding the
formulation of the strict dance standards by the Coimisiún. Both
dance bodies, the Coimisiún and Comhdháil, are quick to stress that,
while competition etiquette requires the arms to be kept at the sides,
they should not be held stiffly, but neither organisation is prepared to
forego the tradition, as these quotations from the *Irish Times* article,
referred to previously (McNally, 1994), confirm. Séamus MacConuladh, chief executive of the Coimisiún says:

> I suspect that it developed from teachers telling kids not to have
> their arms all over the place. Kids, especially beginners, tend to
> have a very rigid distorted style, and they would be encouraged
> to let their arms hang naturally.

Séamus O Sé, vice-president of the Coimisiún, points out that the
backing dancers in *Riverdance* might have had arm movements:

> But they themselves rebelled against it because they felt more
> comfortable with the traditional way. In any case, with so many
> dancers, if you had everybody waving arms, it would look like
> *Oklahoma*.

In a radio interview in January 1995, Moya Doherty (Doherty, 1994) indicated that in advance of Eurovision RTE received a considerable number of high-level approaches from "lobby groups" expressing concern on what were seen to be prospective dangers to the purity of Irish dance. She said that it seemed antagonists felt that the Eurovision piece would be culturally degenerate — "with the fear that it would spawn a form of Irish 'dirty dancing'", she added jocularly.

A debate was initiated in the "Letters to the Editor" column of *The Irish Times* on the hands-by-the-side posture which is not unique to Ireland, since it is the format adopted in some Breton dancing, another traditional Celtic form of culture. It is interesting that developing arm movement is part of the exploration of dance in Siamsa Tíre, the Irish folk theatre group based in Tralee, which concentrates on a dance idiom unique to its immediate region, North Kerry, under its artistic director, Fr Pat Aherne. He believes that increased travel and competition have combined to merge regional styles, introducing uniform standards like straight arms.

> I'm not decrying it — it's a lovely form in itself. But the old dance didn't have that rigid style. Hands did their own thing, and the whole body was in the dance. So, one of the things we're trying to do is to free it up, to see if the movement inherent in the dance is capable of adaptation, so long as it doesn't do violence to the art form. Foreign influences can be useful in drawing us out of ourselves, but the bottom line is that it has to be recognisable as Irish dancing.
>
> Siamsa Tíre has worked in the recent past with Bill Whelan, contributing one of the principal dancers in the *Seville Suite*, an earlier fusion of Flamenco and Irish dance, so the sexuality of *Riverdance* will not have taken Tralee by surprise. But seen in reviving its own Kerry tradition, the theatre is reclaiming Irish dancing as an adult pursuit (Hosey, 1992).

Siamsa Tíre

Literally speaking, "Siamsa Tíre" means "rural friendly gathering" or "country amusement". The Kerry-based organisation began its life in 1964 as an experiment to interest a group of young people in their native music and traditions. Its founder and director, Fr Pat Aherne, says:

> The guiding philosophy of Siamsa Tíre has remained constant over the years, namely to make accessible our culture and traditions, our music, song and dance through the medium of the theatre. It has developed from its early amateur status to having a small professional core company which regularly invites guest choreographers and directors to devise new shows (Hosey, 1992).

Siamsa Tíre has, over the years, evoked its share of criticism. Much of it, according to Colm Ó Briain, former Director of the Arts Council, stems from metropolitan envy at Siamsa Tíre's independent development and achievement, and the discomfort of an urban audience at a rural ethos and value system (Hosey, 1992). Some critics have deemed Siamsa to be folksy and slow to move away from the international successes of their early shows. Such critics contend that the company depicts rural Irish life as all sweetness and light, providing only an antiseptic view of Irish culture, which ignores the darker sides.

The following extract from Hosey's 1992 article provides insights into the role of Siamsa, with perspectives of its founder and a prospective vision of the company's future:

> Dance critic Carolyn Swift does not believe there is anything phoney or ornate about Siamsa Tíre. It is, she maintains, remarkably authentic and as our self-professed National Folk Theatre cannot be expected to fulfil the role of a national contemporary dance company. Further, Fr Pat Aherne adds, nostalgia is not necessarily an invalid way of looking at our past. His work with Siamsa Tíre over the years has grown out of a deep desire to share the traditions and culture he experienced growing up in the Ireland of his youth.
>
> For the future, all agreed that Siamsa Tíre must continue to explore the world of modern dance, based on the tradition of inviting new choreographers and directors to explore a wider world that will engage urban as well as rural themes. By combining the strength of tradition with the excitement of invention, Siamsa Tíre will continue to forge a National Folk Theatre of which we can be proud.

Since 1991, Siamsa Tíre has been based at the National Folk Theatre in Tralee, Co. Kerry. Conceived architecturally to provide aspects of a ring-fort structure, it is attractively situated beside the town park. Built at a cost of £1.5 million, it was opened by the then Taoiseach, Charles Haughey, in 1991.

Anticipating the Future of Irish Dance

Like the Liffey from which it derived its theme, *Riverdance* seems destined to surge onwards on its relentless way, as the following epilogue section suggests. Regardless of the destiny of *Riverdance* itself, however, it is useful to try to interpolate the potential culture/arts spin-off effects from media commentaries. In "Fast Forward", an *Irish Times* New Year Guide to the year ahead (Woodworth, 1994), the case was made that:

The arts in Ireland have probably never been more vibrant in almost every medium than they are today. But every renaissance needs patronage, and contemporary Irish arts activity has shot upwards and outwards on a suicidally narrow funding base.

One of the major gaps identified by this commentator was the absence of a national dance company. Interestingly, State support may be close at hand — for purely pragmatic reasons rather than for laudable cultural considerations, since the arts have been officially recognised by the new Government in December 1994 as part of an overall strategy of job creation. It is significant that the former French culture minister Jack Lang, dubbed "Monsieur Fun" because of his efforts to popularise the arts, emerged as a leading Socialist contender to contest the 1995 French presidential elections (Allen-Mills, 1994). The media have commented favourably on the artistic vision of the Irish "Monsieur Fun", Michael D. Higgins (Finlan, 1994), Minister for Arts, Culture and the Gaeltacht. Perhaps *Riverdance*'s success will encourage him to ensure that this form of the performing arts is officially recognised and, more importantly, properly endowed.

With tongue in cheek (perhaps), the "Go Jump in the Lake, *Riverdance*" article (Courtney, 1994) attempts to foresee the future in the following vein:

> What can we expect when the year 2000 comes? *Riverdance Part II, or Return to the Crossroads*? How about "Comhaltas Ceoltóirí *Riverdance*", where you can study both the history and the theory of *Riverdance*, along with the céilís and set dancing?
>
> Or perhaps, *Riverdance* will enter the school curriculum with young people eager to try out this new, sexy arm-viewing eye-contact version of Irish dance? Will the Taoiseach of the day open a new *Riverdance* Summer School, with the immortal words "we've been dancing with the yoke of repression for too long — it's time to wave those arms and be free!" *Riverdance* would become a symbol for Ireland's long awaited psychological independence (Courtney, 1994).

An Epilogue: *Riverdance* — The Show

Following its Eurovision début, *Riverdance* was developed as a theatrical production in its own right — *"Riverdance – The Show"* — again held in Dublin's Point Theatre for 20 performances in February 1995.

In January 1995, Moya Doherty (Doherty, 1995) gave an indicator of the immediate future for *Riverdance* when she announced that, owing to public demand, it had been decided to extend *Riverdance* — The Show to run for a further week, and that West End and Broadway angels, theatre benefactors and sponsors and impresarios were being invited to see the show.

The following advance comments (Corr, 1994) on the show give interesting insights into the evolutionary process that can apply in the performing arts:

> In the new show, *Riverdance* — The Show, Whelan's original tale of Butler and Flatley as embodiments of water and land evolves into a journey where the main players learn to love each other and their surroundings on an even higher level. Flatley explains:
>
> "The show we did (for Eurovision) at the Point was really a teaser. There's not an awful lot I'm in a position to disclose right now about the stage show, but I can say that it gets an awful lot more heated up. It will be a little bit plainer to see what came before *Riverdance* and what comes after *Riverdance*. I think people will be surprised by the number of influences we bring in this time."

Those influences included the skills of tap dancers Marcel Peneux and renowned Spanish dancer Maria Pages, along with a dance troupe from Russia, tap-dancers from England and Spanish Flamenco dancers. Flatley did not want to get excited too soon, though *Riverdance* — The Show had the potential to hit the bright lights of New York. He picked his words carefully (Corr, 1994):

> I believe that there is room in the marketplace for an artists' show like *Riverdance*. I'm absolutely certain with the number of people involved, the hard work and the expertise that we have that we can bring *Riverdance* to the top. We're certainly considering an awful lot of things, even *Riverdance* — the Movie. I would imagine if the show is successful after the opening night, the powers that are driving it would be prepared to take the next obvious step, which would be touring and/or movies. We want to take what we've done to another level and showcase a new flavour of what this particular form of Irish art has."

Particular features of the stage presentation have been the star performances of the two Irish-Americans, Michael Flatley and Jean Butler, and the originality of the former's choreography for the show. Unfortunately, due to a dispute over his "intellectual property" rights and his "appearance fees", Michael Flatley was abruptly dismissed from *Riverdance* in October 1995 and lauched his own show, *Lord of the Dance*, in July 1996. But, as they say in Irish, "sin scéal eile".

APPENDIX 1: *RIVERDANCE* CREDITS
Riverdance
EUROVISION SONG CONTEST
The Point Theatre, Dublin, April 1994

CREDITS
* Music composed and produced by **Bill Whelan**
* Guest dancers and Irish dance choreography: **Michael Flatley/Jean Butler**
* Dance troupe: **The Eurovision Irish Dancers**
* Choreography: **Mavis Ascott**
* Assistant choreographer: **Belinda Murphy**
* Choir: **Anúna** — Lead singer: **Katie McMahon**: Directed/conducted by **Michael McGlynn**
* Orchestra: **RTE Concert Orchestra** — led by **Michael d'Arcy,** conducted by **Noel Keleghan**
* Eurovision production: **Moya Doherty**

Source: Listed credits for *Riverdance* video, augmented with acknowledgement to Katie McMahon, Anúna.

APPENDIX 2: LETTERS TO THE EDITOR

The Irish Times, Tuesday, 3 January 1995

Riverdance — The Show
Sir, when I started to read Kevin Courtney's piece on this subject (December 20th) I thought that at least there might be an
alternative critique. Regrettably it seemed only to be an extended statement as to how good the Eurovision "interval-filler"
was. Instead, might he not consider the claims made with regard to the sexiness of *Riverdance* and the novel use of hands as
contrasted with the tradition?

Obviously, traditional solo dancing has no arm movements.
Hands are usually by the sides — not a unique posture, as I
have seen the same in some Breton dancing. At the turn of the
century, one or both hands on the hip was a common posture
which in the case of girls enabled them to hoist their petticoats
and liberate their legs: which is why the arms direct your gaze
away.

Crucially, the art of Irish dance must be therefore to move the body and legs upwards without the aid of the arms to provide leverage. The requirement is for strong back muscles and a refined sense of balance. That is where the artistry lies. Traditional group dancing, in contrast, makes considerable use of the arms and hands. Typically a boy may hold one or both hands of his partner, entwining her body closely under his arm while her legs and feet move in unison and at the same angle.

They get close, but ideally never touch each other, except of course at their hands. It is in fact a subtle and elaborate form of tease. What was choreographed in *Riverdance* was almost the exact opposite. The use of arms and hands was at its most flamboyant when the two principals danced solo, but thereafter diminished. When the couple joined together, there was a brief moment of brush and explicit sexuality but very little interaction of arms. The ensemble dancers at the finale did not use their arms at all.

Riverdance was not, I suggest, a development of Irish dancing; if that was intended, then choreographer Mavis Ascott and the producers did not understand what they were dealing with. But did they claim it? It was, instead, an imaginative use of Irish traditional footwork, superbly performed by two graceful principals and by a talented but regrettably anonymous line of ensemble dancers.

Hopefully, The Show will be a development. I look forward to it. Yours, etc.

Gerard Murphy, Marley Avenue, Dublin

The Irish Times, Thursday, 5 January 1995

Dance in Ireland

Sir, Another year, another review of the arts, *Irish Times* critics "sorted out the great from the ghastly" for us in the visual arts, theatre, music, records, classical traditional, pop and jazz — but alas not a mention of dance. This is even more unforgivable given that 1994 produced an unprecedented amount of performance and a consequent rise in attendances (flying in the face of the recent *The Audience and the Arts* report, which could find no rise in attendances over the past 13 years).

Dance in Ireland has emerged from the dark years of axed companies, minuscule grants and scared producers, and this bullishness is reflected where it seems to matter most these days, in the box office. It has also given rise to a culture of contrition on the part of funding bodies. We have an Arts Council which has stated that it has treated dance poorly in the past, and it recognised that it needs to show positive discrimination towards dance in the future.

This culture seems also to be seeping into the media. Whilst there seems to have been no shortage of column inches spared for outlining the problems for dance, it would appear that little weight is thrown behind the art form within the overall arts coverage. A general review of the arts that omits dance is the clearest manifestation of this.

There's much evidence that the growth in 1994 will continue into 1995. Hopefully, this will include the nuzzling of dance into a holistic arts coverage in all the media. In the meantime, some positive discrimination might come in handy. Yours etc.

Michael Seaver, Editor, *Dance News Ireland*
65 Fitzwilliam Square, Dublin 2.

References

Allen-Mills, Tony (1994): "Monsieur Fun Joins Presidential Race", *The Sunday Times*, 18 December.

Conniff, Richard (1994): "Ireland on Fast Forward", *National Geographic*, 183(3), September: 16

Corr, Alan (1994): "*Riverdance* — The Musical", *RTE Guide*, 30 December: 8–9.

Courtney, Kevin (1994): "Go Jump in the Lake, *Riverdance*," in the "Second Opinion" column, *The Irish Times*, 20 December.

Doherty, Moya (1995): in interview with Caroline Erskine, *The Sunday Show*, RTE Radio, 8 January.

Finlan, Michael (1994): "Higgins May Be Let Frame Policy to Protect Heritage" in the "Out of the West" column, *The Irish Times*, 19 December.

Hosey, Seamus (1992): "Siamsa Tíre — Tradition at the Crossroads", *Dance News Ireland*, Spring: 3.

Jackson, Joe (1994): "Anúna: *Riverdance*'s River of Sound", *The Irish Times*, 23 December.

McNally, Frank (1994): "Ripples over *Riverdance*", *The Irish Times*, 15 June.

Ó Cinnéide, Barra (1993): "Noel C. Duggan — The Best is Yet to Come?", paper presented at European Foundation for Management Development Case Development Workshop, Paris, September; published also at the European Case Clearing House, Cranfield, UK with teaching notes (393-144-8).

Woodworth, Paddy (1994): "Michael D. Presents Portrait of the Artist as Poor and Short of Money" in "Fast Forward", *The Irish Times*, 29 December.

5

Irish Breeze

Barra Ó Cinnéide and Ambrose Downey

Introduction

A chance remark about an "Irish" product in California led to an entrepreneurial venture by a Co. Cork woman, Peggy Connolly, on her return to Ireland in 1985. The remark concerned a soap product with an Irish name which was very popular in California. However, on further investigation, Peggy found that, in fact, the soap was manufactured in America (see Appendix 1). Determined to bring this to the attention of an Irish soap manufacturer, she brought back a sample only to find that no equivalent soap was manufactured in Ireland. Surprised at this obvious gap in the market, Peggy set about redressing the situation and, today, her product, Irish Breeze, is establishing itself in the Irish soap market.

Once she had fleshed out the project idea, she approached the IDA (Industrial Development Authority) and received a feasibility study grant. She then went to the Irish Goods Council to find out about other soap manufacturers and spent hours in the library of EOLAS (the State's Science and Technology agency, now incorporated in Forbairt), researching recipes for her potential product. "I knew nothing about soap when I started," she says.

She was amazed to discover that the public is extremely particular when it comes to soap. Irish people like soap which is lightly perfumed — about 1 per cent per tablet. The Americans, by comparison, like their soap to have 10 per cent perfume and they like it to come in giant-sized bars. Colour is also important. White is the most popular, then comes pink, and green runs a poor third although increasing in popularity since the introduction of avocado-coloured bathroom suites. Shape too, is important — people hate soap that goes mushy, so considerable time was spent researching a new soap shape and Irish Breeze developed a special design using Italian technology.

According to Peggy Connolly, her project could have died when her study showed that it was not feasible to establish a costly plant in

Ireland without a strong market presence first. "I decided that if the plan was going to die, it would die in America and not in Ireland," she says. Convinced that she could corner a share of the market, she went back to California and revisited the supermarkets and drugstores where she had seen the Irish soap. She got the names of the stores' head-office buyers and telephoned them.

> I got through to secretaries who told me to call back in three weeks or three months, sometimes, but I persisted and told them that I was only visiting the US for a short time and it worked. My accent certainly helped. They knew I was Irish straight away, which did me no harm. They could see I had a genuine product and, in a way, I was getting in on the coat tails of the other so-called "Irish" soap.

Her assessment, however, following an initial feasibility study, was that it would be extremely difficult for her to go ahead with her planned dream, given the heavy capital investment such a project would necessitate and bearing in mind the small size of the Irish market. Undaunted, she returned to the US and did the rounds there with a prototype of the product. It was well-received and the idea of subcontracting emerged as a solution to the problem of manufacturing. With the help of the Irish Goods Council, Peggy Connolly found an international cosmetic company based in Ireland that was willing to make the soap on a subcontract basis for her.

> I have been very lucky to find a company which is already making exclusive soaps for export. The company has the most modern technology which produces very high quality soap.

Distribution is handled nationwide by Gillespie & Co. Irish Breeze now employs 13 people and plans are afoot to enlarge the business further. Peggy Connolly has spent considerable time on research, gaining an in-depth knowledge of the soap industry. Visits to soap manufacturers and discussions with suppliers in several countries followed, until she satisfied herself that she had sufficient background knowledge of the industry. Having negotiated the manufacture and distribution of Irish Breeze through the recognised producer, she undertook the dual roles of marketing the soap and looking after the administration of the business.

The initial challenge for Peggy was to establish her product in the marketplace. With the IDA, the "Young Ireland Movement" and AIB Group (Ireland's largest retail bank) all aiding the promotion, and with many households conscious of the "Buy Irish" campaign, sales of the soap rose dramatically. Guesting at seminars and promotions also helped. A great boost was her appearance on one of Ireland's most

popular TV programmes, the *Late Late Show*, which dealt with the theme of Enterprise. As part of a panel of successful Irish people, Peggy was able to promote the soap to a wide audience which soon brought increased demand at home and interest from abroad.

Superquinn stores in Dublin organised a special reception for recent "Great Irish Success Stories", which included Irish Breeze. As their salute to these successes they exhibited many life-size posters of business personalities and their products in all their stores and on billboards at transportation sites in Dublin.

Peggy Connolly, keen to exploit the overseas potential of Ireland's imagery, philosophises about the future of the business:

> Having done so well in Ireland, the obvious expansion must be into export markets. Germany and America are two countries that have shown interest in Irish Breeze. I am also about to launch a range of shower gels, thus increasing the scope of the business.

However, due to the increase in the demand for Irish Breeze at home, Peggy felt it necessary to postpone initial thoughts of overseas development in order to consolidate her efforts on the domestic market.

Looking back on the progress of the company, Peggy Connolly says that if she had not left Ireland she would never have succeeded in getting the idea off the ground. The spirit of optimism in America, and the competitive spirit there, was a definite spur. In retrospect, she realises too, her timing was appropriate, although the enterprise was conceived and launched in the middle of a sharp recession. But, in a sense, she says the company's success was born out of the recession.

> There was a lot of goodwill around and people were receptive to products. In particular, mothers of secondary school children were very emotional about it. They wanted to see the establishment of jobs, here, that would mean a better future for their own children.

Peggy Connolly says she is angry at the apathy that exists in Ireland, with so many basic commodity products being imported that could be replaced. She would like to see many more people following her example. Peggy Connolly makes it all sound very easy — one suspects she has a flair for that too!

Why "Irish Breeze"? As Peggy explained:

> We wanted to get a name that was firstly synonymous with Ireland and secondly illustrated the cleanliness and freshness of the product. Having listed many possibilities, we settled on

"Irish Breeze" and, on reflection, we are delighted with the success of both the name and the product.

The Enterprising Female

Peggy Connolly's achievement has demonstrated how a woman's insight can identify a market opportunity that a man might overlook. Her initiative and sense of enterprise confirm that women have an important contribution to make in the drive to promote new Irish-based industry. As part of a self-development process, she undertook a "Start your own business" course run by AnCo (now incorporated in FÁS), the Irish employment/training agency, and was "Student of the Year" on the course.

There has been a significant increase in the number of women setting up their own manufacturing enterprises in recent years, with more than one-third of small industry projects in 1994 being promoted by women, according to a spokesperson from Forbairt:

> The public campaigns to encourage women to set up their own firms and convince women of their potential as entrepreneurs had paid off in the clearest possible way. It is time to finally lay to rest the myth and stereotyping which seems to hold that only men go into manufacturing enterprises while women are "more suited" to the service sector.

(It is of interest that almost 75 per cent of women who contact the "Women in Business" freephone information service, backed up by a free nationwide business consultancy service, are interested in setting up businesses in the service area.) This trend is projected to continue, and the "equality barrier" could be broken over the coming years as more than half of the attendees at recent Forbairt Small Industry information and promotional seminars were female.

The "Women in Enterprise" Scholarship was funded and co-ordinated by the then Department of Industry and Commerce, Aer Lingus (Irish Airlines) and the IDA. The award scheme was based on the applications for IDA Feasibility Study grants to assist new business ideas. The annual winner receives a cash award of £2,000 together with Aer Lingus travel valued at £1,000 to research overseas markets.

Announcing that Peggy Connolly, a specialist teacher by training, was the 1987 winner, the then IDA managing director, Padraic White, said that her feasibility study had been chosen because of its innovative and professional approach to all aspects of setting up a business from production requirements to financing and marketing the product. Born of farming and fishing stock, on Cape Clear, off Baltimore, in West Cork, the closest brush Peggy Connolly had with business before this was running a Montessori class!

It had taken almost two years to bring her idea to fruition — Irish Breeze being officially launched in January 1987. At its launch, the product retailed in Ireland for between 30–35p per tablet. The project cost in the region of £16,000 to establish, with an IDA grant of £7,000 for machinery (a new mould was required) and £2,000 expended on the feasibility study. Peggy Connolly put up the remainder from savings and a small business loan from ICC (Industrial Credit Corporation), the State's industrial bank.

She is determined that the product will be a "national brand" that will:

> . . . give pride to our country and put money back into the economy. It just galled me to walk into a shop in the United States and see the soap "Irish Spring" which was actually made in America.

Peggy is determined to make money in the US and in Ireland with her Cork enterprise. Initially she felt that 3 per cent of the domestic market might be a realistic target in the short term, but support has convinced her to change that target to 10 per cent. "Young Ireland" agreed to assist Irish Breeze by creating nationwide awareness of the product through its 10,000 youth members and attempting to ensure that it is stocked throughout the country in both supermarkets and smaller retail outlets. An extensive distribution network would suit Peggy Connolly as she deliberately does not want to specialise in an ethnic product line, deciding instead to go for an everyday commodity soap.

Pointing to "stickability" as a vital ingredient in initiating an enterprise, she says that any business is difficult and one has to be particularly resourceful to be anyway successful:

> A lot of hard work has gone into establishing the enterprise. I gave up my Montessori school and devoted myself full-time to the venture, particularly in relation to testing and developing the product concept.

> You have to have a plan, the ability to get on with people and you need to believe you're going to succeed. It's all about hard work. You won't get anywhere without it.

She found an American agent who was surprised that she had managed to achieve a breakthrough with professional buyers by convincing them she meant business. Her agent already claims to have a market for her soap, not only in California, but coast-to-coast. "The prospects are for annual sales in the region of seven figures," Peggy

Connolly says. (See Appendix 2 for further background information on Irish Breeze.)

Appendix 1: Extract from the *Miami Herald*

> You can almost smell the blarney. Everything about the TV commercial spells I R I S H. There's a horse drawn cart, green hills, and the "young" man, who uses a pocket-knife to slice a sliver from the green-and-white soap, speaks with a brogue. The only thing about Irish Spring that isn't Irish is the product it-self. It is made by Colgate Palmolive Corp., in the United States.
>
> *Miami Herald*, June 21, 1987.

Appendix 2: Background Information on Irish Breeze

1. The Company

Corporate Status

Irish Breeze Ltd. is a private company incorporated under the Companies Act on 9 April, 1986.

Aim

Its aim is to produce hygiene products for the home market and for export to Europe and America. To this end it has registered its trade mark in Germany, Canada and the US, using a different brand name. It claims to be market-led with the objective of promoting a product range that will achieve a distinctive brand image. The company aims to give a choice of colours and fragrances in the commodity soap range, and also to establish a steady demand for dermatologically formulated soap for problem skins. Its shower gel range consists of two products with different formulations. Irish Breeze plans to target its products to specific sectors of the market. Its bath foam range gives customers alternative fragrance options.

2. Peggy Connolly

Her Profile

Peggy Connolly, the managing director, has become synonymous with Irish Breeze, and has succeeded in generating a high profile as an entrepreneur. By recounting her success story through the media, she has managed to focus valuable attention on Irish Breeze products.

Awards

Peggy has won many awards for her achievements.

- *Adult Trainee of the Year* Award 1985/1986, presented by AnCo, now FÁS, for participation in a "Start your Own Business" course.

- *Women in Enterprise* Scholarship Award 1986/87 presented by the IDA, Aer Lingus and the Department of Industry and Commerce. This award was presented in recognition of her feasibility study on the soap market.

- *Checkout* Award for the outstanding "New Irish Company 1990", presented by the publisher of Ireland's major retailing magazine.

3. Irish Breeze Operations

The following details provide a "snapshot" of the company at an early stage of its development.

Finance

Capital equipment was bought through the aid of an IDA grant, and a term loan from ICC. The cash flow is augmented by an overdraft facility. Credit arrangements with suppliers and the distributor allow for sales revenue to be generated ahead of payment of purchases. Major costs include product development, packaging, promotions, carriage and travel. Ever-increasing calls are being made on the company's financial resources for its marketing communications endeavours, especially to test the effectiveness of above-the-line promotion — for example, outdoor advertising. It appears as if there is a high level of goodwill towards the Irish Breeze brand and, by stepping up advertising, it is believed that the market share can be doubled from 10 per cent to 20 per cent over two years.

Manufacture

The price per unit from the supplier has been arranged to include all manufacturing costs and, as such, while Irish Breeze has personnel indirectly employed in the manufacturing process, there are no financial commitments involved in this functional area.

Initially, it was intended in 1985 that Irish Breeze would supply the Irish market with a commodity toilet soap. Up to that point, all such soaps were imported. (It is believed that in the region of 2,000 tonnes of commodity soap are imported into Ireland annually.)

Irish Breeze sub-contracts its main manufacturing to Arlington Ltd., Portarlington, Co. Laois. This agreement is planned to continue until Irish Breeze has sufficient market share to manufacture its own products. Peggy Connolly concentrates on marketing, product development and new business generation.

Administration / Office Facilities

Administrative services are provided at the Connolly home. This arrangement has necessitated both physical and personal adaptation to the family setting. Facilities are provided rent-free, except for normal office maintenance and outgoings.

Product and Market Features

- The national launch of Irish Breeze occurred on 16 June 1987. It was announced that Irish Breeze had been established to create a new European product range, by adding a unique property to the soaps and bathroom toiletries, through developing a natural fragrance that communicates a message of green freshness.

- Manufacturing is undertaken by an automatic process in a modern soap plant, with a finishing line that is the property of Irish Breeze. The soaps are sold in both single units and value packs.

- The principal market is the family sector of the commodity soap market. The Irish Breeze trade name is now protected in several countries.

- The product range incorporates four different soap types with green, pink and white variations, and dermatologically-formulated soap. The dermatology range, which is allergy-tested, has achieved sales of 5,000 bars per month. The customer buying this product is not shopping around for variety but is potentially brand loyal, since "she has problem skin and sticks to what suits her", according to Peggy Connolly.

- Irish Breeze has 10 per cent of the soap market, with volume turnover of 1 million bars per year. The objective is to increase turnover within two to five years by 100–150 per cent in soaps only, from IR£200,000 to IR500,000. It is planned to build up a bathroom range, initially comprised of three fragrances, to match the soaps, and to add an Irish Beauty feature to make the products unique in Ireland and internationally. The bath additive market in Ireland is valued at £7 million. Irish Breeze plans to capture 20 per cent of that market in two years. The market for bath additives and shower gels is growing, while the soap market has matured and is segmenting.

- Irish Breeze believes it is now necessary to add value to products, introducing unique concepts to its range.

- To date, Irish Breeze has obtained its market share through in-store promotions and PR initiatives. Irish Breeze uses a national distributor, Gillespie & Co. Ltd. The main competitors are well-known multinationals such as Unilever, Proctor & Gamble and Colgate Palmolive.

- It is intended to use an advertising agency for new products and re-designed items in the range. The intended target audience is the 25–50 age group, especially those buying for the family. In undertaking market research, Irish Breeze has engaged a marketing consultant.

- According to Peggy Connolly:

  > The competitive advantage of our new products is that we offer the customer a property in the soap that is unique. It is tied into tradition and folklore, and it also introduces the customer to the purity of the environment by adding this distinctive property.

  > We have already proven that there is a demand for a quality Irish-made soap. We are now enhancing the soap and offering a complete range to complement the initial product items.

Source: Presentation by Peggy Connolly at the University of Limerick.

6

Kingspan Group plc

Thomas N. Garavan, Fergus Walsh and Mary Garavan

Introduction

Kingspan Group plc is an Irish building materials supplier whose main products — pre-engineered cladding systems and insulation products — are used in the exterior frame of industrial and commercial buildings. Kingspan commenced trading in 1970 and, by 1972, had 14 employees and a turnover of £100,000. The group continued to grow and received a stock market listing in 1989. By 1995, Kingspan had increased turnover to over £80m and its number of employees to 476 through strategic organic growth and acquisitions. The case is a good illustration of entrepreneurial activity.

History of Organisation

In 1960 Gene Murtagh commenced a five-year fitter apprenticeship with Gypsum Industries in Kingscourt, Co. Cavan. After four years, Gene left and joined General Steel Products (GSP) in Carrickmacross, Co. Monaghan as a draftsman, but spent most of the time supervising the installation of grain dryers all over the UK. After six months, he resigned as the company was going through financial difficulties.

In 1970, Gene and his friend, Lansy Carolan, received an IDA grant and set up a small workshop in Kingscourt and Kingspan became a registered company. Murtagh and Carolan had identified a market for waste disposal skips and became the principle fabricator in Ireland. Gene's brother, Brendan, saw potential in the business and joined him in 1972.

At that time, the outer cover of industrial buildings was constructed with galvanised or asbestos-cement roofing sheets and block walls. Gene believed that plastic-coated steel cladding was an effective alternative. The purlins (steel beams for supporting cladding) used in Ireland at the time were hot-rolled steel standard sections.

The Ward Group in the UK had developed a lighter and more efficient cold-rolled purlin section. Gene and Brendan went to visit the that the acquisition would supplement its existing range of products and enhance Kingspan's image in the panels market.

Kingspan made a failed take-over bid for Ward Group plc in May 1992. The acquisition of Ward would have, on the grounds of sheer scale alone, represented a major undertaking for Kingspan.

The main competitors in this area are PAB Profeil, Hoesch, Rome-kowski and Forge d'Aironville.

Thermal Insulation Division

In 1978, the insulation materials predominantly used in Ireland were fibreglass and cork. Rigid polyurethane insulation board was introduced to the Irish market by Plaschem and Celotex, both with manufacturing facilities in the UK.

In 1978, anticipating the future growth in products with thermal insulation properties, Kingspan contacted ICI to negotiate a technology transfer for the manufacturing of polyurethane insulation sheets. However, ICI's subsidiary, Coolag, which also manufactured polyurethane products, objected on the grounds that Kingspan could be a potential long-term threat to its position in the UK market.

In 1980, Kingspan purchased manufacturing equipment and technical advice from a company in San Antonio, Texas. Kevin Kidney was transferred from the Buildings Products Division to head up the new division. A manufacturing plant was commissioned in Castleblaney, Co. Monaghan in 1981. In 1982, Kingspan concentrated on the Irish market and made losses of £80,000 — primarily because the Irish construction industry was starting to go into decline. Kevin then went to the UK to investigate market opportunities there and soon he was exporting to the UK via the Birmingham Building Products office. In 1985 Kevin set up his own sales office.

A UK company, Torvale Group, based in Pembridge, decided to divest its insulation board division. In 1986 Kingspan acquired the assets for a sum of £350,000. The company, which had a turnover of £1 million per annum had manufactured acoustic insulation board unprofitably. One of the advantages of the Torvale acquisition was membership of the marketing organisation, BRUFMA (British Rigid Urethane Foam Manufacturers' Association). Sales in the UK mushroomed and, by 1988, Kingspan Insulation had a turnover of £3 million in the UK.

The UK base and membership of BRUFMA gave Kingspan more credibility in the market place. It was able to service demand quickly and was not dependent on shipping. Transport costs from Ireland were 10 per cent of UK sales but, from a UK base, fell to 5 per cent. Kingspan was also less exposed to exchange rate fluctuations from a UK base.

Ward brothers in Yorkshire. The Murtagh brothers became agents for the importation of purlins to Ireland. The relationship with the Wards was a major influence in developing the initial business culture within the Kingspan organisation. Plastic-coated cladding was also imported from Uniform Profiles in Wales for agricultural and industrial buildings. Eoin McCarthy had joined Kingspan in 1973 and, in 1976, the company began manufacturing purlins under licence from Ward. The company grew on the crest of the construction boom and the number of employees steadily increased to 100.

In 1978, Lansy decided to leave the group and ICC plc bought his share. Kingspan later purchased a purlin company in London, and Griffin Roll & Tool Ltd., a roll-forming firm for the automobile industry, in Birmingham. While both companies proved to be unprofitable, Griffin supplied the technological support for the rolling of cladding in Ireland. It was also a useful base for launching a subsequent entry into the UK.

The company established two subsidiaries — one in Ireland and one in the UK — to import and distribute farm machinery from the US. This was at a time when the Irish agricultural sector was about to experience some decline. The heavy equipment included combine harvesters which proved unsuitable for Irish conditions.

The Irish construction industry started to go into decline in 1981 and, by 1983, Kingspan was suffering major losses in its core construction business as well as in its diversified farm machinery business. The group's balance sheet showed the company to be technically insolvent. At this time the group owned companies in the following business areas:

- Cladding and purlin manufacture

- Mechanical and electrical contracting

- Structural steel fabrication

- Structural steel erection

- Insulation manufacture

- Agricultural machinery — importing and distributing

- Heating tank manufacture.

Major restructuring was called for. Many of the loss-making businesses were sold off, including the agricultural machinery and the structured steel fabrication business. All construction work ceased. The remaining business were divided into three divisions:

- Building Products Division

- Thermal Insulation Division

- Heating Products Division.

The profit-and-loss account showed an accumulated deficit of £3.7 million by the end of 1984. Financial restructuring was therefore required. £1.5 million of bank loans were converted to convertible (in certain circumstances) loan stock and an additional £1.5 million bank loan was secured which was interest-free for three years. Table 6.1 summarises the main activities in the three business areas between 1976 and 1994.

Table 6.1: Chronicle of Main Events — 1976 to 1994

Year	Building Components Division	Thermal Insulation Division	Heating Products Division
1976	Set up plant for manufacturing purlins and cladding in Ireland		Acquired GSP in Ireland
1977	Manufactured composite panels in Ireland		
1981		Set up manufacturing plant in Ireland	
1982		Exported to UK	
1983	Exported composite panels to UK		
1985		Acquired Torvale in UK	
1988	Set up composite panel manufacturing in Birmingham		Acquired Veha in Ireland
1990		Acquired Plaschem in UK	
1991	Acquired Integration AP in UK	Acquired Coolag in UK	
1992	Failed bid for Ward Group in UK		
1994	Moved manufacturing base from Birmingham to Holywell		Sold Veha to Barlo

Heating Components Division

In 1976, Gene's previous employer, General Steel Products (GSP), went into liquidation and Kingspan bought the company out of receivership. GSP manufactured steel storage tanks for the oil-based central heating market. With limited growth prospects in steel tanks, the company started manufacturing plastic storage tanks for domestic heating oil. Kingspan quickly developed a 50 per cent market share but, by 1989, there were ten manufacturers in Ireland primarily due to low entry costs and Kingspan was starting to lose its market share.

Veha, the Wicklow-based radiator manufacturer, had gone into receivership in 1986, after a long and bitter strike against the Dutch owners. In 1988, Kingspan acquired a 49.9 per cent interest in Veha for £1.25 million. The remaining 50.1 per cent was held by a consortium of Business Expansion Scheme (BES) investors.

In 1994 Kingspan sold its stake in Veha to Barlo, Veha's chief competitor. The sale was prompted by Barlo's resurgence and Kingspan's inability to achieve the economies of scale necessary to compete effectively in the radiator market.

Building Components Division

Kingspan commenced manufacturing trapezoidal plastic-coated single-skin cladding in Kingscourt, Co. Cavan in 1976 and in its Birmingham plant in 1979. However, this was a mature product and competition in Ireland and the UK was very strong.

Kingspan recognised that a major opportunity in the future would be cladding products with thermal insulation properties. This was given added impetus by the oil crisis in the late 1970s, and the resultant emphasis on energy conservation. The division commenced manufacturing double-skin insulated composite panels in Ireland in 1977 and, in 1983, it entered the UK market. The divisional director Eoin McCarthy, and his team quickly built up its market share in buoyant UK market by adopting strong production and sales-oriented strategies. In 1989, composite panel manufacturing facilities were established at Kingspan's plant in Birmingham. In 1993 Kingspan transferred its operations to a new custom-built location in Holywell, Wales.

Kingspan Building Products had expressed an interest in diversifying into the architectural panel business in 1988 because of higher added value. These products were high-technology products with design responsibility and warranty implications. Integrated Architectural Panels Ltd was a small company, based in Liverpool which manufactured medium- to high-specification architectural panels. Kingspan purchased the company for £550,000, envisaging

Kingspan acquired one of its main competitors, Plaschem, in June 1990. By December 1991 Kingspan had effectively gained control of the thermal insulation industry with the acquisition of another major competitor, Coolag (see above). The Coolag acquisition gave Kingspan increased access to the market and improved its image within the industry.

Kingspan Goes Public

In May 1989, the group joined the USM (Unlisted Securities Market) with a 4.3 million share placing at 76p (£3.3 million). The company had a market capitalisation value of £19.8 million. In an interview with *Aspect* magazine in June 1989, the Kingspan CEO and chairman, Gene Murtagh, when asked about the big losses to the Group in 1983 and 1984, replied:

> We got involved in the businesses then without giving them enough consideration. At this stage we have learned to walk around the hole rather than walk into it — that's for certain. It was possibly because some of the projects lacked market research or it was partly the timing. We got involved in farm machinery and made a diabolical mistake — the timing couldn't have been worse for us; had we done it two or three years before that it would have been a good decision. That is the "one big mistake" we made. Every other business has still continued as good business and expanded. The other businesses in the Group at that time were not strong enough to carry the error.

The new Kingspan Group plc was headed up by the following key individuals:

- Gene Murtagh: Founder of the Group and has served as group chief executive and chairman since the incorporation of the Company in 1970.

- Brendan Murtagh, B.Comm: Marketing director and deputy chairman joined the Group in 1972 and became a director in 1979. He is a member of the North East Regional Board of the IDA.

- Eoin McCarthy: Chief executive of Kingspan Building Components since 1973, with overall responsibility for the Group's building products activity in Ireland and the UK. He joined the Board in 1982.

- Dermot Mulvihill, FCA: Finance director and secretary. Joined the Group in November 1985. He was formerly a partner in Owens

Murray & Co., chartered accountants, and has been a director since 1986.

- Jim Paul: Joined the group board as executive director of corporate development in June 1990. He previously worked with Tarmac in the UK and Middle East and with the Ward Group in the UK and France.

- Kevin O'Connell, BE, MBA: A non-executive director, who joined the Board in 1983. He is a general manager of ICC, a director of ICC Corporate Finance United and other ICC subsidiaries of L&P Financial Trustees of Ireland Ltd.

The Strategic Development of Kingspan Plc

Kingspan's development from a small workshop in 1970 to a large publicly quoted company with a turnover of £82 million in 1995 emphasises that decisions are often made quickly, based on experience and intuition as well as through analysis. Kingspan's primary source of growth was by acquisitions bought abroad. However it did employ other strategies such as market development and lower cost manufacturing, but it was the acquisitions that were the most significant in developing Kingspan.

During the early years of Kingspan's existence there was little, if any, formal planning. The company was in its infancy and, therefore, had little money for expansion. This lack of capital was the dominant influence on strategy and the reason why Kingspan developed the way that it did. Manufacturing waste disposal skips, mechanical and electrical contracting and structural steel erections all had one thing in common — they all had low entry costs. Gene and Lansy had a working knowledge of these areas and knew, to a fair extent, what they were letting themselves in for.

Despite the absence of a plan, the two were employing sound business judgement — stick to what you know best, and invest as little capital as possible initially. Only the most basic of pre-acquisition research was completed when Kingspan took over General Steel Products in 1976. Gene had worked there, he saw potential, it was cheap, so they bought it — simple as that. GSP still is an important contributor to the group's profitability today.

Although no formalised strategies existed at the time, it would be wrong to think that the entrepreneurial venture drifted aimlessly through the 1970s into the 1980s. Senior management in Kingspan had a general direction in which they wanted the company to go. However, they were also prepared to follow other paths that would provide the capital necessary to attain this desired growth. For example, Kingspan made a fortune in structural steel. It got into the business at just the right time and gained a reputation for quality and workmanship. Although management were aware that this would be only a short-term success, they milked it for all it was worth and used the profits to fund expansion in the Cladding Division.

It was partly this desire to "make easy money" that led Kingspan into dealing with farm machinery — a decision that almost caused the company to collapse. When Kingspan acquired GSP, not only did GSP manufacture heating tanks, but it also produced a small range of farm machinery. Kingspan believed that agriculture in Ireland was going to boom, and so it decided to set up an importing and distributing company (Landman) in Ireland to import farm equipment from America. Moving into farm machinery was a critical mistake for the Kingspan management to make. Previously they had got away with minimal planning as they stayed within areas that they were familiar with, so they knew the underlying trends within the industry. Detailed research would have shown that the agriculture sector had reached its peak and was now about to go into serious decline. Management also seemed to overlook the fact that machinery suitable for the prairies of the United States would most certainly not suit the small, predominantly wet fields of Ireland. Large orders were placed with US manufacturers, but when these arrived in Ireland they soon realised that no customers had actually ordered them. To make matters worse, the punt/dollar exchange rate had plummeted in the meantime, so the machinery ended up costing much more than had been anticipated. Kingspan tried unsuccessfully to off-load Landman to the major agricultural dealers in Ireland. Despite the fact that all other areas of the business were holding their own, Landman was pulling the company into insolvency.

The major restructuring that took place in 1983 changed the nature of the company completely and introduced business-level strategic planning. Gone was all involvement with structural steel, all contracting work ceased, and there was to be no more dealing in farm machinery. The effect of this restructuring was to streamline the group into three strategic business units. Each of these units would be run by a Managing Director, who would also be a member of the company board.

Deciding which businesses to dispose of, and which to keep, did not prove to be a difficult decision to make. Management knew which areas of the business offered the greatest potential for development — the only reason that they stayed with structural steel or entered farm machinery was to provide finance for these areas. This was the first conscious attempt by management to adopt structural planning within the organisation.

Ideally, when Kingspan decided to restructure, resources should have been invested into formulating some sort of long-term strategy for the organisation. Instead the organisation merely seemed to have noted the mistakes it made and endeavoured not to repeat them again. This reflects the reality of running a small entrepreneurial business in the competitive marketplace. Management believed that they had enough problems at that time trying to get the group back on its feet without worrying about hypothetical future scenarios. Management style in Kingspan was very much "hands-on", so objectivity was not one of their characteristics. If Kingspan folded, the Murtaghs would lose their company and the local community, of which they were a part, would lose a major employer

Kingspan survived the restructuring and, in 1985, acquired Torvale in the UK. This was a good move. The Thermal Insulation Division had begun manufacturing in Ireland in 1981 and started exporting to England the following year. Torvale was a good base from which to attack the British market. Once the acquisition went through, Kingspan immediately set about bringing the company back to profitability. No integration plan was implemented with the result that there was a major clash of business cultures. It took a number of years before Torvale became part of the group.

Throughout the 1970s and 1980s the Heating Products Division had built up a dominant position in the market for heating tanks — both industrial and commercial. In 1988, Brendan Murtagh took control of this division with the view of expanding its interests in the heating product market. The decision to acquire Veha was opportunistic. There was no strategic planning involved. Although the synergy between manufacturing radiators and producing heating tanks is questionable, Brendan was keen to broaden the division's interests. Kingspan acquired a 49.9 per cent stake in Veha at a time when Barlo, its main competitor, was weak. In fact, Kingspan was at one time less than an hour from taking over Barlo when negotiations broke down. Barlo managed to recover, and soon Kingspan-Veha found itself trapped. The market for radiators is very competitive. In order to survive it is imperative that cost is kept to a minimum, through economies of scale in steel purchase, and a widespread manufacturing base which keeps transport costs down. Barlo had plants in Ireland, UK and the Continent, whereas Kingspan were fighting a losing battle from its one manufacturing base in Wicklow. With little chance of acquiring another manufacturing base and the costs associated with installing a new production line being very prohibitive. Kingspan sold its stake in Veha to Barlo in 1994.

The decision to go public in 1989 was a business decision aimed at providing the capital needed for expansion. This capital was then put to immediate use. Between January 1990 and July 1992 the group formed a joint venture with a Dutch distribution company, acquired two leading competitors (Plaschem and Coolag) through Kingspan's Thermal Insulation Division and engaged in a failed take-over bid for the Ward Group plc, a principal competitor of Kingspan's Building Products Division.

In Summer 1989, the Group's Board produced a corporate plan, which had its roots in the restructuring that took place in 1983. The fact that it took six years to create emphasises the realities of attempting to increase the role of strategic planning in an entrepreneurial organisation. The objectives of the plan were to:

- Improve co-ordination between divisions

- Ensure reasonable allocation of resources

- Achieve successful diversification

- Anticipate technological changes.

The Group's Board decided that "the number one component in the Group's strategic plan over the next five years must be to dominate the markets in which we have been market leaders and to become market leaders in the markets that, up to now, we have only been followers". They defined their business as the mass production of goods, using process technology and using steel and chemicals as raw materials, for all customers in the European construction industry. The Group's acquisition strategy was summarised as follows:

- Diversity by acquisition either into a market with which we are familiar or into industries that use technologies with which we are presently familiar.

- Any new markets we enter must have a potential of £100 million turnover.

- Geographic spread is important.

- In mainland Europe, it may be necessary to acquire distribution outlets to support exports from our existing manufacturing plants.

- Must improve EPS within 3 years.

- We must be able to improve the performance of the companies we acquire.

- An acquired company must have substantial market share, unless it is complementary to what we are doing.

- If the company acquired is outside our existing markets, it should be of a size that can support a full management structure.

The Group drew up a list of areas in which it was interested in making acquisitions and circulated this list to merchant banks and accountancy firms. The new product areas considered included partitions, cold-storage panels for food storage and processing, energy-efficient roofing, external insulation for refurbishment, architectural walling and ceilings and aluminium-framed window systems for commercial buildings.

A new planning system was put in place. The Group initially issued guidelines of expectations from each Division. The system worked in this way. The Divisions would prepare the next year's budget by October for approval by the Board. Each month the divisional managing director and the financial director would consult with Gene Murtagh and Dermot Mulvihill (group finance director) to assess progress. Quarterly strategic planning meetings were also held between the divisional functional directors and the Group Board. All capital expenditure had to be approved by the Group Board. There was no formal performance appraisal of divisional managing directors by the Group Board.

The lessons from the Torvale acquisition seemed to have been put to good use in the acquisition of Plaschem in 1990. A detailed pre-acquisition plan was produced, which paid dividends in the medium-term as the integration of the two cultures went smoothly. There was good strategic planning and this transformed Kingspan's position within the industry. In a short period it became the market leader.

Table 6.2: Competitive Position of Kingspan Group plc

Competitor	1989 % Market Share	1990 % Market Share	1995 % Profit Share
Coolag	28	25	n/a
Celotex	24	23	20
Plaschem	16	n/a	n/a
Kingspan	15	35	32
Others	17	17	14

The fact that Kingspan now researched and strategically planned their development much more so than previously may be attributed to the fact that Jim Paul joined the Group Board from Tarmac in 1990, becoming director of corporate development for the Group. Kingspan now seemed to be embracing corporate planning much more vigorously than previously.

In 1991, Tarmac plc was in serious financial trouble. In an attempt to rationalise, and reorganise, Tarmac decided to divest Coolag, a major competitor to Kingspan in the thermal insulation industry. Coolag had not seen Kingspan as a serious rival until after the take-over of Plaschem. Whereas Kingspan always had difficulty in convincing the industry of their quality, Coolag had a strong brand name that commanded premium prices in the market place.

In preparing the preliminary analysis for the Coolag acquisition, Kingspan management had:

- Compared the performance of Kingspan with Coolag and estimated market figures for the combined businesses.

- Identified synergy potential between Kingspan and Coolag using the value chain.

- Assessed the effects of the Coolag acquisition on competitive dynamics using Porter's framework for industry analysis.

- Identified the potential for organisational fit by using the "seven S" model (Structure, Strategy, Systems, Style, Staff, Skills and Shared values)

- Prepared an integration plan.

On 6 December 1991, the acquisition was complete. The strength of the Coolag brand was verified when Kingspan issued its product selector. Even though Kingspan Thermaboard was listed as the same price as Coolag standard roof board, there was no demand for Kingspan's identical product.

Kingspan Building Products Division entered the architectural panel market in 1991 by buying Integration AP. In contrast to the successful detailed planning that went into the Plaschem and Coolag acquisitions, Integration AP was not a success. Kingspan entered this sector blind, without identifying the competitive dynamics of the industry. Warranty costs for faulty work were considerable. Kingspan was trying to follow a low-cost strategy in a market where a quality orientation was required. There was also a lack of culture compatibility between the Building Products Division and Integration AP.

In 1992 Kingspan's role model, Ward Group plc, was in serious financial trouble. In June 1988, Ward had diversified away from its traditional businesses with drastic consequences. The Belgian company it acquired did not perform well, requiring considerable write-offs against a number of contracts totalling £20 million.

When Gene heard of the Ward Group's insolvency, he was shell-shocked. Gene's vision for Kingspan had always been to emulate Ward's efficiency and reputation as a quality supplier of building materials. The Ward operation had been admired within the Kingspan Group. Jim Paul had spent his formative years with the Wards. Gene was attracted by the excellent fit between Kingspan and Ward. The largest and most profitable part of the Ward operation was the

Building Components Division, which manufactured purlins, composite panels and cladding. The combination of the two businesses would provide market leadership in all these products in the UK and Ireland, and would create a business with the critical mass to penetrate Continental European markets. The acquisition would double the size of Kingspan in terms of both sales and profits. Overnight, the geographic spread of the Kingspan Group would be improved, with about 50 per cent of its sales in Europe, 40 per cent in the UK and 10 per cent in Ireland. Overall, the emotive element in acquiring the Ward Group was strong.

Kingspan made an initial bid of £12 million, and reduced this to £9 million after meeting the administrators and looking at the records. The required capital was as follows: inherited debt £4 million, redundancy cost £4 million and bid price £9 million. However, the bid failed.

The Future

In August 1992, a board meeting was called to prepare a five-year Corporate Plan. At this stage, the Group had decided to "focus on our present range of products", and "instead of product diversification to concentrate on international expansion". Kingspan had been eager to acquire a manufacturing base in Europe for some time. A joint venture with Kuiper van der Kooij in 1990 was to facilitate this planned expansion.

The historic development of Kingspan has been licensing, followed by manufacturing for the home market, and then entry, by acquisition, into the UK markets. It is, therefore, expected that Kingspan will acquire some small to medium-sized company, most likely in the Benelux countries, in the not-too-distant future. The decision to concentrate on international expansion would appear a prudent strategic move. The construction industry is cyclical, but downturns and upturns do not always occur simultaneously in different markets. Increasing its expansion in Europe would, therefore, shield Kingspan from recession in the UK or Irish markets. The decision to move Jim Paul to Germany to drive the development of the European market for Kingspan's products highlights just how determined Kingspan is to break its reliance on the UK market. It is indeed a measure of how well the mistakes of the past have been learned that Kingspan will not rush into any acquisitions. Management have been involved in quite a few negotiations in recent years with foreign companies, but no deals have yet been made.

Sources: Annual reports and interviews with company personnel.

7

The Irish National Lottery

Thomas N. Garavan and Anna Cunningham

Introduction

In March 1987 the National Lottery was launched by the then Taoiseach, Mr. Charles Haughey, T.D. Within 10 weeks, 82 per cent of the adult population had played the National Lottery instant games. After only nine months, ticket sales had reached £100 million, with an average of £1 million per week being paid out in prizes.

"Lotto" was launched in April 1988 in conjunction with the Instant Games. The turnover figure for both instant games and Lotto at the end of 1988 was £110 million. This achievement caused the Lottery world to sit up and take note. These figures suggested that 0.588 per cent of Gross Domestic Product was being spent on lottery products. When compared with the 28 North American lotteries (upon which Ireland's Lottery is based), Ireland ranked in tenth and eleventh place among lottery start-ups in the previous 5 years.

Ireland was merely a follower in its establishment of a lottery. Of the 10 countries with the largest economies, nine have government-sanctioned lotteries. It was investigation of the success of these lotteries abroad, and market research of different socio-economic groups in Ireland which indicated significant potential, that led the Irish Government to announce its approval in October 1984 in the White Paper, "Building on Reality". It was stated that a prime objective in establishing a lottery was to provide funding. However, due to pressure from other political groups, Section 5(1) of The National Lottery Act 1986 deemed that Lottery surpluses should be provided for:

- Sport/Youth/Recreation
- Health/Welfare
- Arts/Culture
- Irish Language
- Any other purpose as the government may determine from time to time.

The Act also provided for the creation of a State agency which would be the sole provider of lottery products. Under Section 3(1), the Minister for Finance was awarded the power to grant this sole licence which he gave to An Post in 1987 to be operated by its subsidiary, "An Post National Lottery Company". In providing a sole licence the Government established a monopoly. In the case of lottery products, other than those sold by the National Lottery, a £10,000 limit a week on total prizes was provided for under the Gaming and Lotteries Acts 1956, 1986. However, the National Lottery Act 1986 placed no cap on prizes to be awarded by the National Lottery. In doing so the Government allowed no real competition for its lottery products thereby enabling the National Lottery to provide a very attractive prize structure to the customer.

The Instant Games were launched in March 1987. This involved the player scratching a rubber latex section on the ticket which revealed instantly whether the ticket was a winner. These games now form 35 per cent of total sales for the National Lottery. Since 1987 the National Lottery has significantly expanded its product line and has provided variety to the player with the launch of over 56 instant games to the end of 1995. Table 7.1 gives an example of its product line.

The National Lottery has also raised the payout rate (gross percentage of revenue returned as prizes) from 42.4 per cent in 1987 to 54.2 per cent in 1994. This was done in a bid to produce more winners. It is estimated that, in 1994, there were 23 winners per minute and 33,000 winners per day.

The launch in September 1990 of the successful TV game show, "Winning Streak", with its grand prize element based on 3-star instant games, and prizes ranging from £5,000 to £250,000, was a major success and helped stimulate sales.

The Launch of Lotto

Lotto was launched in April 1988 and involved the player selecting six numbers from a field of 36. The jackpot was awarded to the player, or players, who selected the correct combination from the numbers drawn — additional prizes are also awarded to those who matched four or five numbers of the winning combination. Prizes were paid on a *pari-mutuel* basis, in which all the winners shared the prize pool in proportion to the amount bet. The coverage rate is the percentage of all combinations that a person covers when they play the "Lotto". It is a rate watched closely by the National Lottery since 1 minus the cover rate indicates the probability that there will be a winner. If there is no winner, the jackpot rolls over to merge with the

Table 7.1: Expanding the Product Line

	Instant Game	Month of Launch		Instant Game	Month of Launch
1.	Instant 3	Mar. 1987	30.	Christmas Extra	Dec. 1992
2.	Windfall	May 1987	31.	Winning Streak 6	Jan. 1993
3.	Extra Chance	July 1987	32.	Three of a Kind	Jan. 1993
4.	Double Up	Oct. 1987	33.	Stars and Cars	May 1993
5.	Cash Drive	Dec. 1987	34.	Aces High	June 1993
6.	Celebration Bonus	Mar. 1988	35.	Winning Streak 7	Sept. 1993
7.	Cash Splash	June 1988	36.	Eyes Down	Sept. 1993
8.	2 Plus 2	Oct. 1988	37.	Cue for Cash	Sept. 1993
9.	Whirl Win	Jan. 1989	38.	Christmas Special	Dec. 1993
10.	Twice as Nice	Apr. 1989	39.	Winning Streak 8	Jan. 1994
11.	Top Score	May 1989	40.	Jokers Wild	Feb. 1994
12.	Eureka	July 1989	41.	Bon Voyage	Mar. 1994
13.	Lucky Numbers	Sept. 1989	42.	Summer Million	May 1994
14.	Joker's Delight	Oct. 1989	43.	All Ireland	June 1994
15.	Megadraw	Sept. 1989	44.	Bingo	Sept. 1994
16.	Carnival	Jan. 1990	45.	Winning Streak 9	Sept. 1994
17.	Cash Chance	Apr. 1990	46.	Hampers & Roses	Oct. 1994
18.	Gold Rush	July 1990	47.	Cashcade	Dec. 1994
19.	Winning Streak	Sept. 1990	48.	Winning Streak 10	Dec. 1994
20.	Winning Streak 2	June 1991	49.	Aces High	Jan. 1995
21.	Win 'n' Spin	Apr. 1991	50.	Millionaire	Apr. 1995
22.	All Cash	Apr. 1991	51.	Noughts & Crosses	Apr. 1995
23.	Star Trail	June 1991	52.	Bingo	May 1995
24.	Winning Streak 3	Sept. 1991	53.	Big Match Cash	June 1995
25.	Winning Streak 4	Dec. 1991	54.	Winning Streak 11	Aug. 1995
26.	Zodiac	Jan. 1992	55.	Hampers & Roses	Oct. 1995
27.	Spin & Deal	Jan. 1992	56.	Christmas 3	Dec. 1995
28.	Eurochance	June 1992			
29.	Winning Streak 5	Sept. 1992			

next jackpot thus producing larger jackpots and fewer winners resulting in a significant stimulation of sales. The size of the jackpot appears to be the most influential factor in the decision to play the "Lotto".

In 1995 Lotto sales were £202 million, an increase of 6 per cent over the record sales achieved in 1994, accounting for two-thirds of

total sales. It is the National Lottery's most successful product and one that it has enhanced significantly through enlarging the jackpot.

Prior to August 1992, 70 per cent of all combinations were being played as opposed to 30 per cent when "Lotto" was launched in 1988 — thus increasing the number of winners but reducing the payout to each. Therefore in a bid to revive interest and raise jackpots the lottery changed the format from six winning numbers from 36 to six from 39. This raised the probability of winning from 1 in 1.9 million to 1 in 3.3 million — the addition of every 4 numbers approximately halving the chances of winning. This resulted in a lower percentage of combinations being played, fewer winners and more rollovers and, therefore, larger jackpots. In conjunction with this the National Lottery also made jackpots more attractive by adding sums of £0.5 million and £1 million to the jackpot on such occasions as Christmas and

Table 7.2: How the Jackpots Varied

1993 Lotto Jackpot Statistics		1994 Lotto Jackpot Statistics		1995 Lotto Jackpot Statistics	
Value IR£	*No.*	*Value IR£*	*No.*	*Value IR£*	*No.*
Over £1 million	6	Over £3 million	1	Over £4 million	1
Between £750,000 & £1 million	8	Between £2 million and £3 million	2	Between £3 million and £4 million	2
Between £500,000 & £750,000	15	Between £1 million and £2 million	9	Between £2 million and £3 million	3
Between £250,000 & £500,000	42	Between £750,000 & £1 million	10	Between £1 million and £2 million	21
Between £100,000 & £250,000	50	Between £500,000 & £750,000	19	Between £750,000 and £1 million	4
Between £50,000 & £100,000	17	Between £250,0000 & £500,000	38	Between £500,000 and £750,000	12
		Between £100,000 & £250,000	14	Between £250,000 and £500,000	15
				Between £100,000 and £250,000	3
Total	**138**	**Total**	**93**	**Total**	**61**

St. Patrick's Day. Again, this resulted in larger jackpots, and an increase in consumer demand. The largest jackpot in 1987 was £721,566 while in 1995 it was £4.43 million. The number of significant winners has fallen from 138 in 1987 to 61 in 1995. Jackpots have risen from just under £0.75 million to between £2 and £3 million. This has been a most effective strategy (see Table 7.2).

The record jackpot of IR£4.43 million in May 1995 was noteworthy because the winner had used the "Quick Pick" facility to select the winning combination. Quick Pick was introduced with the 42-number formula in September 1994 and accounted for an average of 10 per cent of all Lotto plays up to May 1995. Following the publicity associated with the record win, the popularity of Quick Pick doubled and, by the end of 1995, it accounted for almost 1 in 4 of all Lotto plays. Quick Pick winners accounted for 12 of the 61 Lotto jackpot winning tickets in 1995.

Another stimulant to demand was the launch in May 1990 of Mid-Week Lotto, which raised the frequency of draws and resulted in the biggest ever increase in sales of 42.9 per cent in 1990. It also laid the basis on which to enhance the impact of rollover on the size of the jackpots.

Profile of the Customer

Two major surveys have been undertaken on the National Lottery by Behaviour and Attitudes Limited in 1989 and 1991. Both consisted of a series of three surveys, each carried out for three months of that respective year, in 60 different sampling locations. Each of the three surveys comprised a sample size of approximately 1,100 adults, aged 18 and over. The samples were quota-controlled to reflect the known demographic characteristics of the State. Due to the consistency of their findings, they were aggregated into one, giving total sample sizes of 3,258 and 3,231 respectively.

The key findings of these studies suggested that:

- Females were slightly over-represented in relation to their share of the population.

- The 18–24 age group and 65+ group were slightly under-represented as opposed to the 25–64 age group which was slightly over-represented.

- Rural residents were slightly under-represented, with a tendency in 1989 towards Instant Games.

The results for the two years are similar and reflect very little change in terms of participation. However, the results dispel the myth that old age pensioners are prone to excessive participation in lottery games. Both surveys show that they were slightly under-represented in terms of their share of population.

Farmers and the upper-middle class are slightly under-represented, while the skilled and unemployed remain slightly over-represented. Those at work and with home duties are slightly over-represented. The unemployed reflect their population size.

Awareness and Motivation of Lottery Participants

There is a generally held view that the motivation for participating in Lotto is the size of the jackpot. The bigger the jackpot the more likely consumers are to participate. In America, two studies looked at this issue. The results of both studies indicated that the size of the jackpot is the major determinant of demand for lottery tickets.

In 1991 Behaviour and Attitudes conducted a survey which questioned respondents on their awareness of the chances of winning the jackpot (see Table 7.3).

The public know that their chances of winning the jackpot are low but they over-estimate their absolute chances. In 1991 59 per cent over-estimated their absolute chances and only a small percentage placed it within the correct probabilities.

Table 7.3: Awareness of Winning Jackpot, 1991

Perceived Chance of Winning 1 in	%
1 to 900	1
901 to 2,000	4
2001 to 10,000	2
10,001 to 50,000	2
50,001 to 1 million	8
1,000,001 to 5 million	46
5,000,001 to 10 million	25
Don't Know	5
Not Stated	7

Impact of the National Lottery on Voluntary Fundraising Organisaitons

Voluntary fund-raising organisations have argued that the National Lottery has had an adverse impact on their fund-raising activities. Four studies have looked at this issue.

The first — "Attitudes to Fund-raising" — was conducted by Irish Marketing Surveys Ltd. (IMS) in October 1990 on behalf of the Rehab Lotteries. It aimed to establish the current issues that were facilitating and hindering fund-raising in Ireland and consisted of interviews with key individuals in 26 charitable organisations. Twenty-two of the 26 respondents stated that the National Lottery constituted a major hurdle towards satisfactory fund-raising. Of these, 19 stated that the National Lottery had had a very negative (7) or a fairly negative effect (12) on their activities. Three said that it had affected them to a minimal degree. The 22 were asked to specify by what proportion they believed they could have increased their income in the absence of the National Lottery. On the basis of these answers and taking all charities into account, IMS reported the increase would have been in the region of 39.5 per cent.

IMS also found that there were other external factors that hindered voluntary body fund-raising activities. Reasons offered included the increasing number of organisations engaged in fund-raising activities, the degree of professionalism adopted by many of the larger organisations and the declining level of consumer disposable income. The IMS study concluded that, while the National Lottery was a significant factor on the falling level of fund-raising, the overall deteriorating climate in fund-raising was the major factor.

DKM Ltd., in a survey carried out on behalf of the National Lottery, questioned respondents on alternative uses of Lottery spend. Four per cent of respondents indicated they would have spent it on charitable donations — amounting to about £20m of Lotto turnover. People tended however to overestimate their charitable donations or were unwilling to concede that they gave less to charitable organisations. Because the average weekly expenditure of adults was £3.07 per week, some people would be unable to account for this level of expenditure. It was estimated that the real diversion of lottery expenditure from charitable organisations would actually be 7–10 per cent — £35 million of National Lottery turnover in 1995.

DKM Ltd. also approached a number of leading charities and asked them for details of private fund-raising from 1986 to 1990 to determine whether revenues had declined over the lifetime of the National Lottery. The research indicated that charities' income rose from £16.5 million in 1986 to £24.2 million in 1990 — an increase of 47 per cent in nominal terms and 30 per cent in real terms. DKM Ltd. concluded, given that the fund-raising income of these organisations had increased, that the National Lottery did not have a major negative impact.

The third study, conducted by the National Council for Voluntary Organisations (NCVO), surveyed 100 voluntary organisations. Two-thirds of these indicated that the National Lottery had a negative impact on their fund-raising activities. Of these, 26 per cent considered the impact to be substantial, 55 per cent moderate and 14 per cent rated it slight.

The National Lottery increased its payout rate from 42.4 per cent in 1987 to 51.1 per cent in 1993 and, in doing so, it generated greater personal disposable income in the Irish economy. Since its initiation in 1987 the National Lottery has had a net expenditure of £654.6 million on its lottery products which accounts for 0.59 per cent of total consumption expenditure.

The proportion of consumer expenditure on lottery products has increased from 0.46 per cent in 1987 to 0.73 per cent in 1994. However this only amounts at its highest level to three-quarters of a percentage point of total consumer expenditure for 1994. Thus while the level of consumer spending on lottery products is high, it is not high in absolute terms. Expenditure on lottery products equates to 20 per cent of the amount spent on tobacco products and 6 per cent of the amount spent on alcoholic products in 1993. However it would equal the amount spent on drugs and medicine and is seven times the amount spent on records, tapes and CDs in Ireland.

The Lottery Surplus

In 1995 £100.7 million was raised through the National Lottery for beneficiary projects. This brings to IR£622 million the total amount generated since the Lottery's launch in 1987.

Net proceeds to the National Lottery Fund were reduced from 40.7 per cent of turnover in 1987 to 32.5 per cent from the period 1990 to 1993. This fall in the level of proceeds to the Fund is directly due to the increase in the payout rate from 42.4 per cent in 1987 to 51.1 per cent in 1993, a tactic aimed at stimulating sales.

Youth/Sport/Recreation are amongst the primary recipients of these funds, receiving 34 per cent of all beneficiary funds since 1987. Health/Welfare received 35 per cent and Arts/Culture/National Heritage received 24 per cent of funds. The Irish language received 7 per cent of funds. Within each of these subdivisions, the proportion of funds allocated to sport has fallen since 1988. In 1989, sport received almost 50 per cent of these funds; however, this had fallen to just under a third in 1994. Youth received the highest allocation since 1993 at 41 per cent. The proportion of Arts/Culture/Heritage funds allocated to arts/culture has fallen from nearly a third in 1988 to just over a fifth in 1993. The Arts Council has received most of the funds at 24 per cent, with grants to higher education ranked second at 14 per cent. The proportion of funds allocated to health/welfare has increased significantly from 32.3 per cent in 1987 to 40.2 per cent in 1993. Grants to organisations in the health area accounted for 64 per cent of funds, while funds given for hospital buildings accounted for 24 per cent of funds since 1987.

The Future of Lottery Sales

The National Lottery, with an average growth rate of 18.3 per cent per annum, experienced its first-ever decrease in sales in 1995 following the introduction of the UK lottery. Ten per cent of sales in 1993 (£27 million) are accounted for by Northern Ireland residents, which presents the National Lottery with its most vulnerable market segment in the face of competition from the UK Lottery. Despite the National Lottery being prohibited from marketing, distributing or selling its games in Northern Ireland, it has nonetheless succeeded in attracting a significant market share for its lottery products. National Lottery residents close to the border pay as much as £1.30 for every £1 lottery ticket and the price rises as high as £1.70 in places further North such as Belfast.

However, lotteries are jackpot-driven and the UK Lottery is offering jackpots in the region of £17 million. This has resulted in an informal cross-border trade-line in the opposite direction. Since winnings are tax-free in both States, a resident of the Republic could win the UK lottery and import the winnings without having to pay tax.

In a bid to keep its market in the Republic, the Irish National Lottery shifted its advertising campaign in 1994. Its advertisements concentrated on the beneficiaries of the Lottery, with the implicit message to the public being that they are doing good. Though it is too early to measure the impact of the UK Lottery on Irish operations, it can be surmised that its presence will undoubtedly have a negative impact on the Irish lottery's turnover figures.

The National Lottery's product mix will continue to change and evolve, especially in the face of competition from the UK Lottery. Ireland's lottery is modelled upon those which operate in North America and thus it is reasonable to assume that it will follow trends evident in the US. In the US, lottery agencies have experimented with betting machines that allow customers to make a bet without entering a retail agent. However these have been found to be little better than vending machines and are only suitable for busy shopping areas. More innovative variants include Player Activated Lottery Machines (PALM)s and Video Operated Lottery Machines (VALs). These are similar to commercial video games, except that winning is randomly preordained and not related to the player's skill. However agencies in the US have been slow to adopt these, due to their similarity to slot machines which are outlawed in many states.

Another threat to the National Lottery's monopoly in recent years has come from private betting agents, whose "Lucky Numbers" game allowed customers to bet on between one and five specific numbers, with fixed odds on winning. These odds were slightly more favourable than those of the National Lottery, and allowed a greater range of chances. In 1997, the National Lottery introduced "5-4-3-2-1", its answer to the "bookies' game".

The biggest potential to influence sales is through the use of machinery to take on-line bets. In 1993 the National Lottery's most successful development in its Instant Games operations was the introduction of a new on-line validation system which facilitated the operation of six simultaneous Instant Games in the market. Significant advances in communications technology are being made in the US such that the possibility exists for an automated teller machine in a bank to be adapted for use as a self-serve lottery window. This would make betting more convenient to customers, players would be able to make a bet anonymously and it would afford increased availability which could attract new users.

The result could be a European Lottery — not outside realistic expectations considering that in June 1992 Ireland's National Lottery Instant Games players participated in "Eurochance", the first ever pan-European game in which 11 countries participated. One marketing agency has even put forward the idea of a world-wide Lotto through the use of automated teller machines.

Besides expanding its product line and updating its hardware, the National Lottery has a number of possibilities open to it in terms of combating competition from the UK Lottery. It could increase its payout rate in order to make its prize structure more attractive which will inevitably increase sales. However, this is an expensive tactic because, if the National Lottery wishes to increase its payout rate to 60 per cent, turnover would have to increase by 30 per cent in order to produce the same lottery surplus as in 1996 and there is no guarantee that such an increase of sales would occur.

While the National Lottery has succeeded in developing the market over the past eight years, it appears from the reduced growth rate in 1995 that its ability to generate an increasing surplus for the Government for distribution to beneficiaries in future years is under threat. The National Lottery is now facing a changing and more competitive environment in which sustained growth can only be achieved in the long-term by regular game innovation.

8

The LEADER Programme and Rural Enterprise Development

Thomas N. Garavan and Mary Garavan

The Rural Crisis in Ireland

The problems of rural Ireland have been highlighted in a plethora of reports and studies for about twenty years. In general these problems focus on the decline of agriculture as an industry of economic significance. The numbers engaged in agriculture have declined steadily from 255,000 in 1973 to 140,000 in 1996. Furthermore, populations in rural Ireland have been significantly affected by vast migration, depopulation and a general demographic imbalance. This depopulation has resulted in the deterioration of rural physical and social infrastructure. The closure of schools, post offices and creameries has become commonplace in many rural areas.

Some of the more specific rural problems include the following:

- **Over-employment**. In the agricultural sector there is a high degree of over-employment in the sense that on a large number of holdings, the labour available on the farm is far in excess of what the level of agricultural activity would warrant. Many continue to work in farms despite low returns, because there is no alternative job available. Others simply prefer farming to other occupations, while some are locked into the agricultural system through family or social obligations. Farming skills are very sector-specific and this limits the opportunities for occupational mobility.

Teagasc point out that two-thirds of Irish farm households are not economically viable. Teagasc defines economic viability of a farm as the ability to remunerate family labour at the average agricultural wage and to give a 5 per cent return to non-land assets. The "viability" status of Irish farms was judged in conjunction with demographic and off-farm activity. A farm that is demographically non-viable has no apparent heirs to control or own it.

- **Part-time farming**. A significant development in recent years is the growth of part-time farming. Income from farming has declined in importance. The proportion of total household income derived from farming has decreased from 70 per cent in 1973 to 44 per cent in 1994.

- **Rural depopulation**. The aggregate rural population increased generally from 1971 to 1986. However, there was a significant reduction in the population of rural areas over the period 1986–91. Rural depopulation was particularly evident in the north-west, west and midland regions. There was, for example, a higher depletion of the 15–19 age group in western counties such as Mayo and Leitrim than on the east coast.

The LEADER Programme

LEADER (*Liaisons Entre Agences de Développement de L'Économie Rurale*) is probably the best known of the European programmes focusing on the rural community, which was set up under the last round of European funding. The aim of LEADER is to assist and encourage rural communities to develop their own areas in accordance with their own priorities. Financial assistance is made available by the EU and the state towards the cost of implementing business plans drawn up by the rural groups and aimed at the development of their own areas.

LEADER I commenced in 1992 and finished in 1994, at which time LEADER II took over. Under LEADER I, a fund of £35 million was made available to the seventeen local groups to support development initiatives in their local areas. Representatives from co-ops, community groups, tourism, development agencies and local authorities were usually represented on the management of LEADER groups. Each group on applying for LEADER funding drew up a broad business development plan.

For the seventeen groups that were accepted, this plan was then used to direct how the block grant was spent in each area. These plans were generally multi-sectoral, broadly based and coherent. The objectives of the plans would have to have been clearly set out, actions costed and sources of funds identified (i.e. whether state funding or private contribution). The seventeen LEADER groups received proposals from groups/individuals in the region for funding. Those proposals to receive funding would have to be compatible with the business plan. A number of different types of initiatives received LEADER I funding. These included:

- Technical support to rural development (e.g. surveys, assessments)

- Vocational training and assistance for recruitment

- Rural tourism enterprises

- Small firms, craft enterprises, local services

- Development and marketing of local agricultural, forestry and fishery products

- Other activities which contribute to the development of the area.

LEADER I generally grants 50 per cent of the total investment costs of a particular project. The boards were allowed to be flexible when issuing grants, depending on what was required to see each project up and running. However, there was a general rule that each LEADER group must ensure that for every pound it spends in the local area, this must be matched by another pound invested by the local community.

LEADER II came into force on New Year's Day 1995 and it covers a greater area of the State with 30 new local development groups involved on this occasion. The funding which is likely to amount to £30 million over the next five years will cover 47 specific areas. LEADER II may part-fund rural groups who are new to the concept of local development planning. LEADER II will also place greater emphasis on the transfer of information, knowledge and skills between rural regions in Europe (e.g. networking).

The LEADER Programme has not been without its Critics

LEADER critics claim that there is too much bureaucracy and "red tape" surrounding LEADER. Claims have been made that much of the cost of LEADER goes into administration. The involvement of County Enterprise Boards in LEADER II will, it is believed, lead to a "power struggle" between them and the already established local LEADER agency. The plethora of regional and local structures — FÁS, Teagasc, Coillte, local authorities, County Enterprise Boards — that are available at present has resulted in "overlap" and thus may hinder the process of rural development in the long term. In Wexford, the County Wexford Development Forum has been set up to solve this particular problem. It is a partnership of all the major local development agencies and organisations within the county. These organisations and agencies have decided to work together in a co-operative spirit in order to offer a more effective and co-ordinated support service to rural initiatives in Wexford.

LEADER does not always adhere to its "bottom-up" structure and certain projects have allowed for no local involvement.

Since the LEADER Programme was introduced in 1992, the project groups have created 500 jobs. The LEADER I budget for the Republic of Ireland was £35 million, £21 million from the EU and £14 million from the National Exchequer. Since it started, LEADER groups have been responsible for a number of significant developments in agri-tourism. It has also assisted in the setting up of small-scale factories as well as developing industries such as shellfish, horse-breeding and deer farming.

The Role of Co-ops in Rural Development

The role of co-ops in rural development has been much emphasised in recent times. The signs are that co-ops are committed to promoting rural development activities. The Irish co-operative society believes that a number of its affiliated co-ops have the potential to collaborate with the government and the EU using the LEADER Programme as the key vehicle. The following are some of the ways in which Irish co-ops have become involved:

- Making "donations" to community projects

- Providing loan capital or equity to business projects they regard as viable

- Engaging in joint venture projects

- Providing research, technical or marketing assistance to projects

- Partaking in experimental pilot projects in association with the EU

- Establishing an "enterprise development division" staffed and funded primarily by the co-operative to act as a local enterprise agency

- Taking the lead role in creating an "enterprise partnership"

- Acting as the administrator of a global grant on behalf of the Government or EU.

The Waterford Development Partnership

Waterford Foods became involved in rural development in a joint venture with the Waterford Development Partnerships (WDP) to establish the Carrefour (information) centre in Dungarvan. This centre is a rural EU information centre linked by computer to Brussels. Its role is to inform people in rural areas of EU policies and grants. It started operations in January 1994 with a grant of £8,000 from the EU. The Carrefour centre has found itself very busy responding to individual requests for information and it has provided a meeting place where discussion can take place and partnerships between groups in rural areas encouraged.

By the end of 1995 the Waterford Development project had created 150 full-time jobs. In addition over 400 unemployed people had received training and significant community efforts were initiated to aid rural tourism. WDP received £300,000 from the EU and £69,000 from the Enterprise Trust. WDP is now the agent for all LEADER II funds in Co. Waterford.

Wexford Organisation for Rural Development

In 1991, Wexford had the second lowest level of economic participation of all Irish counties. There was, in general, an over-dependence on domestic tourism and there was also a serious skills gap limiting the capacity to expand Wexford's job base. In addition, the imposition of CAP and GATT reforms was significantly impacting on rural areas.

In order to respond to these problems Waterford Foods plc, Teagasc and County Wexford Farmers Co-op decided to form an organisation with specific responsibility for identifying alternative farm enterprises. They founded WORD (Wexford Organisation for Rural Development).

WORD held consultative meetings throughout the county with all significant community interests represented, thus getting a sound base of support in the community. An intensive advertising and publicity campaign was embarked upon to inform people and to encourage them to participate. This resulted in over 1,000 individuals and 100 organisations involving themselves in the preparation of a rural development strategy. The Board of WORD consists of three members from Waterford Foods plc plus ten others.

The principal activity of WORD, since it was founded, had been to act as the agent for LEADER funds in Wexford. WORD successfully implemented its LEADER I programme by 31 December 1994 and had paid out 100 per cent of its budget. £1.6 million was made available through LEADER I in Wexford. The breakdown of expenditure is shown in Table 8.1.

Table 8.1: LEADER I Expenditure in Wexford

Rural Tourism	£755,000
Farming/Forestry/Fisheries	£410,000
Small Enterprise/Crafts	£181,000
Technical Support	£177,000
Training/Employment Assistance	£155,000
TOTAL	£1,678,000

Since its foundation in 1991 WORD has assisted 143 projects, (see Figure 8.1). Waterford Foods were particularly involved in a feasibility study for fruit and vegetables in the Wexford area. The study was conducted in two phases. WORD provided £33,000 for the first phase and £17,000 for the second. The major outcome of this study was to identify a niche market for strawberries that are suited to Wexford's growing conditions. WORD also contributed £30,000 to a quality milk training scheme to ensure that milk suppliers improved quality in accordance with EU objectives.

Figure 8.1: Number of Projects under LEADER I in Wexford

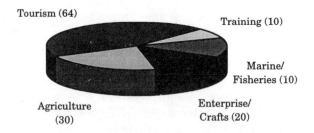

A major programme undertaken by WORD has been a campaign in co-operation with Wexford Food Producers to mount a major promotion to increase awareness and consumption of locally produced food. The brand "The Taste of Wexcellence" is used as a quality label and licensed for a fee to products and services meeting specified quality criteria. In keeping with the brand, the theme of the WORD plan for LEADER II is "Towards the land of Wexcellence".

The most significant achievement of LEADER I in Wexford has been the creation of development awareness throughout the county. WORD received over 300 proposals seeking LEADER II funds even before the programme had opened for applications. LEADER I also had an impact in employment terms:

- 188 full-time jobs

- 121 part-time jobs, and

- 74 seasonal jobs.

Over the 5 years of LEADER, WORD is forecasting total investment expenditure from public and private sources of £5.6 million per annum or £28 million for the total period. Private sector investment is expected to stand at £11 million while the public sector is expected to invest £17 million. WORD plans expenditure of £17.23 million over the next 5 years.

The Mission of WORD is to mobilise individual and community resources to create, promote and assist initiatives in economic and social development aimed at halting the decline in population and incomes affecting Wexford in the post-CAP Reform era. WORD believe that they have learned some important lessons. They must not be curtailed by bureaucracy problems such as fund applications taking eight months to be processed. They have gained experience in the aftermath of LEADER I and feel they are prepared to make a greater contribution over the next five years.

The Boherbue Co-Op

Boherbue Co-op is situated in Boherbue village about 20 miles outside Mallow and was established as a co-operative in 1903. Today, its traditional trading activities are milk assembly, animal feed products and stores trading, and it has 140 milk suppliers who supply the co-op with four million gallons per annum. It has a second branch in Toureen, Co. Cork, a village which is situated about 7 miles from Boherbue. Butter was manufactured in Toureen until the 1970s but today the milk supply goes directly to the Cadbury Plant at Rathmore, Co. Kerry, for the manufacture of chocolate. (Rathmore is only 10 miles from Boherbue.) Boherbue has a reputation of paying good milk prices to its suppliers as they have low overhead costs. At present, the co-op employs 15 people.

Joe O'Connor, General Manager of Boherbue Co-Op, realised that with the introduction of production quotas, super levy restrictions and the reform of GATT and CAP, farmers would find it difficult to survive. The co-op was faced with a decline in its supplier base and its survival depended on a sale to one of the bigger co-ops or expansion into other business ventures. Joe O'Connor's commitment to make it possible for local people to remain in rural Ireland was illustrated by the co-op selecting the latter option. Mr O'Connor and his

Board saw diversification as a means for survival and thus examined the feasibility of alternative enterprises which would add to the future development of the co-op. While Boherbue's main business is still milk assembly, it now has a wider variety of viable interests which include a majority holding in the Irish Venison Co-Op and the opening of Duhallow Retail Park.

The most exciting and potentially most lucrative development undertaken by Boherbue Co-Op is investment in the Irish Venison Co-Op. It was established in 1992 and now has a shareholder/farmer base of about 100. Its producer base is concentrated in Munster, although it does have members throughout the country. Both co-ops in recent times have faced similar survival difficulties and they realised that they could benefit each other. The Venison Co-Op needed capital for product development and capital expansion. Without this they were limited to producing unprocessed venison cuts with poor market returns.

In February 1994, the two co-ops formed a partnership. Boherbue Co-Op became a majority shareholder of Irish Venison Co-Op. Five of Boherbue's shareholders were appointed to the board of nine on the Irish Venison Co-Op. The investment by Boherbue was in the region of £0.25 million. This does not include the cost to Boherbue of marketing the venison product. The dormant Boherbue dairy processing facility is now used as a venison carcass-processing, packaging and marketing facility. Boherbue's four-million-gallon milk supply goes directly to the Cadbury plant at Rathmore. The deer are reared by the various shareholder farmers and it is hoped that in the near future, deer will be slaughtered in satellite abattoirs strategically located around the country.

Boherbue presently exports venison to Germany, but Billy Reddy, Market Manager of the Co-Op, explains that he hopes to supply venison to supermarkets.

The Duhallow Food Training Centre is another initiative by Boherbue Co-Op and is leased out to IRD Duhallow. It is situated in Boherbue village and it was officially opened in October 1994. The aim of the project is to encourage start-up food business by providing the necessary training and expertise to make them succeed. Professor Charles Daly, University College Cork (UCC), when opening the centre, stated that it will play a major role in the growth of clusters of food companies in the Duhallow region. It has already forged links with the local co-ops, Boherbue, Newmarket, Dairygold and North Cork, as well as Teagasc's development centre in Moorpark in County Cork and UCC's Food Science Department. The centre is providing courses run by experts on food technology, manufacturing, quality control, etc. Six jobs have been created operating four units:

1. A food development facility

2. A bakery

3. A venison smoking and slicing unit

4. A research and development unit.

It is in the smoking and slicing unit that the Irish Venison Co-Op intends to develop its new product lines. LEADER funds of £178,000 were invested in the Food Training Centre by IRD Duhallow. it is hoped that Boherbue will become the centre of the Irish deer industry.

The other major development Boherbue Co-Op is involved in the Duhallow Retail Park. It is a shopping centre which is wholly owned by the Co-Op. The building houses a hairdresser, fruit and vegetable shop and a coffee shop and delicatessen, owned by Boherbue. This new Retail Park features Boherbue's new hardware store. The complex comprises c.10,000 square feet and is intended to meet the growing demands of the community. The development, as well as including retail units, consists of an office complex, including computer technology, which will identify and control up to 10,000 stock items and will streamline the entire operation.

These three projects, the Irish Venison Co-Op, the Food Training Centre and the Duhallow Retail Park, cost in the region of £1.25 million to complete. It is the single largest investment in the North Cork area for many years, and it has already created 16 jobs with the potential for additional employment as the projects grow and develop. Boherbue Co-Op is also involved in other "non-traditional" Co-operative activities on a minor scale. Sections of the Co-Op farm have been planted with trees for the Christmas market and a further section is being planted with mainstream forestry.

Boherbue Co-Op believes in the effectiveness of "clustering" different businesses. For example, the coffee shop and grocery shop, both situated in the Retail Park adjacent to the Co-Op benefit from increased traffic coming to Boherbue. Boherbue Co-Op is involved with the local LEADER group, IRD Duhallow in a number of ways. It contributes £3,000 per annum to the funds of the group. 19 per cent of total contributions to IRD Duhallow in 1995 came from co-operatives.

Boherbue Co-Op is trying to create a food environment in the local area and it feels that it has a social obligation to develop the community of which it is a cornerstone. A sign on the office wall reading "Proud to serve our community" proclaims that the Co-Op has retained its identity in the competitive and changing Irish dairy industry.

PART 2

IRISH ENTREPRENEURS

Overview

A major question in the entrepreneurship literature centres around what makes an entrepreneur or small business owner. There is considerable debate about whether an entrepreneur is different from other individuals and whether it is possible for anyone to be an entrepreneur given sufficient resources. Such issues have occupied researchers and theorists for some time, however, as yet, there are few solid answers. Many people equate entrepreneurship with either new or small businesses and with the owner/manager. This rather narrow application is perhaps misleading in that it excludes the establishment of ventures by government. In reality, many new businesses are not truly entrepreneurial in that they are copies of existing businesses.

The ideas and concepts surrounding the entrepreneur have been explored in Chapter 2 of Volume 1 of this series and clearly demonstrate that researchers have spent a considerable amount of time trying to detect traits of successful small business owners and entrepreneurs. This has led to a situation where significantly less effort has gone into focusing on the entrepreneur's ability to learn from problem-solving and to gain from their business experience. There is limited knowledge about what facilitates entrepreneurs to learn.

The case studies presented in this section illustrate a number of important issues. Networks appear to be important in successful entrepreneurial development. There is a limited amount of research which suggests that effective networks contribute to successful entrepreneurship. These networks foster good communications and are important for the on-going success of the venture.

Three of the case studies focus on male entrepreneurs and one concerns a female entrepreneur. Concern has been expressed within the literature about the existence of latent entrepreneurial talent. There are many unanswered questions about the low number of successful female entrepreneurs. It appears to be caused by a combination of social and economic reasons.

[114]

The four case studies presented in this section illustrate that the environment is as significant as the qualities of the individual entrepreneur. All of the business entities which they formed succeeded despite the fact that a large number of new ventures fail within three years of start-up. The cases do illustrate the loss of control of the entrepreneur as the venture grows. This has not, however, happened in the case of Woodlands House Hotel. All of the entrepreneurs faced varying degrees of risk and they tried to minimise this by either limiting their financial stake or by reducing the degree of uncertainty. They took proactive steps to find out what the potential market was, who the main competitors were and then made a careful selection of what strategy would be best in the market place.

9

Ballygowan Spring Water

Barra Ó Cinnéide

Introduction

In 1979, Geoffrey D. Read, aged 24, returned to Ireland from the UK, where over a period of five years he had been, in turn, an electronics technician, male model, landscape gardener, and shoe salesperson.

> When working as a door-to-door salesperson in the UK I first conceived the idea of selling Ballygowan. I was attempting to sell a pair of shoes to a lady in a place called Little Wapping. She was enjoying a bottle of French mineral water at the time and I thought that, if they can sell that with little imagery and lack of proper presentation, there must be a greater opportunity for marketing one of Ireland's most natural resources — pure water.

Read had no idea how to set up a business, let alone an enterprise centred on bottled water. He went to FÁS (the Industrial Training Authority), which was running a "Start Your Own Business" course with the Irish Productivity Centre. He was accepted on the basis that he had two projects — one a study of bottled water and the other publishing. Read's acceptance on the course was justified on the basis of the latter, but his heart lay in the bottled water project. He took the opportunity to undertake a comprehensive study of the market over five months, in the course of which he got a lot of assistance from the market research department of CTT (the Irish Export Board, now An Bord Tráchtála). However, the explosion in the market for bottled water did not really happen until 1979, so up-to-date data was not available. Nevertheless, he was encouraged by the trends.

Geoff Read summarises the outcome as follows:

> So I left this FÁS course with a promising concept and some ideas how to go about it. From then the story of Ballygowan is one of energy, commitment and ignorance. I think that ignorance was the most beneficial part of it.

Ballygowan

If he had not established Ballygowan, Geoff Read feels that he would have developed some other enterprise. His UK experience in selling shoes gave him a unique insight into how consumer markets operate and a desire to develop his own business project some day.

He has an interesting philosophy on the potential for developing Irish marketing:

> There is so much about Ireland that is marketable and under-utilised. The Irish within themselves have perhaps the best basis for marketing in the world. This is probably a reflection of the old "Blarney" characteristic. Because we are less disciplined than say the US and Germany, where it is all formula marketing, we have a particular kind of innovative ability that I think doesn't exist anywhere else. If we could just direct it into appropriate projects we could do extremely well.

Source of Supply

His early analysis of the potential for a bottled water product convinced him that what was really required was a superb source of spring water located near a bottling plant with spare capacity. He set out in search of this unlikely combination.

Geoff Read recalls these events as follows:

> Around this time I heard of a guy in Newcastle West, Co. Limerick, whose ancestors had bottled pure spring water for pilgrims on their way to Mecca. So I thought it must be worth a look if it was good enough for these pilgrims. I contacted the person concerned, Richard Nash. As a result, Dick and I became partners and friends, eventually trading together as Ballygowan. Against a lot of odds, Ballygowan was born.

Spring Water Source — History

The Ballygowan water source is situated upstream of the town of Newcastle West in Co. Limerick. The spring source was originally known as St David's Well and was given its name upon discovery by the Knights Templar in 1184. These Knights Templar received the lands from the Church in return for fighting in the Christian Crusades and built a fine castle (Castle Roe) at the Ballygowan spring source. After the suppression of the order of Knights Templar in 1314, the castle and lands around it lapsed to the Crown and later became the property of the Fitzgeralds of Desmond.

The Earl of Desmond lived there until the death of the 15th Earl, when the lands were escheated to the Queen who, by patent dated

1519, granted them to Sir William Courteray with instructions to plant English settlers there. In 1875 the segment of the castle including the Ballygowan source was bought by the Nash family who used the spring water in the manufacture of their high quality soft drinks, until 1986, when the land and source became the exclusive property of Ballygowan Spring Co. Ltd.

Speaking at the launch of the Marketing Centre for Small Business at the University of Limerick campus in May 1986, Geoff Read commented on the historical connections of the Newcastle West resource and referred to its relevance to the Marketing Centre's core theme — "Enterprise".

> Today, more than 800 years after the discovery, it is fitting that the recent development of this indigenous resource, Ballygowan Spring Water, is enjoyed by many people in different parts of the world and is the same excellent quality as noted throughout history in *Lewis's Topographical Directory of Ireland* and *The Holy Wells of Co. Limerick*.

Catchment Area and Product Protection

The surface water and groundwater catchment contributing to the Ballygowan source is an area of 18.6 square kilometres, rising up 250 metres into the hills to the west of the source. The high rainfall in this part of Ireland provides a potential groundwater yield of some 5,000 million litres of water per year. However, as it is technically impossible to remove all this water from the limestone acquirer, the catchment easily accommodates the extensive production level envisaged at the new Ballygowan bottling facility.

A very detailed field-by-field, farm-by-farm, land-use survey has been made of the catchment area to ensure protection of this natural resource. Over 83 per cent of the area is good quality grassland used as grazing for dairy cattle. The remaining land is lower quality rough grassland and woods. No herbicides or pesticides are applied to the land, and the catchment area is totally free of industry and intensive farming.

Another attractive feature of the Ballygowan source is its geographical location in the south-west corner of Ireland. The strong prevailing winds off the Atlantic ensure that the area is completely free of acid-rain pollution, which is currently destroying much of mainland Europe. Happily, the region was also favourably positioned in relation to the radioactive fall-out from the nuclear accident at Chernobyl in the Soviet Union in May 1986, which so dramatically affected the rest of Europe, especially Scandinavia, and caused high radioactivity levels in water sources on mainland Europe.

Spring Water Characteristics

The geological structure of the aquifer from which Ballygowan source draws its spring water is unique — being almost exclusively limestone. The high calcium, magnesium and bicarbonate concentrations mean that the water is hard. The hardness gives the water its attractive taste and, being low in sodium, the water is useful in combating the incidence of heart disease.

Table 9.1: Analysis of Ballygowan Natural Irish Spring Water

	Parts per Million		Parts per Million
Calcium	132	Chloride	29.0
Iron	0.0	Nitrite	0.0
Magnesium	6	Nitrate (N03)	5.1
Potassium	3	Phosphate	0.0
Silica	1	Sulphate	9.4
Sodium	13	pH	7.41
Fluoride	0	Hardness (CaC03)	335.0

Market Trends

On meeting Dick Nash for the first time, Geoff Read was able to put to him the results of some test marketing that he had completed on Irish spring water. It was enough to enthuse them both about the potential for the future. Some of the items of interest that came out of the research were the reasons why people were buying bottled water. Health and fitness fanatics were emerging in significant numbers and demanding purer, more natural products. Traditional three- and four-course lunches were becoming a thing of the past and the "JWT set" (the sun-bound Irish tourists) were flying off to the Costa del Sol and bringing back many habits, some good and some bad. Among the good was the practice of drinking mineral water. Also, people were becoming concerned about chlorination and fluoridation of tap-water supplies.

These considerations were not unique to Ireland. The growth in sales of bottled water worldwide has been the fastest of any sector for over six or seven years. In 1976 sales of bottled water in the US were approximately 200 million gallons. By the turn of the century, sales are expected to be in excess of 4 billion gallons. Similar growth trends have emerged in the UK.

The Role of Market Research

How much of Ballygowan's progress to date has been the result of market research, and how much has resulted from following an innate "gut feeling"?

Geoff Read did considerable market research while on the FÁS training programme. Basically, this was a five-month planning period during the course of which he was paid IR£40 per week. It incorporated a two-month taught course which concerned itself with the "dos and don'ts" of establishing an enterprise. For the three months that were confined to project investigation, Geoff Read spent most of his time at a desk — using the telephone placed at his disposal, generating a file of correspondence with prospective suppliers and customers, and pestering CTT staff for information on overseas markets. Read explains as follows:

> Market research was very important because I had to determine what the trends were in the market, generally, and to compare our proposed position *vis-à-vis* likely market developments in particular. The trends I found were very encouraging since even in mature markets there were significant upsurges in sales of bottled water. There was a very evident cyclical element in the drinks industry.

Soft drinks started off as water, then manufacturers added some gas (carbon dioxide), then some sugar, caffeine and assorted flavourings. Subsequently, ingredients were eliminated one-by-one to give "sugar-free", "diet/one-cal" and "caffeine-free" products. The cycle is now nearly complete with spring/mineral water coming back into fashion. According to Geoff Read:

> To a certain extent I think you have to be able to see these underlying long-term trends, but also not to be over-reliant on the scientific approach to market analysis. If you have a strong "gut reaction" to a market opportunity you should be prepared to go along with your own instincts.

The Ballygowan Name

When asked how he selected the name of his enterprise, Geoff Read explains that he first went to a number of friends in the advertising field:

> They came up with ridiculous names like "Rinks" simply because it rhymed with "Drinks". Other product names were equally absurd — so much so that they wouldn't help to sell even a washing powder.

So he decided to compose a name himself. After several starts "Ballygowan" seemed to fit the bill, being a name that rolled off the tongue easily. It was only subsequently, when registering it as a trade name, that he discovered that there were places called Ballygowan — insignificant townlands, with the exception of an identifiable cross-roads village in Northern Ireland.

Read admits to minimising on his research into the name's suitability. He merely checked out its acceptance with members of his family and a handful of friends. The main rationale behind choosing such a name was its connection with Ireland and the need to create an image of the rural origins of the product. He freely admits that, even at an early stage, such a name was considered important if exports were to be a prime consideration, especially in "ethnic" markets such as the US:

> Irrespective of what name we would choose, I wished to identify the product as being an obviously Irish one, while avoiding the leprechaun and stage-Irish imagery. What we are trying to sell is a sophisticated Ireland, one that has a great history and culture, yet with the ability to produce a high quality product from a renowned natural resource.

Geoff Read believes that the above image can be successfully created by a determined planned marketing approach so that promotion, packaging and distribution are in tune with the product. This entails gaining access to sophisticated outlets like up-market hotels, restaurants and bars. He believes that in most parts of the world there is a fount of goodwill towards Ireland that has yet to be tapped by Irish business.

The Role of Packaging

The next step was to develop a product that would be sold. Geoff Read believed that the key to success related to packaging:

> The world wasn't out there waiting for Irish spring water. We had to develop a particular product that had the imagery and appeal that people would relate to, not only in Ireland, but overseas. I worked very closely with a designer, Noel Hayes of Aston and Hayes, from our very early test-marketing stage. We developed a type of plastic packaging for our bottled water. We feel we have been innovative within the bottled water market.

Becoming unique, even for a short period, can give an enterprise a valuable head start, but it must work hard at keeping ahead of the posse. With its smaller glass bottle, Ballygowan was the first product in Ireland with this type of packaging.

Geoff Read explains the significance of this:

> We believe we are ahead of places like the United States in de-
> veloping a see-through film for use as a wrap-around label. I
> have always believed that packaging has been the least impor-
> tant concern of Irish manufacturers and I think that this has
> been proven over a number of years, but to us it was a most im-
> portant consideration.

Contact with Retailers

Having developed packaging, the product was allowed to filter on to
the market. Geoff Read had maintained contact with the major forces
in Irish retailing since the early test-market days, and had kept them
fully informed of progress. He explains the benefits of liaising closely
with retailers, particularly multiple store buyers:

> It is important to remember that these particular people, like
> Damien Carolan of Superquinn, Tom Nolan of Quinnsworth,
> Kevin Flynn and Vincent Kenny of H. Williams, are very critical
> in the new product planning process. They are aware of what is
> happening elsewhere and can be far more discerning than your
> consumers. We have had, and continue to receive, great support
> from retailers. At the end of the day their support relates to how
> quickly they move the product off the shelves and how profitable
> your product is to them. It is very encouraging that they are
> prepared to take risks in this area.

Product Range

Initially, Ballygowan produced two main lines: sparkling and still
spring water, responsible for 88 per cent and 12 per cent of sales, respectively. There was the expectation, however, that still water would
generate a larger share of the enterprise's turnover, over a period of
time. Synergy can arise from promoting one product which can re-
dound to the benefit of the other.

The public's palates change and there is a generation phenomenon
where, above a certain age, the gaseous element of drink affects the
digestive system more harshly. Thus Ballygowan has a high profile
among the over-65 age group. This is considered to be an interesting
feature in itself, since it probably reflects the rural roots of the older
urban population, with a sentimental attachment to "natural water"
which they remember drinking in the old days from the parish
pumps!

Geoff Read believed that a generation of consumers had now
emerged with loyalty to vintage water, just as wine aficionados have

developed special taste preferences. He believed that future growth will arise through the public becoming more discerning about what they drink. Ballygowan felt that it offered a unique product. The firm conducted a number of taste-testing studies and Geoff Read claimed that his product came out number one every time.

In 1987 Ballygowan undertook test marketing of sparkling spring water with the addition of natural fruit essence (extracts). These are now available in flavours such as orange, lemon and lime. Ballygowan products are available in a range of convenient packages suitable for both on-premises and off-premises consumption.

Table 9.2: Ballygowan Product Range, May 1987

1. Sparkling		
Pack Size (Litre)	Case Size	Cases per Pallet
0.15 Can*	24	150
0.20 Glass	24	96
0.25 Glass	24	96
0.75 Glass	12	70
1.50 PET	12	52
2. Natural		
Pack Size (Litre)	Case Size	Cases per Pallet
0.25 Glass	24	96
1.50 PV	12	40
3. Flavours		
Pack Size (Litre)	Case Size	Cases per Pallet
0.20 Glass**	24	96
0.75 Glass**	12	70

*   Cans were developed for airlines and promotional use.
** Orange, lemon and lime flavoured.

Publicity

Geoff Read had reason to be thankful for the many column inches written about bottled water and the phenomenon of a small Irish company taking on the might of Perrier, the world leader in the field. He himself has been to the fore in promoting Ballygowan.

> We have produced a product which is superior to the largest-selling bottled water brand in the world and have been unique in actually taking them on in an immature market. We have re-

duced their market share from 80 per cent to approximately 30 per cent, while ours stands around 60 per cent at the moment (March 1986). To get back to the journalist role element, we spent just under IR£1,000 on advertising before we became brand leader in the supermarkets.

Publicity is a very important aspect of marketing and is often the key to success for the launch of a new product, particularly a consumer product. Journalists need something to write about so Read was not slow in providing them with story-line material.

They need to write about you as much as you need them to write about you. In fact, this is worth far more than advertising; it is also free, or reasonably costless.

Advertising

In Autumn 1985 Ballygowan won the National Newspapers Award, which gave the enterprise IR£100,000 worth of free advertising. For a small company this sort of recognition was significant. In March 1986 the company launched a national advertising campaign funded through the award scheme.

The "Table Water for Two" ad was the brainchild of the media buyer in McConnell's Advertising, Dublin. Ballygowan had identified that there was considerable underperformance in sales to restaurants and bars. The company was looking for a medium that would get to the restaurant owner/manager. Up to then, "Perrier" was the generic name for mineral water, and customers would order the French mineral water without thinking.

Therefore the "Table for Two" eating-out column in the Saturday edition of *The Irish Times* became the focus for Ballygowan's advertising effort. With agency help from McConnell's, Ballygowan parodied the style of the regular restaurant column, winning several advertising awards in the process. More importantly, this particular promotional initiative was very effective in achieving its objective, directing the attention of restaurateurs to the product. However, an early colour-ad campaign proved unsuccessful in business terms — though it earned many advertising accolades, and even several more awards. A later colour campaign was to prove more effective.

Distribution

While generating publicity it was important to get distribution moving simultaneously, and this was achieved by a lucky stroke. Ballygowan had become associated with the Canada Dry group, in that Nash's is the franchise element of Canada Dry, which has national distribution. It had no relationship with Nash's, other than an arm's-length arrangement through shareholding, but the trade connection meant that Ballygowan had an inside track in many centres throughout Ireland. However, it did not cover the key Dublin area effectively. The company had to get the product into the outlets where the consumer was demanding it because of publicity and the product's visibility in the larger stores. This was done by a combination of persistent badgering and the offer of respectable margins. Eventually wholesalers and distributors found out that it was an easy product to sell. Geoff Read claims:

> It was perceived to be a better product than the competition, and people wanted it. I would like to think that a combination of efforts on both the public relations and the distribution fronts paid off.

Sales

Sales of Ballygowan on the Irish market have grown rapidly, but there is a lot of dispute about market shares. Ballygowan insists that its information is much more accurate than its foreign competitors "because they cannot monitor our sales but we can monitor their import statistics".

Ballygowan undertook independent market research, through the Lansdowne Omnibus survey and through the Nielsen audit, which confirmed that the brand had a 70 per cent share and was growing at the expense of all others.

Ballygowan was launched in Northern Ireland in February 1986 and received an extremely positive early response in spite of abnormal political conditions there. Geoff Read summarises his international experiences as follows:

> Northern Ireland is a very interesting market and one that hasn't been exploited fully to any degree. We feel that while Ballygowan is an all-Irish product, it is international in appeal. The current per capita consumption for the domestic Irish market is about one litre per head. It is going to take some time before we get close to the 56 and 51 litres per head consumed by the French and Germans, respectively. We have exported to a number of countries including the UK, Belgium, Germany, Australia and the United States, but we are taking a cautious approach. It is very easy to dump a product into a market and achieve early recognition but if one cannot service that market effectively, then alternative efforts will come to nought, particularly in the United States. So we have been spending a lot of time in preparing for market launches abroad. We have initiated market research programmes of which I think CTT would be proud. We are undertak-

ing detailed quantitative analysis to determine what our production requirements are going to be.

Table 9.3: Irish Trade in Spa and Aerated Waters, Value (IR£000)

Imports

	1980	1981	1982	1983	1984	1985	1986	1987
France	121	143	158	212	307	348	246	224
Others	4	80	75	25	147	62	106	146
of which:								
Britain	n/a	n/a	n/a	n/a	*119	n/a	n/a	n/a
N. Ireland	n/a	n/a	n/a	n/a	*16	n/a	n/a	n/a
TOTAL	**125**	**233**	**233**	**237**	**454**	**410**	**352**	**370**

Exports

	1980	1981	1982	1983	1984	1985	1986	1987
EC	n/a	n/a	n/a	n/a	n/a	n/a	41	111
US	n/a	n/a	n/a	n/a	n/a	n/a	60	224
TOTAL	**0**	**77**	**3**	**21**	**5**	**27**	**101**	**344**

Note: Industrial representatives, including Ballygowan, believe that some miscategorisation may have occurred in the compilation of trade statistics.

* It is suspected that lemonade and other soft drinks, often called "minerals" have been included in the data, especially those relating to Britain and Northern Ireland.

Source: Trade Statistics of Ireland (CSO).

It is a quantum leap to take a product from the Irish market to more mature markets with the potential of the US, the UK or Germany. Until mid-1986, Ballygowan only employed three people directly — a woman in Germany, a woman in Ireland and Geoff Read himself. Although a young management team, they showed their ability to select the product, believing that it is the best available. They were anxious to establish Ballygowan's name as being a credible organisation. According to Read:

> It is very easy to be Irish and not to be taken seriously in the international market, because there are very few Irish products that make it overseas. We feel that to be successful overseas re-

quires a lot of investment not only in marketing but in new facilities while monitoring and maintaining quality control at all
times. One of the greatest kicks I have had is sitting in a restaurant in the States and seeing people order Ballygowan at
US$2.75 a bottle. In New York they have experienced consecu-
tive droughts which meant that the tap water supplies have
been diluted with water from the Hudson river. So, not unexpectedly, New Yorkers have been buying bottled water in increasing numbers.

The US Market

Up to 1987, Ballygowan had limited distribution in the US. Originally
it had a deliberate policy of not getting too locked into distribution
deals until it was satisfied that they were serving the market in the
way that best-suited Ballygowan's long-term interests. The tempta-
tion was to do otherwise, but Read warns against the attraction of
short-term strategies:

> It is very easy to sell products on a once-off basis in the US, be-
> cause it is a consumer society. But you must provide continuous
> service to your accounts. You need to back up customers with
> deliveries, as required, and have financial resources for market-
> ing support to justify your shelf-space. You certainly can't dump
> product on the market and run. Traditionally, people go to the
> States about six weeks before St Patrick's Day, get their orders
> in and they aren't seen again until the following year, thus an-
> tagonising the US buyer.

Ballygowan negotiated a distribution agreement with Anheuser-
Busch, which had in excess of 960 wholesalers covering the entire US.
Anheuser-Busch brews Budweiser, among other beverages, and
claimed 38 per cent of the US beer market, with a turnover of $7,500
million.

Over a number of months the relationship grew to the point that
Anheuser-Busch took a major equity stake (just over 50 per cent) in
Ballygowan (see Appendix). The "marriage" was not a happy one, in
either the penetration of the US market or in terms of organisational
capability. Following litigation, the Irish equity owners, Geoff Read
and Richard Nash, negotiated a "buy back" arrangement, with the
introduction of a new shareholder, a UK-based financial institution.

Over the next four years Ballygowan redoubled its efforts on both
the Irish and British markets until, in the early 1990s, the company
was acquired by a large UK-based drinks conglomerate. Geoff Read's
equity sell-out was estimated to be near £3.5 million. He entered a
three-year contract as UK Market Development Manager, domiciled

in the UK. Towards the end of 1995, Geoff Read announced that he was establishing a new drinks enterprise and, as they say in the Irish language, "sin scéal eile" — that's another story!

Growth — Establishing Credibility

Over the years, Ballygowan has received significant support from semi-state bodies, particularly from CTT (now An Bord Tráchtála), in terms of marketing assistance, and from Shannon Development, the regional agency for Ireland's Mid-West. Initially it was hard to be taken seriously but once the new enterprise had established its credibility, generally it became easier to find support for future development plans.

In the early days, the venture capitalists reacted fairly negatively. It was a high-risk venture based not on any asset base, because everything was contracted initially. In the late 1980s, Geoff Read explained:

> Financial investors are becoming more supportive of our ability to market and sell a product for which there was virtually no home market before. It is still difficult for us to present the complete profile of Ballygowan and its future because we have hardly got past the first couple of pages in the story-line, to date.

Perhaps the prospects for tapping the goodwill and favourable image of indigenous products that exist abroad is best summarised in Geoff Read's philosophy when he was the driving force behind Ballygowan:

> The future I see is rich in potential. It poses both opportunities and challenges for Irish food and drink products. On the positive side there is enormous goodwill to things Irish. The first-time entrepreneur welcomes such a "plus" factor since it is difficult to generate the same amount of energy consistently to a project as it grows. One's concentrations get diverted into so many different areas, new product development and new markets. In Ballygowan I see a situation where we don't need an infrastructure that is overburdened with people. We need quality rather than quantity, and that is our intention for the future. We believe that Ballygowan is set on the correct course and that any future investment in the product will be well rewarded.

Asked to identify the most important ingredient for success in establishing an enterprise, Geoff Read commented:

> Commitment is the single biggest factor. If you're not committed, how can you expect people to back you? If you have faith in

something, then keep plugging away, because if you drop it in the middle you'll spend the rest of your life wondering what it would have been like to be successful. But, to be honest, you must be prepared to go through a hell of a lot of rubbish: people saying that you're nuts or crazy. But in the end you've got to satisfy yourself. You'll be proved right or wrong, quickly enough.

APPENDIX

"Sails" Promotion for Ballygowan

Local ocean-going grandfather, Pat Lawless, set sail from Limerick docks on 29 May 1986 in his 8.5 metre boat *Iniscealtra* to cross the Atlantic single-handedly. He successfully completed the journey 57 days later, effecting his landfall in Newport, Rhode Island.

Although he admits to not being a big eater, Pat Lawless carefully planned sufficient provisions for the crossing. He recounts taking liberal quantities of water on board — in all, 48 gallons of fresh water and several dozen litre bottles of Ballygowan Spring Water.

Unfortunately, at mid-point of the voyage, his main water supply had deteriorated to such an extent that almost all of it had to be dumped overboard, whereas Ballygowan remained in perfect condition throughout the entire voyage.

Ballygowan Spring Water Co. Ltd.

Ballygowan Spring Water Co. Ltd. was founded in 1981 by Geoff D. Read. The company was restructured in March 1984 as part of a joint venture agreement between Geoff Read and Richard Nash & Company Ltd. In September 1986, a majority stake in the enterprise was acquired by Anheuser-Busch Beverage Group Inc., a wholly owned subsidiary of Anheuser-Busch, Inc., of St Louis, Missouri, the world's largest brewer. Owners of the Budweiser brand, the world's best-selling beer, Anheuser-Busch purchased 50.1 per cent of the equity of Ballygowan Spring Water Co. Ltd., together with the trademark and distribution rights for Ballygowan products in the United States. As mentioned in the main text, following a judicial review, the Irish minority stakeholder succeeded in arranging management "buy back" with the support of a British financial institution

Bottling Facility

In Spring 1987, Ballygowan completed construction of bottling and warehousing facilities at its source in Newcastle West, Co. Limerick. This state-of-the-art, custom-built water-bottling facility was the most modern in Ireland and Britain and incorporated a modern design into a rural environment. The bottling line operates a speed of up to 600 bottles per minute and is fully automatic.

Figure 9.1: Awards Won by Ballygowan

1985	National Newspaper of Ireland Best Consumer Product Advertising, value IR£100,000
1986	Royal Dublin Society — Allied Irish Banks New Ventures Award
1986	Advertising (International) at ABWA 1986 Aqua Award; Runner-up (best international advertising category)
1986	*Today's Grocer* — Aida Sial Award Best beverage product in Ireland since 1984
1986	Aida Sial International Grocery Oscar Best non-alcoholic and soft-drink beverage in Europe since 1984
1987	*Irish Times* — PA Management Award Runner-up, Best Management of a company in Ireland in 1986

Sources: Presentation by Geoff Read at the University of Limerick.

10

Noel C. Duggan — The Best is Yet to Come?

Barra Ó Cinnéide

Introduction

Before gaining exposure to over 300 million people through hosting the 1993 Eurovision Song Contest — the first time this event was held outside a major European city — Millstreet, Co. Cork typified, in most respects, many small Irish towns that rely on the fortunes of the farming community within their trading catchment areas. However, a number of critical factors exist in Millstreet that distinguish it from similar-sized towns — its vibrant community spirit and, above all, the Millstreet International Horse Show (and its originator, Noel C. Duggan).

Millstreet is situated at the emergence of a natural pass between the Derrynasaggart and Boggeragh Hills that leads to the Blackwater valley. It is situated on the bank of the Finnow river, a tributary of the Blackwater. The many archaeological and historical sites in the locality indicate early and continuous settlement of the area. There are numerous stone circles and ring forts, as well as "holy wells", which may well date back to early Christian, or even pre-Christian times.

The land to the south and south-west is hilly and rugged, offering a poor agricultural environment but affording breathtaking natural beauty. The town itself is dominated by Clara, a conical mountain rising 300 metres, immediately to the south-west. The land to the north and east, extending across the wide Blackwater Valley, is much better suited to agriculture. Dairying predominates, especially in recent years, but the richer alluvial soils nearer the Blackwater are capable of sustaining a wide variety of agricultural use.

Leisure, Recreation and Social Activities

One of the major attractions of the Millstreet area is the availability of a great variety of recreational and leisure pursuits. It abounds in visual attractions, especially among the hills to the south and west. As local promotional literature indicates:

> One is free to trek, on foot or horseback, through acres of solitude, where only the occasional bleat of a sheep or songbird disturbs the silence. The few mountain farmers who inhabit the area are open, warm and welcoming.
>
> The hunter can stalk game, or fish in the lakes and rivers for trout, salmon or coarse fish. The fit and nimble can attempt rock climbs of varying difficulty. The naturalist can study the wildlife. Those interested in archaeology can visit prehistoric dwelling sites or standing stones. The daring can hang-glide from Clara mountain. The poet can find inspiration.

There are over 30 clubs, societies and other organisations in Millstreet. Irish culture remains strong in the area, especially in Cullen. In particular, traditional music and dancing attracts devoted followers, among young and old. As a result, the Millstreet area, despite having a relatively small and somewhat dispersed population, is socially vibrant.

Historical Development

Prior to the catastrophic famine period of the mid-nineteenth century, the rural population of the hinterland was considerably higher than it is now. In recent decades, the population of Millstreet town has ranged from just over 1,300 to a little over 1,450 (for demographic details, see the Appendix). Up to the first half of this century, Millstreet was relatively prosperous, serving as a market town with a range of traditional trades and commercial activities. Its people were employed in small industries such as milling (hence the name), smithing and tanning, or in retail distribution. Its fortunes ebbed and flowed with the relative prosperity of agriculture, and much of the town's prosperity related to its location on the "Kerry butter road".

> From the late 1700s, the "Kerry butter road" had become of growing importance as the Cork Butter Exchange, with its revolutionary system of quality control, had risen to become the biggest in the world, exporting butter as far afield as Jamaica, Brazil and Australia. Until the completion of the Cork–Kerry coach route in the 1930s, Millstreet was a strategic centre on the main highway between Cork and Killarney for the carriers and "carmen" who, with pack horses or "flat carts", had brought

in the 56lb firkins of butter from the small dairies of Munster (*Cork Examiner*, 17 December 1992).

Its over-dependence on agriculture left Millstreet vulnerable and its growth potential limited. The lack of opportunity caused many of its potential entrepreneurs to emigrate, or at least migrate, often to achieve considerable success elsewhere. The last two decades, however, have seen the development of a significant enterprise of both indigenous and foreign origin.

Millstreet's renaissance, and its expectations of better things to come, can be traced to several critical events that have led to the emergence of a particular entrepreneurial spirit in the town.

The Basis for Renaissance

Founded in 1977, Millstreet's Community Council has been a major factor in the town's development. Another critical element in the town's revival has been Noel C. Duggan and his group of companies. Ironically, it was in 1977, the year that the Community Council was established, that the Duggan group suffered a severe set-back. On 12 October, the hardware shop was completely destroyed by fire. Within days, however, it was "business as usual", with trade being operated from what had previously been a warehouse.

Noel C. Duggan immediately started on the construction of a new hardware store. The outlet today, covering 2,500 square metres, is one of the largest stores to be found in any rural town in Ireland. It is fronted by a car park capable of facilitating up to 150 cars. The site includes a large timber store and a steel fabrication shop. In addition to this, there is a concrete-surfaced yard covering approximately two and a half acres.

There are 75 people employed by Noel C. Duggan in his retailing and construction enterprises, in addition to teams of sub-contractors that are employed from time to time.

Pessimism Lifts at Millstreet in the 1980s

In the 1970s a sense of pessimism pervaded Millstreet. Being largely dependent on agriculture, it was hit hard by recession. A decade later everything had changed. Two new industries had been established, and the town was becoming internationally renowned as an equestrian centre. How did such a remarkable transformation take place in such a short time? Many commentators have ascribed the revitalisation of Millstreet to the occasion when people came together to work for the European Junior Showjumping Championships in August, 1980.

At what was scheduled to be the "winding-up" meeting of the Equestrian Committee after the Championships, Noel C. Duggan argued strongly that the group should not disband but should work to take advantage of this initial success in other fields. The members agreed and, with the blessing of the Community Council, the Equestrian Committee, a little changed in personnel, became an Industrial Committee, charged with the task of attracting industry to the area.

Ken Brennan, the Community School principal, recounts:

> The immediate tasks were to convince the Industrial Development Authority, IDA, of the community's credibility, and to prepare the ground locally to attract visiting industrialists. Up to this point, Millstreet scarcely related with the IDA as a potential location for the establishment of an industry.

Background details and statistics were prepared by the Community School personnel, and the task of improving the town's appearance was undertaken by the Community Council.

Potential industrialists were duly taken on coach tours of the area, brought to schools, shown the first-class equestrian centre, already internationally recognised, and introduced to the business community. While, at times, there were significant differences of opinion on courses of action within the committee, a united front was always presented externally, and contrary to the "traditional" occurrences of splits in local voluntary groups, the Industrial Committee remained intact throughout this period.

Millstreet became part of the IDA's itinerary for visiting industrialists. In March 1981, Keyboard, an American company that was later to become part of Apple Computer Inc., announced that it was establishing a factory at the Mount Leader estate — a prime site centrally located in the town, which had been acquired through the intervention of Noel C. Duggan. More good news followed in June, when another US computer components firm, Molex, confirmed that it, too, was locating a subsidiary in the town.

Employment in these two firms at Millstreet progressed to reach its peak of 200 in 1984 but, by the beginning of 1985, the workforce had dwindled to 80, due to a serious recession in the computer industry worldwide. In May 1985, a crisis meeting in the Apple headquarters in California decided the company must retrench or collapse. Three plants would be closed, including those in Dallas and Millstreet. For Dallas, it was but a minor event — for Millstreet, it was devastation! As Apple was the largest employer in the area, it appeared that the platform of future prosperity was irretrievably lost.

Millstreet: Life After Apple

The empty Apple Computer factory provided a daily reminder for the Millstreet community of the task ahead and, as the months went by without any significant development, it was difficult to maintain optimism. Each contact, however tenuous, was followed up.

After a succession of disappointments, a potential breakthrough came in 1987. Craig Chaffee, an American who had managed the Keyboard plant in Millstreet for some time, was then managing a plant for ALPS Electric in California. Chaffee had acquired a genuine regard for the workers and people of Millstreet during his stay and had kept in touch. Knowing his new employers were considering a European location, he gave the Japanese owners the Millstreet booklets and advised them to consider locating there.

The ALPS management, including Mr. Kameoka, now US President of ALPS, visited Millstreet and began negotiations with the IDA. Within a year, ALPS Electric announced it was about to set up a facility in the former Apple plant. With typical Japanese efficiency, the plant was in production just three months later.

Referring in ALPS' corporate magazine to the company's location in Millstreet, Craig Chaffee stated:

> It's the people that make the difference. The quality of the workforce, the spirit of the community and the support the project received from all quarters were major factors in our location decision (*ALPSpeak* magazine, ALPS Electric Inc., USA, July 1990).

Although there are no Japanese managers in the Millstreet plant, the Japanese executives who have visited the area have struck up an immediate affinity with the local people. Today, there are over 400 people employed in the town's two high-tech plants — ALPS and Molex.

While Millstreet has no pretensions to becoming a major resort, tourism is recognised as potentially important in the local economic "mix". A local "Visitor's Guide" has been published and distributed nationally and abroad, with the co-operation of Bord Fáilte, the Irish Tourist Board. It is significant that, until the last decade, except for an occasional reference to Noel C. Duggan in relation to equestrianism, Millstreet scarcely got a mention in the media. Since then there have been numerous articles and features on activities, developments and personalities from the area. This has not been accidental — the value of good publicity has become increasingly recognised by the town.

The Spur for Noel C.'s Initiatives

A key player in the town's industrial development drive has been Noel C. Duggan who, as noted earlier, was involved in his own family firm's development, as well as instituting the Millstreet International Horse Show. His personal ambitions, no doubt, were spurred by the fact that there were ten children younger than himself in the family, and that the family's fortunes had been at a low ebb when his father died, the year the youngest child was born. Noel C. was 13 when his schooling ended. He recounts his early days in business:

> I started my business on a bike which cost 30 shillings. You couldn't buy a pound of nails in the town at the time. I bought £40 worth of hardware with a loan from the local bank manager.

> I had myself convinced it would work. I learned, having convinced myself, it's easy to convince others. The days were long. The business was open in the morning before the people came to the creamery at seven o'clock. My mother was scared of her life; she thought I was going to bring disaster on the family.

> I admit that when I started to work in the family store I was ambitious and a bit headstrong. There was nothing too much trouble. If a customer wanted something that wasn't in stock, I'd send somebody out the back door, down to another shop, to buy it while I kept them occupied. Sometimes you'd make a loss but the important thing was not to let him know you didn't have the stock.

> The town wasn't progressing. More needed to be done. I had a little taste of success in my own business and I was anxious to achieve. I wanted to do more to further the image of the town.

> I felt if it was proved it could be done, others would know they could do it, too. They subsequently have done, and that is why Millstreet is a thriving, ambitious, vigorous little town.

He says he knows every employee personally and has never asked any of them to do anything he was not prepared to do himself. His good humour, friendly disposition and contentment with life are apparent.

> I believe in the maxim, "be happy, for tomorrow you might be sad".

He obviously believes in mixing business with pleasure since he played minor, junior and senior football for Millstreet and did some cross-country running. He was chairman of Cork Hibernians soccer club for two years (1974–75) and was Master of the Dunhallow Hunt, the oldest pack of foxhounds in the country, from 1974–76.

He has a rare capacity to involve everyone in what he is doing. When he married at 22, his wife Maureen, who was a nurse, was involved immediately in the business. She now works full-time in the Duggan Group of enterprises, is secretary of the Millstreet International Horse Show, and still manages to keep house and be a mother.

Origins of the "Millstreet Show"

It all began at a branch meeting of the Cork/Kerry branch of the Show Jumping Association of Ireland (SJAI). Noel C. Duggan had sponsored a jumping league on the condition that the final be held at the old agricultural show in Millstreet, which it was.

Noel C. recalls that, the following year, at a meeting of the SJAI, when they were deciding where the final would be held the next time:

> A certain man from West Cork said: Look, we should go to some other backward place now", and of course, that hurt my pride and I said "Fair enough, you do that and I'll run my own show", and that's how it all started.

Since 1973, the show has become an annual event, quickly attaining international stature. Currently, it costs nearly £400,000 to stage. Noel C. states: "We aim to break even and so far I've achieved that."

Sponsors have included Ford, Bank of Ireland, Kerry Group, Bord Bainne (Irish Dairy Board), Dairygold, Heineken, Irish Cement, Carroll's, Waterford Crystal, Citibank, Volvo, Renault, Coca-Cola, ACC (Agricultural Credit Corporation), and ICC (Industrial Credit Corporation).

Library research undertaken for production of this case indicated that there has been wide media coverage of events in Millstreet over more than a decade. For instance, The *Clara News*, Millstreet's local paper, commented:

> The annual Millstreet Horse Show has been a fantastic exercise in co-operation — one which is worthy of success. The Community School, adjacent to the "Green Glens" complex, is being used as a hotel. On visiting the school I was most impressed with the cleanliness, efficiency and comfort. The rooms were warm and comfortable and the menu was comparable with any Grade A hotel — no "Fawlty Towers" here! (*Clara News*, Sunday August 31, 1980).

> The organisation of this event in a small town like Millstreet can be put on a par with the organisation behind the Pope's visit to Knock — a huge undertaking whose success is guaranteed when undertaken by talented, dedicated and energetic people. The Equestrian Federation of Ireland (EFI) are also to be commended for entrusting the running of this prestigious event to a rural town. Unlike RTE (Irish Broadcasting Authority), which wouldn't even consider Cork or Killarney for the Eurovision contest, the EFI, undoubtedly swayed by Noel C. Duggan and his confidence in Millstreet, showed courage and initiative. It is the opinion of the *Clara News* that their confidence in our town and its people will be justified.

Each year the Millstreet International Horse Show goes from strength to strength. The organisation of such an event is mind-boggling and would prove too much for a lesser mortal, but Noel C. gets great satisfaction when his plans come together and everything comes right on the day.

Quickly after hosting the European Junior Showjumping Championships and with development of the Irish Jumping Derby event, Millstreet began to rival the long established Dublin Horse Show held annually at the Royal Dublin Society, (RDS). When one considers the facilities available to the RDS, it is almost inconceivable that a rival show could be staged in rural Ireland. Up to recently, everything has to be provided for the day; toilets, phones, office equipment, catering facilities, foodstuffs, car parking, stewards, and a myriad of other services.

A lesser person would submit in the face of all the adversities, but Noel C. thrives on the challenge and his show is improving all the time. Such is the high regard in which the event is held that breeders, buyers and riders of the highest calibre make a special effort to be at the Millstreet Show. Of course, like everything else there are ever-pressing concerns. Overheads are massive, insurance alone costs a fortune. (*Clara News*, Sunday, August 25, 1985)

Millstreet Show's Uniqueness

Millstreet Show is held in an attractive "picture-postcard" setting with a backdrop of rolling parkland. A particular format and style has been developed and it has become internationally known for the evolution of distinctive events, and, especially, for its "grand prix" — the Irish Show Jumping Derby. (In 1979, Noel C. Duggan ran the first Irish Show Jumping Derby — an event that put Millstreet squarely on the international equestrian map. At that time, star names competed for the winner's prize of only £1,500. This is a far cry from the current status of the Millstreet Show which attracts over 60 riders from 12 countries, competing for a total prize fund of £250,000, including a qualifying round for the Volvo World Cup.)

The Derby is held on a specially designed five-acre course and contains the inevitable and imposing bank, water jump, "devil's dyke" and other permanent obstacles. It has been likened to the famous Hickstead arena in England. The "Greenvale" Irish Draught Mare Championship was the first of the national events to be promoted at the show. Later, radical showing classes (the brainchild of Noel C.) were introduced. These are the "Young Irelander" for 3-year olds, the "National Discovery" for 4-year olds, and the "Boomerang Finder" Championships for 5/6-year olds.

Although the young 3-year old fillies and geldings are shown "in hand" as at traditional shows, in the "Young Irelander" class they also have to be lunged over poles in a disciplined, obedient and effective manner. Noel C. says:

> The aim of this championship is to identify horses most likely to make top class international show jumpers or eventers.

In particular, the concept of staging a qualifying round at local shows has added a new dimension to the horse classes at agricultural shows throughout the country.

While the public spotlight falls mainly on the international show-jumping events at both pony and horse levels, Noel C. Duggan describes Millstreet Show as the "Farmer Breeder" show of the year. It is a title which equestrian sportswriters have increasingly come to acknowledge as being well deserved.

Developing the Equine Industry's Potential

At the 1984 Olympic games in Los Angeles there were 42 medals to be won in horse events. Eleven of those were won by Irish-bred horses — not one of which was Irish-owned.

Noel C. speaks highly of the equine industry's potential:

> The Irish horse is the greatest single most important ambassador we have. It's the best. None better. I could go to any country and get to meet the King, Queen or Prime Minister almost — through the Irish horse. It would be a very sad day for Ireland if that was to go.

Noel C. Duggan was in the news in 1987 for a first-time breakthrough in a new market for Irish horses — Algeria. Noel C. sold three jumpers, including one of his own, the Grade A jumper "Green Glens", to Algerian buyers. One of the big problems facing the African nations now going into equestrian sports, and into show-jumping, in particular, was the fact that most of them had to start from scratch. Their riders had to be trained in the various aspects of equestrian sports, such as course building, horse management, organisation of shows and, of course, saddlery and farriery. Noel C. feels that countries like Ireland should be attempting to assist less-developed nations through the transfer of equine operations "know-how" and specialist management expertise.

"The Show Must Go On": The Motto at Millstreet

In August 1987, fire heavily damaged 1,000 square metres of the Millstreet Indoor Arena, including the restaurant, bar, viewing balcony, and trade stand area. Forty firemen from Killarney, Kanturk,

Mallow, Macroom and Millstreet were at the scene. Nearly 300 horses and ponies were stabled in the grounds for the four-day show. Many of the stabled animals were released into a paddock but a large number escaped, rushing into the town and countryside. Some travelled as far as Castleisland, Co. Kerry — over 40 kilometres away. However, within hours they were all rounded up unharmed, indicating Millstreet's community spirit and ability to recover from adversity.

The Horse Centre: From Concept to Reality

From the outset, Noel C.'s intention was to build a totally new horse-marketing infrastructure in tandem with development of the annual horse show. With an investment of over £4 million, extensive indoor training and exhibition facilities, a sales arena, and 125 permanent stables have been installed.

The Centre includes a business centre, a laboratory capable of dealing with all the new technical developments in horse breeding — for example, artificial insemination (AI) and embryo transfer procedures — along with a forge and other ancillary facilities to support an international multi-purpose equestrian centre.

Based on the successful marketing centres already established in Germany and the Netherlands, it is envisaged that up to 250 horses will be brought into the Millstreet Horse Centre for training periods of six months prior to the biannual international sales.

Noel C. has visited just about all the top European equestrian centres of this type and has adapted what is best in them to the first major project of its kind to be brought on-stream in Ireland. The plan involved creation of 25 permanent jobs at the centre with double that number, at least, of temporary staff during peak periods like sales shows.

The "Green Glens" covered area has a riding floor space measuring 55m x 35m, making it as large as any indoor show-jumping arena in the world, with seating for 5,000 spectators. An upstairs refreshment area looks out onto the outdoor international Derby arena. The old eighteenth-century stone stables were converted into a cosy restaurant and bar, with a view of the arena.

People did not believe Noel C. Duggan when he predicted that the best was yet to come for Millstreet but, in December 1990, he purchased Drishane Castle, an historic and scenic property on the verge of the town.

> The 100-hectare complex was purchased from the Sisters of the Infant Jesus. Although purchased in December 1990 by Noel C., the girls secondary boarding school of Drishane continued to operate until 1992.

An 18-hole championship golf course, a swimming pool, conference centre, health-farm, tennis courts and other amenities are also planned. It is intended to develop an airstrip as well as a helicopter pad.

He is now preparing to develop it into an international status house (with 120 rooms) and country club, at a cost of £10 million, topping everything he has done in the past (*Cork Examiner*, 18 December 1990).

Noel C. also owns a 90-hectare holding across the road from Drishane which features lakes and landscaped grounds and is close to the Blackwater and Finnow rivers. He says it has been his dream for many years to acquire the property so that he could develop the type of complex he now planned. He felt there was tremendous potential for such a project and was looking further afield for the best method of financing the development which would provide about 50 jobs, rising to 100 on occasions.

Accolades for Achievement

Noel C. Duggan has been honoured with multiple awards in recent years. The Co. Cork Association of New York hailed him as a businessman, farmer, community leader and most notably, as a breeder, trainer and exporter of quality horses. Bord Fáilte, the Irish Tourist Board, made him an Honorary Ambassador for Ireland in recognition of this work for tourism and he has also been chosen for the People of the Year National Endeavour, Duhallow Man of the Year and Special Cork All Star awards.

Noel C. has always paid tribute to the contribution that his wife, Maureen, sons Barry and Thomas, and daughters Martina and Gena, have made to his success, and to the support of the community.

Millstreet Attracts TV Attention

An hour-long TV programme — "I Live Here" — dealt at length with the centuries-old Duggan family connections with Millstreet and its Sliabh Luachra hinterland. It also focused on the logistics involved in planning and managing the 1988 Millstreet International Horse Show.

Most of the broadcast featured personal anecdotes. There were many tributes to Noel C. As he talked about his home town and his plans for the future, Noel C. expressed the view that Millstreet should not depend on external assistance. With self-confidence he explained how Millstreet had tackled life "head-on", giving an example to other towns and cities that have suffered reverses over time.

"Eurovision" Brings Added Publicity

The increasing awareness of Millstreet in sports circles and its attractiveness as a feature for television programming was highlighted when the Screensport satellite TV channel broadcast the 1992 Jumping Derby from Millstreet to 20 countries in four languages — English, French, German and Dutch — to a potential viewing audience of 30 million. However, major commentary on the town's initiatives did not occur until its hosting of the 1993 Eurovision Song Contest was announced.

> It is difficult to exaggerate this achievement. At a time of recession, when businesses everywhere seem obsessed by the idea that nothing can be achieved without State intervention, Mr. Duggan has illustrated what individual effort and vision can achieve, when it has local and even cross-country support. More than most, Noel C. Duggan is living proof of the idea that success in life is possible outside Dublin and that international success can be realised in Millstreet. Whatever the obstacles, he has shown that *"all kinds of everything"*[1] are possible. (*Cork Examiner*, 27 October 1992)

The contest attracted over 3,000 guests, including 800 members of the 23 competing delegations and an international press corps of over 300. Millstreet's indoor arena enabled an audience of 3,500 to be seated comfortably and, for the first time in the history of the Eurovision, members of the Irish public had a chance of being at the huge extravaganza, through a National Lottery competition for tickets.

The song contest was broadcast live by satellite on 15 May 1993 to 300 million people and, for the first time, into Russian homes, and even as far away as Australia and the US. It was the widest audience in the history of the contest.

Planning for Eurovision

Bringing Eurovision to Millstreet had been an obsession with Noel C. since Linda Martin won the contest for Ireland in Stockholm the previous May. He says that, with three countries left to judge, he knew she was going to win. Before the final announcement was made, he was already starting his letter to the Director General of RTE, Vincent Finn, on the back of an envelope:

> The winning song was "Why Me?", so what about Millstreet, and "Why Not?" (*Sunday Tribune*, 1 November 1992).

---

[1] The italicised phrase was the title of Ireland's first winning entry in the Eurovision Song Contest.

RTE said that it would be possible, logistically, to stage Eurovision outside Dublin, but to do so would mean going over budget by £400,000, including the price of a venue. Noel C. wiped £200,000 off the bill by donating the venue for nothing. The local authorities and business interests in counties Cork and Kerry came up with the rest. (According to Denis Galvin, marketing manager of the Hotel Gleneagles, Killarney, the benefits of tourism in the north Cork/Kerry region were immeasurable — the "picture-postcard" marketing from Eurovision being long term. "The value of a single picture of the area beamed to 300 million viewers will be worth a lot more than the entire Bord Failte budget for an entire year.")

The following press comment is of interest, in retrospect:

> And there were those in Dublin and other places who laughed when they first heard that some place called Millstreet wanted to host "Eurovision 93". How corny could they get, they thought. Sure there isn't a hotel in the place, let alone a night-club (*Sunday Press*, 1 November 1992).

The Need to De-centralise Television

The holding of the Eurovision Song Contest in Millstreet represented much more than arranging a sing-song in Co. Cork. It was an important statement by RTE that there is an Ireland outside Dublin — an Ireland with skills, professionalism and facilities. That this decision caused so much attention also gave an important message.

> There is a feeling that any place further than Naas, Maynooth or Balbriggan is very far away from Dublin. This, of course, is nonsense. A couple of hundred miles will take anyone anywhere in Ireland.

> We have not exploited the country's compactness. Because of this compactness the growth of Dublin should have stopped years ago, rather than the position which has now been reached — where virtually one-in-three of our population live in the greater Dublin area.

> This lopsided development is most apparent on a Friday evening if you attempt to drive home from Dublin. Roads are blocked with cars from three in the afternoon to nine at night. Thousands trying to escape from Dublin each weekend. Noel C. Duggan puts it totally in context when he states that "Millstreet is not 170 miles from Dublin, but Dublin is 170 miles from Millstreet". If the RTE decision on Millstreet is an indication of future policy, it is a very welcome trend.

> Television is moving into a new age. Very many of our towns already have a choice of more than half a dozen channels. Very

quickly with new technology, the whole country will have a similar, or even a wider, choice of TV programmes. Then what happens to Irish television? If it tries to compete and gives us a diet of New Zealand, Los Angeles, London or Tokyo-type television, then why look at RTE at all? It is simple to get the outside material of source by just flicking a switch. However, if RTE shows what is happening in Ireland, then its future is secure. That is what the future of Irish television has got to be about — ranging from using the brilliance of Noel C. Duggan in Millstreet to the talents of Dublin's Northsiders as shown in the recent widely acclaimed film *The Commitments* (*Irish Farmer's Journal,* 14 November 1992).

Sources: Interview with Noel C. Duggan.

11

Woodlands House Hotel

Anna Cunningham

History and Development

"Our objective is to provide an all-round top-quality service and excellent accommodation at middle-of-the-road prices," said Mary Fitzgerald, proprietor, at the official opening of the new Woodlands House Hotel, Adare, Limerick, on Friday, 4 October 1991.

The success story began in 1977 when Richard and Mary Fitzgerald anticipated the future development of the Irish economy from one that was highly dependent on agriculture to one in which tourism and the provision of services would become increasingly important. The 1970s also saw the commencement of other aspects of farming, such as agri-tourism, to enhance farm incomes. Richard and Mary Fitzgerald, acting on advice from relatives who had opened similar establishments in Kerry, decided to open their four-bedroomed bungalow to the public by offering farmhouse holidays to tourists. Mary Fitzgerald had some experience of the trade from her time as a receptionist at the Shannon Arms Hotel in Limerick, where she had worked prior to getting married.

In Spring 1980, the intended construction of the Aughinish Alumina plant at Aughinish Island, Askeaton, Co. Limerick, was announced and the Fitzgeralds decided to build an extra 12 en-suite bedrooms — the first of their kind in the mid-west — to cater for the larger market brought about by the construction workers at the Alumina plant. This extension was completed in Summer 1982, when the first of the building work began on the new plant, and Woodlands Guest House enjoyed consistently high levels of occupancy during the period of construction at Aughinish.

By the end of Summer 1983, construction on the Aughinish Alumina plant in Askeaton was completed, and the Fitzgerald family was left with a seasonal tourist market with 12 new bedrooms lying idle for six months of the year. Although the farm was still in operation, work in this area had been scaled down with all efforts being put into the guesthouse, so the family faced a problem. It was decided to apply for a hotel licence, which was granted in Autumn 1983. With the changing of the fire safety laws in the aftermath of the Stardust disaster in Dublin in 1982, many public houses throughout the country were forced to cease operations as they could not comply with these new laws. Woodlands obtained a bar licence relatively easily. The addition of a bar and a banquet room catering for 80 people meant that extra kitchen facilities were developed to deal with the increased capacity.

In 1986, because of the increasing numbers of clients, the Fitzgeralds decided to build again, with the main emphasis being put into the restaurant and banqueting rooms. An extra 80 covers were added to the restaurant, bringing the capacity up to 120 covers per setting, and 120 covers were added to the main banquet room — the Fitzgerald Suite — bringing capacity here to 200 covers. The increase in the size of the main banquet room led to a greater focus on the wedding business, which was seen to be very profitable. Additions were also made behind the scenes — the kitchen was doubled in size to cope with the extra business. The early parts of the week, however, remained relatively quiet, especially in the winter months, so two bedrooms were sacrificed for the construction of a meeting room to cater for 50 people. This was used extensively by local farming and other organisations, which boosted bar and food sales during the quieter periods.

In Spring 1990, the banqueting facilities were further extended to cater for up to 250 people. That summer, Richard and Mary Fitzgerald unveiled their £1.8 million plan to redevelop their grade B premises totally into a new modernised Grade A hotel. Work began that autumn, following the announcement that the Irish National Ploughing Championships were to be held in Limerick as part of the Treaty 300 celebrations. The National Ploughing Association showed great faith in Richard and Mary by choosing Woodlands House Hotel as the headquarters for the ploughing championship, even though the Association had only seen the plans for the extensive redevelopment of the hotel. This put a deadline of October 1991 for the completion of the building work. With work being carried out day and night during the last few weeks, the new Woodlands was completed on Friday, 4 October 1991. All of this development was funded without State aid or BES funding and was privately funded by Richard and Mary Fitzgerald. Apart from the quality product, service and friendly atmosphere which were always present in the hotel during its developing years, Woodlands, after the large development, offered a number of key features to its customers, which added to their overall comfort and general relaxation, as well as enabling the hotel to maximise revenues and profits.

These included the new development of 18 mini-suites and two executive suites (two bedrooms, a small meeting area and a jacuzzi, as well as all of the standard features), bringing the total number of rooms to 32. The emerging conference market was also catered for with the addition of a new fully air-conditioned conference room, aptly named the Treaty 300 Suite, which can cater for up to 100 delegates, and which boasts all of the most modern facilities. The new restaurant, the Brennan Room, catering for up to 108 people and offering the best of local quality food with exceptional value, and an extended bar facility, the Woodcock Bar, were also added to deal with the extra demand at the hotel.

In 1993, the banquet room, the Fitzgerald Suite, was extended again to cater for the growing wedding market. This has become one of the core areas of business of the hotel, and because trends were running toward larger weddings, the extended room was designed to cater for 320 people.

The year 1994 brought more changes to the hotel, with the addition of a further 24 mini-suites and two more executive suites. These were was seen as necessary, as the hotel had been running at close to 91 per cent occupancy since the official opening in October 1991, and the amount of business that was being turned away justified the new extension. This development began in September 1994 and the new rooms were opened to the public in March 1995.

Target Market

Eighty per cent of the business of the Woodlands House Hotel is generated locally, with the other 20 per cent coming from foreign tourists and the greater Irish market. In the Limerick region, Woodlands House Hotel is considered by many of those in the industry to be the wedding specialist and, because Adare is the "Wedding Capital of Ireland", the hotel caters for between 200 and 250 weddings per year. This large wedding trade is a highly repetitive business, with many couples holding their wedding reception in the hotel because their brothers, sisters or friends held theirs there. The large wedding trade does not allow bedrooms to be left unoccupied as special rates are offered which range from £16 to £35 per person, bed and breakfast, depending on the room occupied by the guest. The local target market draws from a 50–60-mile radius stretching from north Cork to north Kerry to south and east Clare and across to west Tipperary. This radius also includes Ireland's third largest city, Limerick, which has a population in the region of 250,000 people. The local trade is made up of family outings and dinners, as well the vibrant wedding business. Currently, weddings constitute 43 per cent of the hotel's revenue.

The hotel also enjoys good relationships with all of the local farming organisations, through the Fitzgeralds' involvement in the farming business. This provides a ready market for the hotel. The situation of the hotel on the outskirts of Adare and close to Limerick city, but also in the middle of the county of Limerick, allows for ease of access for all events organised by country-wide organisations such as the IFA, ICMSA and Macra na Feirme.

The remaining 20 per cent of the market is made up of tourists (both Irish and foreign-based), and there is also a strong commercial market. The competitive rates offered by the hotel to the commercial market — £25 per room, bed and breakfast — have led to very good occupancy levels when the wedding business is slack in the earlier parts of the week. The tourist market features mainly during the summer months, and the new rooms allow the hotel to cater better for this market — and tourists pay better room rates than anybody else. Tour business is also catered for, but only when the bedrooms would otherwise be empty, as rates in this sector are not as attractive as "rack" rates received from other tourists. The number of tourists visiting Adare is largely a result of the efforts of Adare Innkeepers, which promotes the town as a holiday destination, rather than a place to pass through on the way to the west of Ireland.

Organisational Structure

The hotel employs 82 full-time staff and 40 part-time staff. The organisational structure is illustrated on the following page.

Owner/Manager Profile

Mary Fitzgerald has an entrepreneurial nature and describes herself as innovative and constantly searching for new ideas. She comes from an agricultural background and had no exposure to the hospitality industry during her school-going years. She has an enthusiastic and outgoing disposition. She describes herself as a leader and one who would actively seek out responsibility.

Her route to the position of owner/manager started when she trained as a receptionist in a hotel in Limerick, where the general manager acted as a mentor. She acquired general business skills, particularly in the area of book-keeping.

Figure 11.1: Woodlands House Hotel Organisational Structure

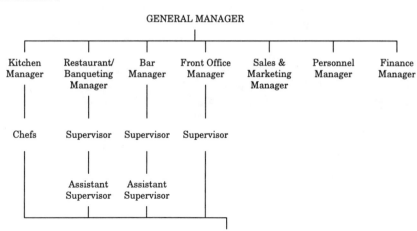

When questioned on the perception of her own role in the business, she describes herself as a listener, very much in touch with each department and somewhat of a matriarchal figure. She believes in participation and meets representatives from the various departments on a regular basis. She sees herself as a problem-solver when it came to staff problems. The hotel is non-unionised but a works committee exists which represents the staff.

The Woodlands House Hotel is very much a family-run business where Mary Fitzgerald acts as general manager and her husband Richard takes care of public relations. Their eldest children are pursuing qualifications in hotel management and are very much involved in the day-to-day running of the organisation.

Future Direction of the Hotel

At present, the hotel is concerned with maintaining market share. As a result, management strategies are very much repeat-business-oriented. There are no plans to build a second function room to cater for the ever-expanding wedding market. The hotel operates strictly on a "one wedding per day" basis.

It is felt by the Fitzgerald family that, in order to develop the long-term profitability of the existing hotel, and to increase its market share in the Mid-West region, something new must be created in the immediate vicinity of the hotel. With this in mind Shannon Development was approached with a view to gaining an insight into the long-term plans for the region in general, and especially in regard to the developing leisure industry. At the time, Shannon Development was near the completion of its grant-aided facility at Waterworld in Tralee, Co. Kerry, and plans were also on-stream to develop a similar facility in Kilkee, Co. Clare. The main reason for these leisure facility developments was to increase the length of the peak tourist season, and so to increase the length of the shoulder season, through the attraction of greater numbers of tourists. As there was no such facility between these two leisure pools within the mid-west, Shannon Development was delighted with the proposition that was on offer at Woodlands House Hotel. All of these leisure complexes had, or were to have, leisure pools, as opposed to the conventional tank pools, and therefore were seen to be a more attractive investment, which would increase tourist numbers to the region and would be financially viable.

The development of a leisure centre is currently being considered by Woodlands House Hotel. The main objective in the development of the leisure centre would be to increase the overall profitability of the hotel through the inflow of increasing numbers of people to the new attraction, and then to the hotel. The development of the leisure facility would greatly enhance the opportunity of the hotel to enter the "family leisure holiday" market which is emerging rapidly both in Ireland and abroad.

Source: Interviews with Richard and Mary Fitzgerald.

luate at that time. However a return on capital em-
ulated to the best of their efforts.

risk, Pat McDonagh states that no huge financial risk
ong-term loan was sought. Supermac's was already
enerous cash-flow. The gearing of the company was
creased.

gh stipulates that a management risk factor was their
states:

t risk factor of course is the management risk factor
expand too fast you mightn't have the management
trained or enthusiastic enough to go along with you.
e biggest snag I found.

najor boost for Pat McDonagh that he didn't have to
loan. His brand name and reputation for quality
imprinted in the minds of people in the Galway

s fast-food restaurant in Eyre Square is extremely
ble and clean and offers a wider menu-range than
ast-food restaurants in Galway. Supermac's is, no
reins" in Galway.

ow Ireland's biggest chain of family restaurants.
ntly has 22 restaurants nationwide in Ballinasloe,
arleville, Galway, Dublin, Ennis, Gort, Kilkenny,
, Nenagh, Tuam, Portlaoise, Thurles, Tullamore
of the restaurants already operate on a franchise

d its first Dublin restaurant in 1992. Opening in
ajor venture for Pat McDonagh. He agrees that
e of the Dublin restaurant is due in large part to
travelling from the country are already familiar
refore constitute much of the trade. So much so
urant has become known as "Culchies' Corner"!
d Ltd. currently employs approximately 1,400
f staff are trained to a very high standard on an
re of the training programme concentrates on
ustomer service with time also given to man-
and strategic planning.

s, Pat McDonagh:

eady on the market.

12

Supermac's

Thomas N. Garavan and Mary Garavan

Introduction

Pat McDonagh is the owner and managing director of Supermac's Ireland Ltd. The company currently operates at 21 locations nationwide. Supermac's "key players" include Pat's wife, Una, who takes a major interest in the training aspects, marketing manager, Paula Clarke, and other key staff members. The start-up story is quite an interesting one in that it was only by chance that Pat McDonagh entered into the fast-food business.

Background

Pat McDonagh was born and raised in the parish of Kilturragh, Co. Galway. He qualified as a primary teacher, but became interested in setting up his own business. In 1977 he purchased a premises in Ballinasloe, Co. Galway with the intention of setting up a business. Originally he intended setting up a pool-hall cum amusement arcade. This plan did not come to fruition, because planning permission was not granted. Pat McDonagh was forced to look at other alternatives and saw an opening for either a furniture or a fast-food business. A furniture business seemed initially promising as his premises were of substantial size. Following investigation he discovered that the furniture market in Ballinasloe was already well catered for. At that time Ballinasloe had few fast-food outlets. Pat McDonagh was convinced there was a definite niche in this market. He set up his first business there as the proprietor of a small-scale take-away in 1979.

The large premises was divided into two halves — one let to Michael Ward, a clothing retailer, and one-third of the other half at the front of the building was used for the fast-foot outlet. As Pat McDonagh was operating on a "shoe-string" budget, only minimal staff were employed. He employed a chef from the local area, who was an expert on food and had broad experience in catering. Pat

McDonagh himself had no experience. The second person hired was also a local man. He was really the "handy man", though he became involved in many areas of the business — working at plumbing, carpentry, lighting, and even assisting in the kitchen. Thereafter other part-timers joined, bringing the total employed to five people on the first day of business.

Market Research

Pat McDonagh confesses that he did no thorough market research at the outset. What he did amounted to a brief investigation into the general business scene in Ballinasloe. He believes that "if you keep your ear to the ground and your finger on the pulse, market research is merely cop-on". He claims that one can always see an opportunity and that very little market research is necessary. He illustrates his point by reference to his successful outlet in Thurles. Pat McDonagh had seen Thurles as a town with only three or four fast-food outlets. The town had a population of 8,000 people and a good hinterland. Pat McDonagh believed that all the ingredients needed for a profitable outlet were there without conducting major market research.

Sources of Finance

The purchase price of the premises in Ballinasloe was £35,000. Pat McDonagh states that approximately 43 per cent of that amount was raised from his own funds. He had previously been involved with a pool-table business in Dublin and had generated quite a substantial cash-flow from it. The balance of the cost of the premises was borrowed from the Bank of Ireland. Supermac's received no government grants as Pat McDonagh believes canvassing for grants is a "waste of time, energy and finance". There were no other investors in the business.

With respect to grants, the government at that time were less eager to provide finance compared to today. Government funds were tighter in the 1970s and the emphasis on new business development was not so pronounced. When Pat McDonagh entered into business, Ireland was in a relatively poor economic state and, more importantly, could not depend on EU aid — unlike today.

Supermac's accepted no advice from accountants or consultants. Pat McDonagh is of the opinion that one must learn about the fast-food trade by oneself — and, as he says, "get your hands dirty". Financial reasons have also shaped his actions, since consultants tend to charge very high fees.

First-time Recruitment

In terms of hiring first-tim[...]
he had the advantage of kr[...]
had no need therefore to e[...]
checking, curriculum vita[...]
recruitment was benefici[...]
type of system, he believ[...]
company, possibly incre[...]
consuming.

Management Style

Pat McDonagh profes[...]
within the company in[...]
vital importance for h[...]
his premises. He still[...]
involvement improve[...]
ment/employee relati[...]
consultants who adv[...]
they themselves ha[...]
McDonagh has, ho[...]
which give benefici[...]
successful compan[...]
had adopted and t[...]

Initial Costs of [...]

He explains how[...]
which lay ahead[...]
lying idle", wh[...]
McDonagh exp[...]
costs, construc[...]
for example, ir[...]
penses, bank [...]
foresee the ir[...]
costs can, in f[...]

The Comp[...]

Pat McDon[...]
the opening[...]
1991. This[...]
chip-shop i[...]
be Superm[...]
vides, in t[...]

He ex[...]
broad me[...]

difficult to eva[...]
ployed was cal[...]

As regards[...]
existed as no[...]
generating a g[...]
therefore not in[...]

Pat McDona[...]
greatest fear. He[...]

The bigges[...]
that if you[...]
necessarily[...]
That was th[...]

It was already a[...]
seek a long-term[...]
were already wel[...]
area.

Pat McDonagh[...]
spacious, comforta[...]
any of the other f[...]
doubt, "holding the[...]

Supermac's is n[...]
The company curre[...]
Ballina, Carlow, Ch[...]
Limerick, Loughrea[...]
and Waterford. Ten[...]
basis.

Supermac's open[...]
the capital was a m[...]
the high performanc[...]
brand loyalty. People[...]
with its style and th[...]
that the Dublin resta[...]

Supermac's Irelan[...]
people. All members [...]
on-going basis. The c[...]
quality, hygiene and [...]
agement development[...]

Market Factors

Marketing

In choosing his product[...]

- Looks at products al[...]

12

Supermac's

Thomas N. Garavan and Mary Garavan

Introduction

Pat McDonagh is the owner and managing director of Supermac's Ireland Ltd. The company currently operates at 21 locations nationwide. Supermac's "key players" include Pat's wife, Una, who takes a major interest in the training aspects, marketing manager, Paula Clarke, and other key staff members. The start-up story is quite an interesting one in that it was only by chance that Pat McDonagh entered into the fast-food business.

Background

Pat McDonagh was born and raised in the parish of Kilturragh, Co. Galway. He qualified as a primary teacher, but became interested in setting up his own business. In 1977 he purchased a premises in Ballinasloe, Co. Galway with the intention of setting up a business. Originally he intended setting up a pool-hall cum amusement arcade. This plan did not come to fruition, because planning permission was not granted. Pat McDonagh was forced to look at other alternatives and saw an opening for either a furniture or a fast-food business. A furniture business seemed initially promising as his premises were of substantial size. Following investigation he discovered that the furniture market in Ballinasloe was already well catered for. At that time Ballinasloe had few fast-food outlets. Pat McDonagh was convinced there was a definite niche in this market. He set up his first business there as the proprietor of a small-scale take-away in 1979.

The large premises was divided into two halves — one let to Michael Ward, a clothing retailer, and one-third of the other half at the front of the building was used for the fast-foot outlet. As Pat McDonagh was operating on a "shoe-string" budget, only minimal staff were employed. He employed a chef from the local area, who was an expert on food and had broad experience in catering. Pat

McDonagh himself had no experience. The second person hired was also a local man. He was really the "handy man", though he became involved in many areas of the business — working at plumbing, carpentry, lighting, and even assisting in the kitchen. Thereafter other part-timers joined, bringing the total employed to five people on the first day of business.

Market Research

Pat McDonagh confesses that he did no thorough market research at the outset. What he did amounted to a brief investigation into the general business scene in Ballinasloe. He believes that "if you keep your ear to the ground and your finger on the pulse, market research is merely cop-on". He claims that one can always see an opportunity and that very little market research is necessary. He illustrates his point by reference to his successful outlet in Thurles. Pat McDonagh had seen Thurles as a town with only three or four fast-food outlets. The town had a population of 8,000 people and a good hinterland. Pat McDonagh believed that all the ingredients needed for a profitable outlet were there without conducting major market research.

Sources of Finance

The purchase price of the premises in Ballinasloe was £35,000. Pat McDonagh states that approximately 43 per cent of that amount was raised from his own funds. He had previously been involved with a pool-table business in Dublin and had generated quite a substantial cash-flow from it. The balance of the cost of the premises was borrowed from the Bank of Ireland. Supermac's received no government grants as Pat McDonagh believes canvassing for grants is a "waste of time, energy and finance". There were no other investors in the business.

With respect to grants, the government at that time were less eager to provide finance compared to today. Government funds were tighter in the 1970s and the emphasis on new business development was not so pronounced. When Pat McDonagh entered into business, Ireland was in a relatively poor economic state and, more importantly, could not depend on EU aid — unlike today.

Supermac's accepted no advice from accountants or consultants. Pat McDonagh is of the opinion that one must learn about the fast-food trade by oneself — and, as he says, "get your hands dirty". Financial reasons have also shaped his actions, since consultants tend to charge very high fees.

First-time Recruitment

In terms of hiring first-time employees, Pat McDonagh explains that he had the advantage of knowing the majority of them personally. He had no need therefore to employ interview methods such as reference checking, curriculum vitae analysis and so on. The system of "local" recruitment was beneficial for the business at the early stages. This type of system, he believes, leads to better internal relations in the company, possibly increased productivity and is certainly less time-consuming.

Management Style

Pat McDonagh professes to using no distinct management style within the company in the first few years. He maintains that it was of vital importance for him to occasionally work behind the counter in his premises. He still believes in doing so today. He believes that such involvement improves staff morale and enhances general management/employee relations. He admits that he never had any respect for consultants who advise on management matters and claim that often they themselves had already failed in their own business plans. Pat McDonagh has, however, regularly attended management courses which give beneficial advice to employers. He also investigated other successful companies regarding the kind of management style they had adopted and their suitability to his business.

Initial Costs of Start-Up

He explains how his initial enthusiasm blinded him to the difficulties which lay ahead. One major cost was "funds tied up and buildings lying idle", while awaiting necessary planning permission. Pat McDonagh explains that there were other costs such as purchase costs, construction and equipment costs, plus "the invisible costs" — for example, insurance, legal fees, rates, continuous maintenance expenses, bank charges and so on. He believes that most people do not foresee the invisible costs or budget for them at the outset. These costs can, in fact, account for three or four percent of turnover.

The Company's First Major Expansion

Pat McDonagh states that Supermac's first major "expansion" was the opening of the spacious fast-food outlet in Eyre Square, Galway in 1991. This development enabled the transition from the "traditional chip-shop image to that of a fast-food restaurant". This outlet was to be Supermac's largest, comprising ten thousand square feet. It provides, in total, seating for over 300 people.

He explains that his decision to expand was assessed against two broad measures: return and risk. He admits return on the project was difficult to evaluate at that time. However a return on capital employed was calculated to the best of their efforts.

As regards risk, Pat McDonagh states that no huge financial risk existed as no long-term loan was sought. Supermac's was already generating a generous cash-flow. The gearing of the company was therefore not increased.

Pat McDonagh stipulates that a management risk factor was their greatest fear. He states:

> The biggest risk factor of course is the management risk factor that if you expand too fast you mightn't have the management necessarily trained or enthusiastic enough to go along with you. That was the biggest snag I found.

It was already a major boost for Pat McDonagh that he didn't have to seek a long-term loan. His brand name and reputation for quality were already well imprinted in the minds of people in the Galway area.

Pat McDonagh's fast-food restaurant in Eyre Square is extremely spacious, comfortable and clean and offers a wider menu-range than any of the other fast-food restaurants in Galway. Supermac's is, no doubt, "holding the reins" in Galway.

Supermac's is now Ireland's biggest chain of family restaurants. The company currently has 22 restaurants nationwide in Ballinasloe, Ballina, Carlow, Charleville, Galway, Dublin, Ennis, Gort, Kilkenny, Limerick, Loughrea, Nenagh, Tuam, Portlaoise, Thurles, Tullamore and Waterford. Ten of the restaurants already operate on a franchise basis.

Supermac's opened its first Dublin restaurant in 1992. Opening in the capital was a major venture for Pat McDonagh. He agrees that the high performance of the Dublin restaurant is due in large part to brand loyalty. People travelling from the country are already familiar with its style and therefore constitute much of the trade. So much so that the Dublin restaurant has become known as "Culchies' Corner"!

Supermac's Ireland Ltd. currently employs approximately 1,400 people. All members of staff are trained to a very high standard on an on-going basis. The core of the training programme concentrates on quality, hygiene and customer service with time also given to management development and strategic planning.

Market Factors

Marketing

In choosing his products, Pat McDonagh:

• Looks at products already on the market.

- Investigates what other companies are doing and "piggy-backs on their actions".

- Visits other companies in the USA and Great Britain, and observes trends there. In his view Irish people have always been demanding in relation to quality of products. Supermac's therefore ensured that, from the start, its products were of top quality.

Price Determination

In terms of pricing the products, he analyses the production cost and then adds whatever mark-up he deems necessary. In such pricing situations, the basic principle is the same — the application of mark-up to a cost to determine an appropriate price.

The Decision on Suppliers

When choosing suppliers, Pat McDonagh adopts the following criteria in order of importance: Quality, Consistency and Price. He states that most companies he deals with are reliable and consistent and show a high standard of integrity. He states that his ultimate concern is customer satisfaction.

Advertising

Pat McDonagh states that he relies mainly on word-of-mouth to advertise his outlets initially. He established different outlets ensuring high-quality service and standard of products and service. He then hoped the word would spread. He also placed advertisements in local newspapers.

Paving New Roads to the Future

In recent years, Supermac's has become involved in diversification of its business. Pat McDonagh states that he diversified internally as he does not believe in mergers or acquisitions. He believes that Supermac's can manage its operations independently. Three internal diversification strategies were employed.

McSandwich

Supermac's opened its independent sandwich-shop, "McSandwich", in Galway city in 1992. By opening McSandwich, Pat McDonagh made use of part of his Eyre Square premises which up to then had been idle. Pat McDonagh explained how he had conducted market research on the sandwich business by visiting London, Belfast and Dublin where it was clear to him that the main customers in those cities were office workers and builders on sites. He wanted to attract the same type of people in Galway city. McSandwich, however, was not successful; demand for sandwiches fell far short of what Supermac's expected. It subsequently closed as an independent shop in 1994.

Peaches and Cream

This is an ice-cream parlour that Supermac's opened in 1991 in its Eyre Square Restaurant in Galway City. Supermac's had begun to stock a vast variety of ice-creams and therefore establishing Peaches and Cream was, Pat McDonagh felt, a "natural development". Peaches and Cream is now operating successfully nationwide.

Funworld

Supermac's established Funworld in 1993 in Galway City. Funworld is a family entertainment centre as opposed to an arcade. It markets video games and other games, including pool. It epitomises Supermac's diversification into the leisure industry. Funworld, with its "new and bright decor" attracts families and groups alike. It is seen as the ideal venue for a company outing, clubs, or any group event "in search of an adventurous and exciting evening" as outlined in their prospectus. Funworld is at present performing well.

The diversification into Funworld was prompted by Pat McDonagh's previous experience of the leisure industry (pool tables) and also by the availability of idle space.

Plans for the Future

Supermac's has recently opened a leisure centre on the Ennis Road in Limerick. The centre contains a bowling area, kiddies play-area, adventure-play area for children, pool, snooker and a health gym. Apart from this development, Supermac's has no other plans for expansion.

Source: Interviews with Managing Director.

PART 3

ENTREPRENEURSHIP AND FIRM GROWTH: MANAGEMENT ISSUES

Overview

Following the creation of a new venture, many entrepreneurs discover that the venture they are now in charge of is quite different from the one they initially created. As the business expands, initially successful management practices may become obsolete. Recognition of this fact is of central importance to the continued survival of the business. Hofer and Mahon (1980) point out that it is essential for the owner/manager to recognise at an early stage that radical changes in the way the business operates will most likely be required if the venture is to survive in the long term. This admission tacitly accepts the need to change from an entrepreneurial management approach to a professional one.

There is a considerable body of evidence and research which suggests the types of modifications necessary before a successful transition can be made. Some of the areas to be modified include:

- A reliance on a highly centralised decision-making system

- An over-dependence on one or two key individuals for the venture's survival and growth

- An inadequate repertoire of management skills and training

- An over-paternalistic atmosphere

- A shortage of working capital

- The inability to innovate on a continuous basis.

There is also clear evidence to suggest that if the venture is to continue to strive for growth and profitability it must give attention to efficiency-related goals and activities. This adjustment in goals does not mean that the start-up goals of creativity and innovation should be abandoned, but rather that additional goals should be set. This may well involve the venture attempting to balance sometimes incompatible goals. To achieve efficiency it may be necessary to make adjustments in a venture's human resource strategy and structures. A helpful strategy in this situation is for the manager to put together a management team and delegate authority to team members.

A key issue relates to management behaviour. Denning et al. (1978) and Jones and Woodcock (1983) suggest that the owner-manager should be better able to cope with change and growth in the organisation. They point out that the owner and the firm are inextricably linked in that, as far as small business is concerned, the owner often *is* the firm. Therefore, it follows that an improvement in management effectiveness will improve the performance of the venture.

The need for competent owner/managers is illustrated in the first set of cases in this section. This describes the training and development initiatives of four owner/managers. The case scenarios illustrate that this development may be undertaken in a very unsystematic and haphazard way, whereas most of the literature points out that it should be undertaken in a systematic fashion. Training and development should not be viewed as just one particular activity but rather the sum of a number of activities. It should also not be something which is engaged in by the owner/manager in response to a crisis but used as a proactive strategy to help the owner-manager successfully manage the business.

The second set of case scenarios in this section focuses on the exporting decision process of the small firm. Exporting is often chosen by small firms when it lacks the resources to engage in foreign joint ventures or international direct investment. There is, however, considerable evidence to suggest that small firms are slow to consider the exporting decision and the case scenarios illustrate that there are many ways in which this task can be accomplished.

New product development is essential for any new venture; however, it carries a greater significance for the small high-technology venture. One-product ventures are quite common, but they are extremely vulnerable to competition. Having only one product can limit the growth potential of the new venture. The third set of cases in this section describes how a number of high-technology ventures tackled the new product development task. In all cases they were trying to broaden their product base and ensure continued success.

Many entrepreneurs think their problems are over once customers start to roll in. A large increase in sales, however, brings with it additional expenses and outgoings. Generally, these expenses have to be met before the customer pays up. Such overtrading has major implications for long-term survival. The final case selection in this section focuses on how three new ventures dealt with cash flow and working capital issues, how they managed to establish accounting and credit control systems and ultimately managed to walk the fine line between overtrading and undertrading.

13

Four Entrepreneurial Start-Ups

Briga Hynes

EIRELEC LTD.

Company Background

Eirelec Ltd. was established in 1978 in Dundalk by Tom Meers to manufacture and export a range of electronic digital thermometers for industrial and laboratory applications. In 1992, as a result of growth, the company moved to its own refurbished premises, a facility of 10,000 square feet. This also resulted in the creation of a new company called Advanced Manufacturing Technologies (AMT). Eirelec Ltd. is engaged in the manufacture of electronic instrumentation — for example, digital thermometers — while its sister company AMT is heavily engaged in the domain of contracts and electronic design assembly. The establishment of this new sister company provided CAD and surface-mount technology facilities for Eirelec Ltd.

AMT Ltd. is now in a position to offer spare design and surface-mount assembly capacity to other companies on a subcontract basis. The companies have developed a range of products and services, which they are continually updating because of dynamic market changes. Seventy per cent of the products are exported to Europe and Eirelec has recently opened a sales office in the UK. The company has achieved the ISO 9000 award.

Eirelec appears to have overcome all the initial teething problems associated with starting a business. It has now established structures and systems that allow smoother running and accommodate the now growing firm. The firm is still suffering some of the problems of delegation, which needs to be increased as the owner/manager still wants to have total control. It is also in the process of sourcing extra finance for the company, which now employs 30 staff.

Entrepreneurial Profile

Tom Meers comes from a middle-class, non-entrepreneurial background. Both parents worked in professional occupations. Tom progressed to a third-level college where he completed a diploma in management. He emigrated to the UK where he initially worked with Rolls Royce in a very junior position. Tom's family did not encourage him to look at entrepreneurship as a career option nor did he consider it himself at this stage. His primary motivation was to gain relevant experience that would provide him with career progression and promotion. To achieve this progression, Tom defined career objectives, which he achieved successfully by gaining experience in a variety of engineering and electronics companies. Tom's personal characteristics can be described as confident, shrewd, decisive, resourceful, and determined. He is also willing to take a "reasonable degree" of risk. He considered these attributes to be very important when starting up and establishing a business.

His educational qualifications did not appear to be major influencing factors in his decision to enter self-employment. However, once up and running, he often found himself referring back to his education and what he had learned.

Experience was critical in influencing his decision to "go it alone". The experience provided him with the knowledge of how to deal with people, developed his negotiating abilities and also made him "streetwise". It also resulted in him being a much more decisive, confident and resourceful individual. However, Tom did not have any specific management experience — his main experience being in the functional areas of industrial relations and engineering — which he considered to be a disadvantage in the early stages of business development.

After a number of years' experience, Tom felt that he needed another avenue to promote his career. Analysis of his experience and business knowledge to date led him to consider self-employment. Tom believes that the following were also important:

- The influence of "role models" — other individuals he met who had started businesses and operated them successfully

- The desire for independence, and the ability to be his own boss

- The desire for greater financial rewards.

He also mentions the level of personal satisfaction and the sense of achievement as being important factors in the decision to start in business. He enjoys the work he does, plus the challenge a small firm poses.

Tom spent two years evaluating his business idea, undertaking research and completing a business plan for funding. He chose the option of starting up on his own, as sole owner/manager of the firm, as it would allow him to operate with considerable flexibility and control. Tom's decision involved the trade-off between risk and the security of existing employment. Support and advice from family, friends and state organisations greatly assisted his final decision to start a business.

Organisational Structure

The management structure of Eirelec follows the traditional functional structure, where each function of the business is managed by one individual who reports directly to the owner/manager (see Figure 13.1). This structure accommodates the requirements of the firm and allows for improved communication throughout the firm. Tom considers that he has a balanced view of the overall business and emphasises the importance of having an understanding of functions such as marketing, finance, people management, etc.

Figure 13.1: Eirelec Ltd. — Organisational Structure

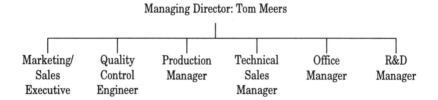

Managing Director: Tom Meers

| Marketing/ Sales Executive | Quality Control Engineer | Production Manager | Technical Sales Manager | Office Manager | R&D Manager |

Market Conditions

Eirelec is faced with volatile and rapidly changing demand patterns in the marketplace, which put pressure on the competitiveness of the company. Eirelec has reacted by implementing new technology and new product development. A critical element contributing to its success was the establishment of a sister company to provide essential back-up services and facilities for the firm. This provides a broader product/service range and gives Eirelec a competitive edge in the marketplace. Eirelec serves both the domestic and industrial sectors. Customer demands change, and updates and innovations in the products are required frequently. This puts pressure on the company for an effective customer and competitor evaluation process. Personal selling and active promotions are also important to ensure that awareness and knowledge of the company are high. R&D is an important function in the organisation as it takes responsibility for new product/technology development. The R&D section constantly tests new ideas and communicates with other sections to obtain new ideas.

The company is performing well, considering the many environmental factors which affect it, and is now involved in exporting, which accounts for approximately 70 per cent of overall sales. The decision to export was taken because of limited growth in the Irish market. Market research and analysis indicated greater potential for sales and profitability in the UK market. The trend to export will continue as the company intends to expand its international efforts to other European countries, such as Germany and France. The marketing/sales executive is currently evaluating market entry strategies for these markets.

Training and Development

Tom Meers believes that an involved management approach which motivates staff in the firm is essential. Heavy emphasis is placed on staff development and training. He encourages teamwork and involves staff in decisions. This has resulted in reduced turnover of staff. To achieve the correct management approach, he considers training to be very important. Tom had undertaken some professional programmes before starting in business, including:

• Diploma in Management (Part 1), provided by the Institute of Industrial Management

• A number of short-term part-time courses on personnel/industrial relations issues.

Tom considers that this training provided him with the business and management knowledge needed to ensure the growth of the business. This emphasis on training and development continues today in the organisation and is emphasised at all levels of the firm. Employees are encouraged to participate in relevant training programmes, which are often sponsored by the company, including:

• Induction training

• Customer awareness

• Telesales

• Techstart Programme

• Personal development (Creative management)

• Operator training

• Clerical training.

Tom is very satisfied with the results of the training undertaken by staff. These programmes not only provide increased technical and managerial knowledge, but also develop individuals personally, increasing their confidence and motivation. The programmes were structured very well in that they accommodated the time requirements of the company, while providing the mix of structured and unstructured learning situations. The unstructured learning involved role-playing, discussions and analysis of cases. Training needs of management and staff are reviewed at least once a year.

Tom places heavy emphasis on ensuring that staff in his firms have an opportunity to participate in the development of the business. This is achieved through open communication channels, suggestion boxes, meetings, etc. Performance evaluation indicates that staff are satisfied and motivated and no industrial relations problems have been encountered to date.

Future Developments

Eirelec realises that it is in a growth market with future potential for increased sales and market penetration. For the company to capitalise on this market, product development and quality are critical — this poses financial problems for Eirelec. Management now needs to decide what position it will take in the market and devise an appropriate strategy to achieve this position.

BHP LABORATORIES

Company Background

BHP Laboratories was founded in 1978 in Limerick by three entrepreneurs, each with different backgrounds. Two of the partners were engineers and the third was involved in the science area. The entrepreneurs were acquainted with each other before starting in business. Dermot Purcell is the focal point of the business.

The business was registered as a partnership, with each partner having an equal share. The ownership structure remains intact today, and is operating successfully. The company is involved in providing a range of technical services:

- Quality engineering

- Welding engineering

- Laboratory services

- R&D.

Services are also provided in design, verification, quality auditing, quality control and inspection. Quality and consistency are critical elements of the production process because of the service nature of their operation. It is critical that customers receive the same high level of quality each time. The company's services are exported to the UK through the establishment of an office in London. The company will continue its efforts in exporting and market development. A structured approach to market development is achieved by delegation of the marketing function to marketing departments in the various offices.

The company is expanding into new markets both domestically and internationally. It is also involved in developing new services to broaden its customer base. A structured management team has been implemented which accommodates the geographic composition of the company. The company now employs 35 staff.

Entrepreneurial Profile

Dermot Purcell is the main innovator in BHP Laboratories. Dermot is a member of a comfortable middle-class family — his father was involved in a professional occupation and his mother was a full-time housewife.

Dermot's family background encouraged personal and career development, resulting in Dermot attending a third-level institution, where he completed a course in the engineering field. While his parents encouraged him to be independent, confident and career-oriented, they did not specifically encourage Dermot to seek entrepreneurship as a career option. However, the development of the above characteristics, plus the completion of a third-level qualification were beneficial and contributed to his eventual decision to start a business of his own.

Dermot is an independent individual who has no problems making decisions quickly, is assertive and willing to take risks. He gained experience in a number of engineering companies, which provided him with job satisfaction and career enhancement. However, Dermot felt that he needed something else, which would allow him to work for himself. The following factors helped him to make the decision to "go it alone":

- The influence of other people who managed their own businesses successfully

- The availability and encouragement of individuals who were willing to act as partners and become involved in the business

- The desire to be independent, be his "own boss", which would allow him to pursue personal objectives

- Financial considerations — he wanted to ensure, as far as possible, that the financial gain of the business would at least be comparable to his existing financial position.

Dermot, now having satisfied his need for independence and being his own boss successfully, would never consider working for somebody again. Factors such as status, or recognition by others, were not important influencing factors. Once Dermot decided to start a business, he established it very quickly as he was young, single and did not have family or financial commitments. He did not consider job security as an issue. Encouragement and support, both financial and non-financial, assisted him greatly in the pre-start-up stage.

Organisational Structure

Management organised the company to accommodate the geographical requirements of the firm. There are three main locations: Limerick, Dublin and London. Each location is assigned a manager who has responsibility for all the functions and aspects of the business. Each location has the managing director's office as its final reporting centre. Centralised control is maintained. Dermot considers it important to be aware of, and involved in, all aspects of the business. This reporting structure facilitates the requirements of the market and the need to be flexible and provide all facilities to cater for each customer's requirements. Dermot considers that the organisation structure will also facilitate the growth and expansion of the company (see Figure 13.2).

Figure 13.2: BHP Laboratories — Organisational Structure

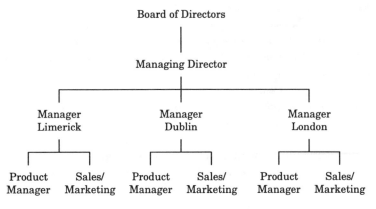

Market Conditions

BHP Laboratories operates in an industrial market. Customer orders vary between very large continuous, repeat purchases, to the one-off customer-specific jobs. Because of the changing nature of the market, it is critical that constant market research is undertaken to identify potential needs of existing and new customers. The customised nature of the market requires a heavy concentration of sales people in the firm. Competition in this sector is severe; therefore BHP needs to be innovative and to ensure that it has a competitive edge in the marketplace. To achieve this competitive strategy, the economic and technical environment is constantly monitored and evaluated. Because of the international nature of the company it is essential that constant monitoring of demographic and economic factors is undertaken in Europe.

Management Style

Dermot had an open and positive approach to management from the early stages of business. He realised that his main weakness was in his lack of management experience, and was happy to undertake training and development programmes to deal with this.

Prior to starting his business, Dermot had undertaken some professional academic programmes, obtaining a degree in engineering. This programme provided him with a very preliminary introduction to the concepts of business, but not in sufficient detail to allow him to manage a business.

Having started in business with the other two partners who were also technically knowledgeable, but did not have a business background, Dermot realised that while the production side of the business was running smoothly, major problems were occurring in the other areas — that is, there was a very high staff turnover and an inability to meet customer requirements. At this stage, Dermot decided to go on a development programme. He completed the Business Development Programme organised by the Irish Management Institute, which he considered very beneficial and relevant to his situation. The combination of in-class induction, workshops and in-company counselling allowed him to translate his learning into his everyday management activities.

Later in the company's development, Dermot attended the Export Development programme also run by the Irish Management Institute. This again was a combination of in-class lectures and in-company counselling, which provided the company with a detailed export strategy that facilitated successful exporting. This was critical as exporting is a major aspect of the business.

The combination of these programmes resulted in a critical turning point for the company's development. The results of the programmes were evident throughout the firm, resulting in changes in the following areas:

- Personal development

- Leadership style

- Greater employee participation

- Staff learning and development

- Emphasis on marketing and product development.

Dermot's approach is now more structured and organised, with improved analytical and decision-making skills. As a result of the improved organisation of work, Dermot has more time available to sit back and take an overall view of the firm's progression. He believes that this development process allowed him to become a more democratic manager.

Future Developments

Management is confident of the future of the firm, and realises the need to innovate continuously in order to capitalise on opportunities in the market. This innovation has to be driven by all staff within the organisation and will need to be formalised through the development of appropriate strategies.

SMITHSTOWN ENGINEERING

Company Background

Smithstown Engineering, located in Smithstown Industrial Estate in County Clare, was established in 1974 by Brian King, a trained fitter, together with two other individuals. The company was formed as a partnership, each having a one-third share of the company. However, as is often the case with partnerships, problems occurred, eventually resulting in Brian being left as sole owner and manager of the operation in 1980. Brian was faced with a very daunting task as he was a fitter by profession and did not have any previous managerial experience. The first few years of company development proved very difficult for Brian, as the firm had been left in a very poor financial position after the dissolution of the partnership. The company began to turn around by developing new products and markets.

Smithstown Engineering is involved in injection moulding, tooling, general fabrication, design and manufacture of machines to customer specification. The company supplies a broad range of products to different industry types — medical, chemical, health, etc. It has successfully obtained the ISO 9000 quality standard. Quality is a critical element of its production and is the main selling point for its products. Orders are produced to meet the specific requirements of individual customers, which results in technology being an important aspect of the firm. Smithstown Engineering is in the process of developing a standard line of products to ensure continuity. Brian has less day-to-day direct involvement in the firm and is more heavily involved in the strategic issues. The company now employs 45 staff.

Entrepreneurial Profile

Brian comes from a lower middle-class background and is the middle child in a family of three. He received second-level education but did not pursue a third-level qualification, as it was not encouraged by his parents, who felt that he should gain some form of trade, which would ensure that he would be able to gain employment easily. This resulted in Brian completing an apprenticeship course as a fitter. He obtained employment in a local company.

Brian's personality can be described as self-conscious, not outgoing or extroverted, which often caused him discomfort, especially in the early days of business. He is quietly decisive and determined, and does not consider himself a high risk-taker. He has the ability to make decisions and stand by those decisions, combined with the determination to see results achieved.

Brian had no problem obtaining work once trained as a fitter. However, as he gained experience, he found few promotional prospects. Work became routine and monotonous, and the monetary benefits associated with work became less motivating. For about 18 months, he considered the idea of starting in business. Originally, the idea was a concept that was neither very realistic nor viable. He also did not feel very confident or comfortable with implementing the idea on his own, so he mentioned it to a friend, who became interested. Eventually, Brian and two other fitters came together to work consciously on developing a business. As the business idea became more developed, it presented a daunting and frightening task for the promoters, as none of the individuals involved had any experience of managing a business.

Brian's primary motivations for entering business were:

- Dissatisfaction with his existing job, and a desire to rectify this

- A wish for independence "to do his own thing"

- A feeling of being very knowledgeable and comfortable in his area of expertise.

Brian had also developed a number of contacts which he considered would be beneficial when starting up. Overall, he wanted to undertake a challenging task that would provide job satisfaction while also giving him the independence he wished for. He wanted to follow through, with determination, an idea he considered viable.

Brian's final decision was based on an evaluation of the level of risk involved, both with regard to job security and financially, a risk that he finally considered to be manageable. Family commitments — wife, children and mortgage — also influenced his decision. Family support was very important at this stage of business development.

Organisation Structure

The marketing and sales function is maintained at the apex of the organisation, with Brian assuming these responsibilities. He is considering the employment of a financial director who will manage and provide greater control over the financial side of the business. Brian concentrates on quality and the technical side but also realises the importance of the business elements. He considers it important to have a clearly defined line of communication in the organisation, which will ensure that all employees know who they are reporting to and what their area of responsibility is. All major decisions have to be passed to the top management before being acted upon. Tight control over decisions and employees is maintained at the apex of the organisation.

Figure 13.3: Smithstown Engineering — Organisational Structure

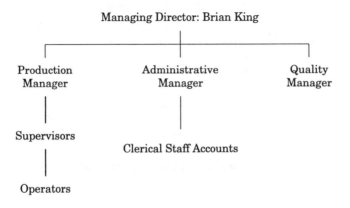

Market Conditions

Smithstown Engineering has changed in the past number of years, because of both internal and external influences. The internal influences have mainly arisen from the improved management skills and Brian's innovativeness. However, external forces have also caused the company to change.

Perhaps the most influential factors causing change are the rapidly changing requirements of the customer, which demand that the firm be proactive and be able to perceive these changes and plan accordingly. Very high levels of quality are required by customers, leading to the installation of a rigid quality control process, which is governed by the ISO 9000 quality standard.

Changes in technology have posed problems for Smithstown Engineering. It is critical that the firm has up-to-date technology to ensure that it can produce the product at a competitive cost and quality. This imposes financial pressures.

For the first few years of business, Smithstown Engineering was protected from severe competition, which was beneficial as it provided the company with an opportunity to develop a reputation in the marketplace. However, in the past few years, competition has become a problem, forcing the company to identify unique selling points and a distinct competitive advantage. Brian considers the company's emphasis on customer service and flexibility to be its main competitive advantage.

Management Characteristics

As the company progressed and increased its number of employees to 45, Brian found that his role in the organisation needed to change. He was indifferent to the area of management development, mainly because he did not perceive it to be important in the early stages of formation. His main priority was to ensure that the business was operating at least at break-even point. His early attitude to management development would be similar to his attitudes to education, which were generally negative.

Brian did not participate in any management development or enterprise programmes prior to starting up in business. His technical knowledge was not sufficient to expand and direct the business. The company had potential because demand existed for the product though management did not have the skills to meet this demand.

The project officer from Shannon Development working with the firm decided that the company had reached a crisis stage. While the company's products and services were in great demand, problems existed in co-ordinating the activities of the firm. Therefore, he recommended that Brian should attend some form of management development programme. Brian opted for a Business Development Programme organised by the Irish Management Institute, as its flexible nature facilitated his time constraints. He had also heard very positive feedback from individuals who had participated in the programme.

Brian was hesitant about attending the programme as he felt conscious of his lack of academic background, assuming that others on the programme would come from more progressive companies and would not identify with his particular problems.

The programme had the advantage of providing one day in-company counselling each month. This, in conjunction with two residential days each month, provided the ideal combination, because it did not force Brian to be away from his company for long periods. It also provided an opportunity for in-company development, which was critical for this company. Brian is now very positive about the programme as it provided him with a knowledge of what is required to manage a business efficiently, and accommodated his learning style. The in-company counselling provided him with the ability to take an objective view of the methods used in managing the business. The existing management style had many weaknesses including the lack of delegation, too high standards, lack of planning and poor co-ordination.

On completion of the programme, a number of changes were introduced. Changes were made at all levels of the company. For example, a job costing system was put into operation, employees had to clock in and out of work, quality levels were improved, increased delegation occurred throughout the organisation, more efficient sources of raw materials were evaluated, orders were processed and completed in a more logical format, records were maintained, and customer lead time and service improved.

These benefits convinced Brian of the need for training and development throughout the organisation. The programmes undertaken by key staff were in the areas of marketing, finance and R&D. Each year a training budget is allocated for management and staff training.

Future Developments

Smithstown Engineering is continuously seeking new customers and markets for its products. The development of a standard line of products has provided the company with considerable revenue, which has enabled it to match the market requirements in terms of new customer-specific products. Greater emphasis is now placed on marketing and customer service. Staff turnover has been reduced, providing a more motivated workforce.

OVELLE LTD.

Company Background

Ovelle Ltd. was established in Dundalk in 1975 as a result of a buy-out by Sean Gardiner who identified an opportunity of turning into a profitable company one that was operating in a growth market, but was loss-making.

The company originally manufactured a range of pharmaceutical products. In 1982, after undertaking market and product research, a decision was made to manufacture a range of dermatological products. To facilitate this expansion, the company moved into a new purpose-built factory. Ovelle now employs 50 full-time employees.

Ovelle supplies both branded and generic products, mainly to the domestic market. Because of the fluctuations in demand in this market, new product development is a constant concern. The company has a variety of products at different stages of the product life-cycle. At present, the majority of products are in the late introductory/growth stages, which provides the company with a balanced portfolio of products.

Competition is a critical element that is constantly monitored and evaluated by the marketing department. This provides feedback to the firm, which forms the basis of its marketing plan. The company now sells both generic and branded products to accommodate varying market requirements. It is currently involved in the export market, selling its generic products to Denmark, UK, Holland and Germany. Attempts are also underway to get branded products into the UK and German markets.

Entrepreneurial Profile

Sean Gardiner comes from a middle-class background, of non-entrepreneurial parents. Sean progressed to become a pharmacist, and secured his early work experience in this area. While not ruling out the potential of starting a business, he did not seriously consider the option until the late 1970s.

His educational experience tended to be very scientifically oriented, concentrating specifically on pharmacy. No business education was received. He gained experience as an industrial chemist, and also worked in the area of brand development. This provided him with an insight into some aspects of management, especially marketing.

Sean is confident, decisive, enjoys a challenge and variety in work, has the ability to take a risk, but not just for the sake of taking risks. He enjoys working with people, and integrates well with his peers and staff.

Sean Gardiner was employed in his specialist area when he became aware of a business opportunity. This opportunity arose at the same time as redundancies were occurring in his original employment. Further contemplation of the business opportunity, plus discussions with friends, pushed Sean to evaluate the possibility of self-employment as a career option.

Research was conducted into the business opportunity, which indicated that a viable potential market existed. Once Sean was satisfied with the financial viability of the business opportunity, he then examined his personal circumstances and ability to manage a new business. The final decision was based on the following:

- The opportunity to avail of a redundancy package in his existing firm

- Availability of an appropriate opportunity (buy out)

- A challenge in entering a new field and job

- The importance of personal satisfaction and a sense of achievement

- The perceived financial benefits.

Organisational Structure

The structure of the organisation is well defined and provides a logical reporting system. The owner/manager still maintains control and is the eventual decision-maker. This requires that Sean be available in the company for the majority of the time, often resulting in long working hours and less time for planning and strategy development. As the organisation increases in size, the main challenge is to ensure that communication is maintained effectively (see Figure 13.4).

Market Conditions

The company is involved in the pharmaceutical industry, which is competitive and dictated by very high quality and safety standards. His experience as a pharmacist made Sean aware of this, resulting in a very stringent quality control and testing department in operation in the company. The quality manager in the firm needs to be up-to-date to implement the many EU standards.

As plans to export progress, management will be faced with much more severe competition. The firm does not appear to have a specific plan of action to devise a competitive advantage or unique selling point. The constant changing market requirements plus regulations impose pressure on Ovelle's technology requirements. Sean considers this a strength of the firm as it has access to sophisticated technology and computerisation which ensures constant quality.

Figure 13.4: Ovelle Ltd. — Organisational Structure

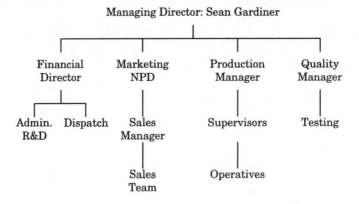

Management Characteristics

Prior to the company acquisition Sean's experience and qualifications were primarily in the field of pharmacy. While this was critical in the development of the firm, Sean soon began to realise that it was not sufficient to deal with the many varying and often complex business and market issues that needed to be addressed.

Experience in running his new business resulted in Sean realising his many areas of weaknesses. Initially, he envisaged that it would be sufficient to recruit business staff who were qualified in their relevant areas. However, this did not relieve the need for Sean to obtain some sound business knowledge.

After a period of time, Sean participated in and successfully completed a number of management development and business development programmes. The practical element of the programmes encouraged him "to think on his feet". This developed his confidence and decision-making abilities. In-company counselling also provided many benefits, as it forced him to observe his own firm on an objective basis; it also assisted him in implementing some of the learning experience from the programme.

However, Sean found it very difficult to find the time to attend the programme and to complete the out-of-class assignments. The cost of the programme was a factor that restricted participation in further programmes. It was considered that this money could perhaps be better allocated to more tangible expenditure.

Nonetheless, Sean's training and development activities have provided a number of benefits to the firm:

- He has been helped to understand the basic business functions and how they should be managed.

- He has been forced to sit back and take a more objective view of the company, to highlight the problem areas.

- He has been helped to understand the basic aspects of finance which had been a major problem.

- He has been assisted in planning, and therefore creating a focus for the company.

- He has been helped to develop personally, and has been provided with improved communication and negotiating skills.

The importance of the non-technical side of the business and how to integrate these two areas is now more apparent in Ovelle.

Future Developments

Sean considers that the main teething problems of the company have been successfully overcome. It has increased market share, increased employment and is placing emphasis on new product development. This growth has led to the need for increased financial resources.

Sources: Interviews with company personnel.

14

The Small Business Exporting Decision: Seven Case Situations

Briga Hynes and Thomas N. Garavan

Introduction

One of the major challenges facing small Irish indigenous businesses is the need to enter the export market to attain long-term growth and success. There is considerable evidence to suggest that many Irish small businesses have a poor record in this area — largely due to the inability to innovate and develop appropriate product ideas, a lack of financial capability and limited market information and assistance. The cases that follow illustrate how seven small Irish micro-businesses approached this task.

THE FRAGRANCE BOUTIQUE

In 1991, Roy Donaldson set up "The Fragrance Boutique" in Dublin as a small business venture, whose prime motivation was the import substitution of potpourri and related products, the market for which had been increasing steadily in the past five years. Initially two people were employed. There are currently nine and turnover is forecast at £250,000 for 1995, up from £120,000 in 1994. In 1992 domestic and foreign sales were evenly divided. However by June 1995 the home base had increased to 70 per cent.

The Fragrance Boutique had approximately 30 per cent of the home market when it began exporting. Exporting was an ambition but not a conscious decision at the time — the export destination was not visited at all, since Fragrance Boutique was satisfied with the foreign distributors with whom they dealt. Distributors were seen as the most suitable method of both domestic and foreign distribution. They are given a 28 per cent profit margin on sales. The use of foreign distributors saves Fragrance Boutique having to set up a sales team, transport and large accounts, which would all amount to substantial costs for a small producer. Foreign distributors also exhibit the company's products abroad.

Table 14.1: The Fragrance Boutique — Sales

Sales	1992	1994
Domestic	50%	70%
Foreign	50%	30%

Product Research

Product research was carried out in Birmingham before the business was set up. Results showed that there had been a large increase in potpourri demand since 1980. In addition, having worked in the retail trade for several years, Donaldson knew where products were imported from, which distributors were used and which retailers were targeted. This knowledge formed the basis of his market research and encouraged him to move forward, confident in the venture he was undertaking. Market research was not carried out when entering the foreign market as it was not deemed necessary, given that foreign distributors had approached the company initially. Fragrance Boutique operates a "30 day net monthly" credit control policy, but payment is always nearer to 60 days. Distributor credit worthiness is assessed by looking at their current size, turnover and retail destinations.

Figure 14.1 shows the initial financial aid and advice received by the company and what it currently requires.

Export Destinations — Sales, Marketing and Competition

The main destination, and the most successful, apart from Ireland, is Germany. Fragrance Boutique met a large distributor who was immediately prepared to distribute its products. Other destinations include Abu Dhabi, Canada, America, Japan, the Channel Islands and the UK. Many of these destinations were not consciously chosen but occurred through various encounters at trade fairs and exhibitions.

The Japanese and Abu Dhabi destinations were suspended as orders were too small to justify market placement. The Italian and UK markets are being actively pursued at the moment. Thus far, Ireland has been very successful. Donaldson now supplies his products to all Irish potpourri distributors except one.

Sales promotion and brochures are the most used form of advertising but trade fairs and exhibitions are the lifeblood of the company. In addition, foreign sales are increasing with the expansion of distributors. Distributors are given incentives to promote the product. Competition, at home and abroad, is considerable. Many foreign competitors have cheaper prices and Donaldson believes that Chinese competition is considerable because of its lower labour costs.

Donaldson believes that he should have pushed for a new factory sooner, as a lot of money was wasted on renting. However, he also realises that he may not have received the finance for such an undertaking. He sees capital as the biggest single obstacle to setting up and believes in operating the business on a shoe-string for the first 12 months.

Figure 14.1: Initial Financial Aid and Aid Now Required

Initial Financial Aid and Advice

- Personal resources
- Bank of Ireland provided an investment sum equal to that of Mr. Donaldson. The rate charged was 14% at one stage, it is currently 10.5% p.a.
- An Bord Tráchtála (ABT) provided an advertising grant towards the cost of producing labels and brochures. ABT also provided a travel grant.
- ABT gave advice on how to approach certain markets.

Financial Aid and Advice currently sought

- Personal resources
- ICC are providing a 10-year loan, fixed at 6.75% p.a.
- Forbairt want equity to equal any investment on its part. It will provide a 25% grant, if new premises are obtained at the Enterprise Centre in Malahide Marina.
- ABT is currently seeking out the location of potential distributors in the UK market.

SUZANNE MAY POTTERY

Suzanne May set up as a sole trader in pottery manufacture in 1983, employing one person. She has subsequently become a limited company and now employs 10 people in Dublin. In 1995, 15–17 per cent of production was exported with the remainder sold on the home market.

Entry into the export market was not planned — it just happened. In the past the majority of overseas buyers were interested only in large manufacturers but this has changed in the last few years with more foreigners coming to "Showcase" and other similar Irish exhibitions (indicating that small business promotion is paying off). It was through contacts at exhibitions that Suzanne started exporting. She exports direct to independent high-profile retail outlets, or else uses distributors. However, she believes that most buyers want direct contact with their suppliers for such a specialised product, since resulting sales may depend on how the product style fits in with the "image" or "look" of that outlet, be it at home or abroad.

Market research was undertaken by travelling to various shops to see if there was a market for pottery. Any customer referral was helped by Suzanne's preliminary display in a showroom of Bord Fáilte. She attended three seminars held by An Bord Tráchtála (ABT), but felt they were not tailored for her specific needs, but more for larger manufacturers. She also attended a management development course but found that very few speakers dwelled on the small business area, thus rendering the programme largely unsuitable.

Suzanne went on two field trips organised by ABT — the first in February 1993 to Frankfurt, the location of the largest consumer craft design fair in the world. The mission was extremely successful, providing much information on customer needs and competitor styles. The second field trip was to Denmark in February 1994 where similar information was acquired. Both trips were more for design purposes than selling. Product ideas were noted for future R&D. The trips were very focused and worthwhile, primarily because ABT worked with one medium — the craft industry. On start-up the IDA provided a 45 per cent grant on all new equipment and rent charged, and employment grants from various bodies such as FÁS and ABT were obtained. She also received a travel grant from ABT.

The business operates cash on collection or cash on delivery for first-time orders; thereafter the policy is 30 days from the invoice date.

Exporting and Marketing

Export destinations include Scotland, Northern Ireland, Italy, Belgium, Austria and North America. The most successful are Northern Ireland and Scotland, largely due to the Celtic and cultural associations. However, Suzanne's success is determined more by the type of outlet in the country than the country itself. In addition, the cost of initial transportation is very prohibitive, especially for small orders.

There is considerable export potential but the issue of extra production and storage space comes into focus once the export option is considered. It is a case of production trying to keep up with demand. If this problem can be overcome, then ultimately, the way to go for future sales is through independent retailers.

Suzanne believes that growth and development could occur at a faster rate were it not for the cautiousness and low risk-orientation of the specialised pottery industry. She believes that product development (design and shape) is very important and could be further developed to suit specific markets.

Publicity is mainly by way of advertising features in magazines and newspapers such as *IT*, *Image*, *Sunday Business Post* and *Irish Interior*. Here the readership is smaller, more specialised and has a more focused target. In the case of postal enquiries, brochures are sent out to customers and are also used in trade fairs and exhibitions.

STUDIO O'GAMHNA

In possession of a unique production technique, four partners set up Studio O'Gamhna in Dublin in 1990 to manufacture collectibles, primarily for the export market. Initially, 15 people were employed and in the first year of business 60 per cent of sales were domestic with 40 per cent exported. In 1995, Studio O'Gamhna is a limited company with only one (Philip Gaffney) of the original partners remaining. It now exports 90 per cent of sales and has six full-time employees and six contractors.

Studio O'Gamhna is now only a trade name but it is promoted heavily in the US for its Irishness. The registered company name is Cultured Collectibles Ltd. which is less ethnic for targeting the Irish and British markets.

The Exporting Decision

Entry to the export market began simultaneously with production — the business was set up to export primarily to the US. Gaffney researched and visited the US on several occasions and the company currently employs two people there. In addition, he entered a joint venture with White-Hurst Imports Inc. which secured the company a place in 12 showrooms, hence further exposing the company name to potential customers. White-Hurst is a large distributor of European giftware. Gaffney also deals with Carisma, which has 36 agents. Monroe Collectibles, which has 45 agents, has agreed a contract for £250,000 per year and additional orders are also processed at various trade shows.

Philip Gaffney researched the giftware business in 1988. Looking at the margins and markets for various products and noting that there were no strong brand leaders, he identified potential for a newcomer to the market. Gaffney also visited "Showcase" and examined the production technique of Irish producers, such as Aynsley and Royal Tara to establish the cost of production and overheads.

Having decided to represent Irish culture by entering the ornamental giftware market, Gaffney travelled to Britain and carried out research in London and Bristol. He then went to the US, where he met Eileen McGrath at ABT, who introduced him to the US giftware market. In researching the US, which included travelling to Disney-world, Gaffney got the idea of producing an ornamental Irish village display. Market research led him to believe that Irish culture was not truly represented and Americans were not educated about differences between Irish and UK cultures.

He decided to go ahead with the production of the ornamental Irish village, selling each collectible part separately. He agreed orders before leaving the US. Each ornament would be accompanied by a different village "story", which Gaffney wrote himself. The objective was to attract customers to the product through the added selling-point of these stories. The product range proved successful.

Since his entry into the export market, Gaffney has added to his collection range as well as devised new ones, such as a Chess Set, prompted by the World Chess Championships.

In order to successfully enter the export market, the business got financial aid and advice from a number of sources:

- In 1991 the IDA approved a £4,000 per job grant.

- Personal investment of £5,000.

- A joint venture with White-Hurst Import Inc., an American company.

- ABT provided advice on showrooms in Ireland and the US and he was introduced to the US giftware market. He also went on an ABT-funded trade mission to Frankfurt.

Gaffney found that many of the existing financial packages had limitations. However the Dublin County Enterprise Board (CEB) agreed to match what he put into the business up to a maximum of £50,000, subject to close monitoring.

Sales and Marketing

Sales and marketing effort consisted of:

- A feature on RTE's "Live at Three" programme

- Direct selling/Cold-canvassing

- 20,000 one-page brochures mailed — 10,000 were sent to US stores and gift shows while the remaining 10,000 went to a US consumer catalogue

- Trade shows in Ireland and US

- In-store promotions — painting the ornaments in a shop to test reaction.

In terms of payment, every new account is cash-on-delivery — thereafter 30 days credit is provided. Payment from the US is quite efficient compared to Ireland because everything is linked to one's social security number. Even public utility supplies may be cut off by the credit bureau if debts are not settled within the required time period.

In the US there are approximately 500 Irish ethnic shops (Blarney, etc.) and 25,000 speciality gift shops (Hallmark, etc.). Gaffney believes that many Irish exporters of giftware start with the 500 and stay there — he has, however, now targeted the larger number having succeeded with the smaller.

UNITHERM PRODUCTS LIMITED

In 1983, Unitherm Products Ltd. was set up in Dublin to manufacture quality hygiene products. It was taken over by Gerard Killen in January 1993 and since then has made very significant progress. Before the take-over there were six employees and 35 per cent of sales were exported. At the end of 1995 it employed 10 people.

The Export Decision

Exporting had already commenced before Gerard Killen took over the organisation but it is now more actively pursued. Distributors/agents are used for sales abroad and an exclusive agreement with each distributor is drawn up. Killen has travelled to all export destinations since his arrival, as he believes that it is essential to establish visible contact with the distribution company. As Unitherm is still a small company, Killen believes it important to deal with a "division two" distributor, effectively a small distributor. The logic behind this is that a small distributor does not make large demands and they cannot control the manufacturer. They may even offer a better deal than a large distributor.

The Australian market was investigated in 1994. Market research was carried out by a private consultant, arranged by An Bord Tráchtála (ABT). Having identified potential distributors from the report, letters were sent to each one. Shortly after, in November 1994, Killen went on a trade mission to Australia with ABT to investigate the market for himself. Follow-up letters were sent to the same distributors together with product samples.

Research on a UK distributor to represent Unitherm Products was pursued at the library in ABT's offices through a yellow pages directory. The outcome is that Britannia Hygiene plc is now an exclusive agent for Unitherm and already its products are in all the terminals at Heathrow Airport.

Research on Thailand and Malaysia illustrated that there are large income disparities among the population. However in the capitals, Bangkok and Kuala Lampur, there are very large hotels indicating a huge market for hygiene products. Unitherm works with a large distributor in Thailand to sell its products — including to the Eastern Orient Express Train.

Sources of Advice and Financial Aid

The company has availed of a large number of financial and information sources:

- **IDA**: Initially the IDA provided a 5-year rent-free policy, but that was 11 years ago. Current requests made by Killen to the IDA took 3 months to respond to and were subsequently rejected.

- **Eolas (now Forbairt)**: "Techstart" programme — which provided 50% of payment costs to recruit a full-time electrical engineer.

- **Bank of Ireland Enterprise Development Loan**: A loan was provided at 6.75 per cent, fixed over 5 years (a good credit rating had previously been established).

- **ICC Business Expansion Scheme**: Private investors provided funds in April 1995.

Exporting and Marketing

The main export destinations are Northern Ireland, the UK, the Benelux and Scandinavian countries, Thailand, Malaysia and Australia. Many of these countries speak good English, making them easier to sell to.

In terms of marketing the following are used:

- National newspaper advertising

- Good relations with its distributors

- Trade shows — including "Vintera", the Publican and Hoteliers' Show.

Environment awareness among customers and potential customers is increasing all the time. In the UK there is currently a move to reduce chemical toxins in hygiene products. Unitherm products are already environmentally friendly and, hence, more user-friendly. Killen believes it is important to be standards-accredited (ISO 9000) for acceptance in export markets. He also believes that product testing, research, analyses and compliance must be observed at all times.

CLARA CANDY

Clara Candy, a soft confectionery manufacturer located in County Offaly, was set up in 1986 with support from the IDA and the Hill Samuel Business Expansion Scheme Fund. Initially it recruited 30 people; by June 1995 it employed more than 140. It exports to 35 countries, accounting for 90 per cent of its turnover. The UK alone represented 36 per cent of production in 1994 and, of that, 35 per cent was for private labels, with 65 per cent brand-oriented. The managing director believes that the success of the company stems from its commitment to market research, its export-orientation and its belief in strategy-building.

The expansion and growth of Clara Candy has been so significant that turnover exceeded the £3 million mark in 1994. However, to arrive at this position, Clara Candy spent several years as a small business in the export market.

Market Research

Before entering the export market, market research was undertaken which indicated that the annual growth rate of the soft eating product area was 5–7 per cent and the total sugar confectionery consumption rate in Ireland, Britain and North European counties was 17 per cent, with significant growth also noted in the US and Canada. These research findings were checked by auditors and by ABT. The research also highlighted that the sugar confectionery industry was not brand-oriented or heavily promoted, hence making it easier for a small operator to enter the market. This provided Clara Candy with the incentive to build a brand. The initial strategy, however, was to build volume (in order to pay for day-to-day expenditure) and then to progress to more sophisticated branding.

Clara Candy was fortunate in that its establishment coincided with the closure of two sweet manufacturers in Dublin — Cleeves Toffees Ltd. and Rowntree's Dublin plant, thus providing the new company with confectionery experts ready to take on new employment. Good luck struck again when a large UK confectionery group — the Alma Group — went into receivership in the early 1990s. Clara Candy acquired one of Alma's brand-names — "Squirrel Horn" — which it used to launch the company into the UK brand area. Distribution was primarily through large wholesalers, buying groups and importers.

Clara Candy is an extremely successful company that very obviously strives for excellence, but its future depends on the development of new products (the product development team meet every two weeks) and packaging concepts and significant growth in export activity, given that 90 per cent of its output is exported. This makes the company totally dependent on the export market for survival.

The company sees two major problems facing it in the British exporting context:

- Slow payment of export refunds is a major disincentive to the future development of sales, especially where payments have not been received at all because they have fallen outside the time-scale allowed. (Export refunds arise to bridge the gap between high European Community price levels and lower world prices. They occur when an EU producer exports an agricultural product, sugar in this case, to a destination outside the EU. Clara Candy's problem is caused primarily by the number of mechanisms through which payment clearance must pass before it reaches the company.)

- Volatility of the IR£, which was revalued against sterling by approximately 5–6 per cent in the two years to the end of 1995. This makes exports expensive and forces the company to cut margins to be competitive. This is quite difficult for a small business where margins are usually quite tight. A continual currency deviation could result in large losses.

BEELINE HEALTHCARE

Beeline Healthcare was established in Dublin in 1989 by Gerry Finn, a chemistry graduate with experience in the pharmaceutical and food industry. Concentrating on vitamin and supplement products, the company initially employed four people but, by June 1995, numbers had increased to 25. Having identified a gap in the sector, the prime motivation of the company was one of import substitution.

Having impressed the IDA with research findings, the company was assigned to a Business Enterprise Scheme (a fast track scheme for companies showing significant potential). The assignment paid off, because in 1995 Beeline held 40 per cent of the Irish market and its product range had grown from six products to 29 with six more in development. Forbairt has now become a shareholder in the business.

Beeline's entry onto the UK market coincided with the sterling crisis, thus forcing it to seek alternative export destinations. While the UK is now a significant market for Beeline, having secured a place with Boots (1,200 outlets) and Superdrug (770 stores), the East European market has also been successfully exploited and the company is currently expanding into the Japanese market.

The company's success can be attributed to the manufacture of a product which is competitively priced and uses a distinctive colourful packaging. Various products are targeted at different national markets based on consumer demand — for example, in Eastern Europe, people eat a lot of meat and less fibre, so fibre supplements sell well while, in Japan, additive-free products are in good demand.

FIACLA

Having obtained the idea of making an Irish toothpaste with an Irish name from an article in *The Irish Times*, Richard Brierley set up Fiacla in 1984. The business began in Connemara but moved to Bray shortly thereafter. This remains its current base. It currently employs 15 full-time staff with an additional seasonal workforce of nine.

Brierley received a small set-up grant from Údaras na Gaeltachta in 1984 to add to his own initial investment of £15,000. At the same time there was a "Buy Irish" campaign, run by the "Young Ireland Movement", which helped with promotion. Fiacla was also promoted on the Late Late Show. All the marketing and distribution was, and still is, handled by Gillespie & Co., which subsequently purchased 51 per cent of Fiacla in 1989. Significant financial investment has since been made by both Gillispie and Brierley without much assistance from the government in terms of grants.

Private label sales now make up 15 per cent of domestic sales and Fiacla claims to hold a market share of 16 per cent in Ireland. Almost two-thirds of total sales are exported — to the UK, Spain, France, Portugal, Finland and as far away as Russia and Saudi Arabia.

The company's success can be attributed to its ability to innovate and their strong sense of focus. Fiacla was the first toothpaste company to introduce the flip-top tube-cap to the Irish market. In 1994 it added the "baking soda" toothpaste to its product line (due to its popularity in both the UK and US). Promotion is mainly by way of magazines, radio and in-store promotions.

For the future, Fiacla hopes to develop an international brand name, as the Fiacla name has limited international appeal, although the Irishness of the brand has been a huge factor in its success to date.

15

Irish High-Technology Companies: New Product Development

Anne Ledwith

Introduction

In 1994, a group of American academics and industrialists calling
themselves the Manufacturing Vision Group (MVG) published a book,
The Perpetual Enterprise Machine. In it, they described a framework
for the management of new product development (NPD). The framework defines Seven Keys for successful product development:

- **Core Capabilities and Core Rigidities**: New products should
  be developed in line with the Core Capabilities of a company. The
  four dimensions of Core Capabilities are: Knowledge & Skills,
  Managerial Systems, Physical Systems and Values. The flip-side of
  Core Capabilities are Core Rigidities. Most companies have some
  rigidities. These should be managed and, if possible, eliminated, so
  that they do not inhibit the development of new products.

- **Guiding Vision**: New product development within any company
  needs three Guiding Visions: A Product Concept, a Project Vision
  and a Business Unit Vision. These visions provide the link between a company's strategy and the day-to-day decisions made on
  development projects.

- **"Pushing the Envelope"**: A company's competitive position can be
  defined by how well it manages its performance in the area of product, process and internal capabilities. Not only is it important to be
  pushing out these performance "envelopes" but it is also important
  to manage the position of these envelopes relative to one another.

- **Project Leadership and Organisation**: The organisation of
  NPD is moving away from traditional functional departments. It is
  now common practice to use cross-functional teams to develop new

products. Cross-functional teams led by senior management are known as "heavyweight" teams; teams led by non-managerial members of staff are "lightweight" teams. The team-leader's level of authority also affects the success of a project.

- **Ownership & Commitment**: NPD projects require strong ownership and commitment from the project team-members, who should feel that they can make an impact on the project and who should link personal success with project success, and senior management, who should link corporate success with project success. Without this commitment, the chances of project success are reduced.

- **Prototypes — Rapid Learning & Early Testing**: Prototyping is a powerful and frequently under-used tool in NPD. The usefulness of prototypes is increased by using them early in the project, building prototypes that are fully representative of the finished project, and involving the production department in building prototypes.

- **Integration within a Development Project**: NPD can no longer be left to the R&D department. Instead, many functions and visions within the company must be integrated into the development process. This level of integration requires a new way of thinking for most organisations.

Successful management of these Seven Keys is fundamental for the success of NPD. This chapter outlines how three high-technology Irish companies approach the process of new product development. The cases are presented within the Seven Keys framework.

BMS IRELAND LTD.

BMS was established in 1980. Its founder, Liam Ryan, ran a distribution company. The company initially manufactured compressors and generators, but expanded into industrial seals, saw-blades and gaskets within a year. By 1987, BMS had taken over Scorpio Diamond Tool Ltd., a company involved in diamond products including grinding-wheels, cutting-saws, and other cutting tools. In 1988, BMS diversified again. Liam saw how Japanese companies were able to develop new products in a fraction of the time, and for a fraction of the price, of their British counterparts. He saw an opportunity for an electronic torque wrench, and, modelling himself on Japanese companies, decided to develop a product that was cheaper, simpler and of a better design than anything on the market. Again taking his lead from the Japanese, he was not concerned with an immediate return on investment but decided that BMS could afford to wait a few years for the project to pay off.

BMS now employs 42 people, 10 (24 per cent) of whom work full time on NPD. The general manager also spends 90 per cent of his time on development projects. In 1994, the company had a turnover of £3.6 million and spent £400,000 (21 per cent) on R&D. In general, upgrades, improvements or modifications, take 12 months to develop, while totally new products take up to three years. On average, the company releases one new product every year. New products are formally launched at trade shows.

Liam was asked to identify two projects for this case study — an NPD failure and a success. He could not identify any NPD project, in the torque wrench business, that had failed. (The NPD failure rate in the diamond wheel business was given at 60 per cent). The company has a very good track record. Its owner has an extremely positive approach towards the companies' products and its performance, and he does not like to focus on failures or weaknesses. This has undoubtedly contributed to the success of BMS.

BMS is described by Liam as a product-development company. Product development is seen as critical to the success of the company. In fact, BMS is interested in taking on development projects for other companies. The particular project that is the subject of this case is the development of an electronic torque wrench. The project was a major success for BMS. It exceeded its market, business and technical objectives and was developed well within schedule.

Core Capabilities and Core Rigidities

The strongest core capabilities at BMS relate to the company's value systems and the skills available at the company. The culture at BMS is very open and flexible. The company is very ready to accept new technology and new ideas. It could also be described as opportunistic — BMS is a company always looking for new opportunities and always ready to take advantage of them. Its managing director is quite comfortable with taking risks. Another element of the value system of BMS that is considered to be critical to success is the level of integration within the company. Staff are kept well informed — in the words of the managing director, "People feel part of the company".

The knowledge and skills at BMS also contribute towards the success of NPD. These skills include expertise in transducer development, software skills, the knowledge of mechanical and materials engineers and the skills of toolmakers and fitters. BMS has worked hard at developing these skills — the company sponsored research at the University of Limerick and employed the student who had worked on their project, once he had completed his degree.

Some of the physical systems at BMS can also be identified as core capabilities. These include information systems, the CAD system used by the engineers and other software systems.

Top management distractions are a core rigidity of BMS. Being an opportunistic company, top management must be constantly on the lookout for new opportunities and open to new ideas. As a result, management is involved in a variety of different activities. This can sometimes limit the time available for its core responsibility.

The company has achieved ISO 9000 status — a quality accreditation which can be thought of as both a capability and a rigidity. A quality system helps a company to identify its process and, by documenting it, inefficiencies can be highlighted and eliminated. Having a quality accreditation is also a great help to sales, as many purchasers will only buy from companies that have quality marks. However, there can be drawbacks to implementing quality systems, especially for small companies. A lot of paperwork must be generated to run a quality system and it imposes an additional overhead by requiring that documented procedures are always followed in full. This can reduce the flexibility that is an important part of the value system of most small firms.

Rigidities relating to skills and knowledge were not identified at BMS. The reason for this was that management has developed the capability of sourcing product and process technologies outside the firm. Specific skills were needed to complete the electronic torque wrench project. These included expertise in designing aluminium-zinc die-casts and multi-layer PCBs. Neither skill was available within BMS but both were sourced externally. BMS has worked with nine different universities in developing and accessing new technologies and has also worked with several large firms.

New development projects are used at BMS to develop core capabilities — usually very efficiently by acquiring the new skill from outside the firm.

Guiding Vision

BMS has a very clear line-of-business guiding vision or mission statement that relates to its torque wrench business. It is to be "an International Centre of Torque Excellence". A second guiding vision that is more general is to develop Partners in Development (PID). This second statement very much captures how the managing director is positioning his company and appears to be something that the company is already putting in practice. These guiding visions originated with the managing director who was guided by several external influences. He has also been responsible for ensuring that all employees in the company are aware of the visions.

Development projects at BMS have also had visions. The electronic torque wrench product line was to be cost-effective, simple and of a good industrial design. Again, this vision was understood and accepted by everyone involved in NPD. The fact that BMS is a small firm with an open culture helps in ensuring that guiding visions are shared by all employees.

Product specifications are normally written for NPD projects at BMS. A specification tends to list the features to be included in a new product, rather than being an accurate description of electronic and mechanical dimensions. Product specifications are normally signed off by the managing director, but they are not always adhered to.

BMS is a young dynamic company with an entrepreneurial managing director. The visions adopted by the company are still very much his visions. This gives the company a great unity of purpose. The fact that the company has prospered to date under this type of management further reinforces the vision of its owner.

Managing Performance Envelopes

BMS has a state-of-the-art product. It has achieved the managing director's objective of imitating the Japanese in producing a product that is simpler and superior technically to other products on the market. The product performance envelope for this product is at the leading edge of technology. However, the other two envelopes relating to the company's process and internal capabilities are not so far ahead. The managing director is aware of the problems with these two performance envelopes and is at present addressing the issue.

An important aspect of managing a company's three performance envelopes is to ensure that they are balanced. When a product envelope is very far ahead of the process and internal capabilities envelope, as is the case in BMS, companies can have problems with quality, delivery times, and cost, because the company is not sufficiently skilled in producing a very high-technology product. The challenge for the company is to improve its process and internal capabilities to match the superior performance of its product. In this way, the new product can help to improve the company's overall position and capabilities. BMS is in the process of improving its process but has not recently made any radical "leaps" forward.

The second aspect of managing performance envelopes relates to positioning them with respect to the industry in general. BMS knows the state-of-the-art nature of the technology that is used in its product. It is also well up-to-date on the state of its competitors' technology. This knowledge is achieved by purchasing and evaluating competitors' products. The one area where the company falls down is in evaluating customer reaction to products. The reason for this is that BMS uses distributors to sell its products. Distributors can form a barrier between a manufacturer and the end-user. It was suggested by the managing director that customer information is the power base of distributors and that they are very slow to give up any of this power.

Project Leadership and Organisation

The NPD teams at BMS are best described as lightweight project teams, which means that project teams span several functional groups and are headed by a team leader who is not a senior manager. BMS has three main project areas and has a project leader managing each. This is a slight variation of the standard lightweight project team where the team only stays together for the length of the particular project.

The project leader's influence on the team at BMS is strong, but the influence of the project leader on manufacturing and marketing is weak. Project leadership skills at BMS are actively encouraged. NPD project teams are located in the one place, and responsibility for the management of the project is focused on one person — the project leader. The link between the NPD project team and the market/customer at BMS is strong, but specific responsibility for ensuring that the new product meets customers' needs is not given to any team member. The managing director generally takes this role.

Projects are frequently organised around specialists. Sometimes a group of specialists will work together on a particular project or a project team will require one or two specialists from different fields. At BMS engineers need to be more than just specialists. While most of the development engineers have areas of specialisation, they also need to have a broad range of general knowledge about the product. This has been described as a T-knowledge profile. Engineers with T-knowledge profiles are very valuable to a company. They allow for greater flexibility in project organisation than pure specialists.

Ownership and Commitment

BMS does not give performance reviews based on project outcomes. Employees are, however, rewarded for corporate success and non-financial rewards are given for outstanding achievements. Both of these actions help to increase commitment to the company, and to develop projects.

Members of NPD project teams at BMS are encouraged to feel that they can make a difference to the outcome of projects. They also feel responsible for the project on which they are working, and are made aware of the consequences to the company of project failure, but at the same time are encouraged to take risk. Top management clearly links project success with corporate success.

Project team members work together and are easily identifiable, which helps them to feel ownership of a project. The result of this nurturing of ownership and commitment to NPD projects, and to the company in general, is seen in the extra effort that employees put into their work. People frequently work weekends unpaid to meet schedules, and one engineer even flew to the US to upgrade a demonstration unit at less than 12 hours notice.

Project ownership was also displayed by an engineer who was working on an electronic spirit-level project. He found it very difficult to walk away from the project even when it was cancelled by top management because of lack of resources.

The culture and organisation of BMS are such that project ownership and commitment are high, not only among members of the project team, but also among other employees. The company is small enough that functional barriers are blurred — everyone can do a bit of everything. For example, the person in charge of purchasing is also responsible for shipping products. He is judged on his performance of both functions. This encourages him to purchase components with delivery time and quality in mind, as well as cost. It also means that his ownership of a project is increased, as his responsibility spans upstream and down-stream functions.

Prototyping: Rapid Learning and Early Testing

Engineers at BMS make extensive use of prototypes. Prototypes are used throughout the NPD process as the following list of prototypes used by the company illustrates:

- Models and mock-ups
- Computer simulations
- Subsystem prototypes
- Mechanical prototypes
- Engineering prototypes
- Production prototypes.

Prototypes are initially used less than 25 per cent into the NPD process, when mock-ups are built. Normally, five copies of any one prototype are made. Manufacturing is responsible for making prototypes — this increases the value of prototyping as it allows manufacturing to evaluate the "manufacturability" of a new product at an early stage. The prototypes used by BMS are not always complete models of the final product. Functions that are not readily visible to the user, or are not used as standard — for example, downloading software — are often omitted from prototype versions of a new product.

While the development department must obviously be involved in making prototypes of new products, it does not have any specific prototyping tools.

Integration within a Development Project

Many functions at BMS are integrated within development projects. Functions outside the development department are involved at an early stage in the process. This integration is managed by the managing director who organises small meetings of different functions to discuss NPD. Engineering and marketing are the most dominant functions within the company, but even the less dominant functions are involved in NPD and are given the power to implement changes. Differences relating to NPD between functions are solved by negotiation, frequently with the help of the managing director.

There is no clear point of hand-over of new products from the development department to manufacturing. Both groups seem to have a certain amount of responsibility for a new product throughout its complete life cycle. Although this is not viewed by management to be an ideal situation, it is in fact recommended by many authors on NPD, as clearly defined hand-over situations can cause a breakdown in communications and can slow down a project.

SCHAFFNER/INTEPRO SYSTEMS LTD.

Intepro was established in 1981 by three Irish engineers. The company designed and manufactured automatic test equipment for power supplies. By 1990, Intepro employed 70 people and was in the top three in power supply testing in the world. The company had a large R&D department and a worldwide marketing presence. In 1991, Intepro was acquired by Schaffner, a Swiss company involved in Electromagnetic Compatibility (EMC) and automotive test equipment. Schaffner was primarily interested in the strong product development team at Intepro. Software development at Intepro — it had recently introduced its first Windows-based software system — was of particular interest.

Since the take-over, the development department at the Limerick division of Schaffner/Intepro has become increasingly involved in NPD for the Swiss operation. It has become the main product development centre for EMC and automotive test systems, replacing the existing Swiss operation. The company is also continuing to develop the power supply test business. Seamus McNamara is technical director at Schaffner/Intepro. He is responsible for the development of all new products.

The two NPD projects that will be addressed in this case are:

a) *The Pizza Project*: This project was to design an EMC test system, for use in the automotive industry. The project was a product update. It was an overall success: it met its schedule, and exceeded its market acceptance, business and technical objectives. One of the reasons given by Seamus for the success of this project was that it was the first project undertaken by the Irish engineers for Switzerland. The team in Ireland was very keen to show that it was capable of EMC design work.

b) *The P-MUX Project*: This project was to design a standard interface for an EMC test system. The project was a radical innovation. The system was the idea of the management in Switzerland. It was an overall failure: it met its schedule, but it totally failed to meet its market acceptance and business objectives, although technically the project worked well.

Schaffner/Intepro employs 60 people, with 20 (33 per cent) people working full time in NPD. The technical director is responsible for development projects. In 1994, the company had a turnover of £3.8 million and spent £700,000 (19 per cent) on R&D. On average, new products take 12 months to develop and the company releases an average of 6 new products every year. New products are formally launched, usually at trade shows.

Core Capabilities and Core Rigidities

Schaffner/Intepro is a company that values flexibility and that readily accepts new technology. Both of these values were very important for the success of the Pizza project and, to a lesser degree, for the P-MUX project. The company has a non-hierarchical, organic structure, and team-work is encouraged. Again, these are characteristics that have contributed to the success of NPD projects. The loose structure at Schaffner/Intepro is evidenced by the fact that there are few clear boundaries between departments and the plant is all open-plan. The dynamism within the company is a core capability that has benefited all development projects.

The company also has a strong technical skills-base. Engineers at Schaffner/Intepro have mixed skills and a broad range of technical abilities. This was particularly useful for the Pizza project. The application of the test equipment that they were designing — EMC for the automotive industry — was new for the engineers. But because they had a good mix of technical skills, the engineers were able to take on the project and make a success of it. Had the design team at Schaffner/Intepro been specialists — for example, in power supplies and power supply tests — this would not have been as easy for them. Technical skills were also necessary for the P-MUX project, but did not have such an impact on its outcome — the project failed in the marketplace.

Within the software group at Schaffner/Intepro there is a very strong knowledge-base in PCs and PC applications. The engineers all have state-of-the-art machines (the PC on an engineer's desk is a status symbol), they use the latest software and are connected to numerous bulletin boards and have CD drives, speakers and all the latest PC gadgets. This may appear frivolous but it is part of a culture that places a high value on understanding all aspects of a PC. The result of this is that the software produced is state-of-the-art — the work done by the engineers in Limerick has revolutionised the technology used in EMC test systems.

The physical systems that are considered to be core capabilities are predominantly software tools: CAD, P-Spice, Computer Network and, more recently, the Internet. Again this re-enforces the value placed on PC technology within the company.

There are also core rigidities within Schaffner/Intepro, which include the fact that engineering is not sufficiently valued at an operations level within the company. Engineering management is dominant but, on a day-to-day basis engineers often find themselves at the bottom of the heap. Inter-company politics is another rigidity that hampers NPD success, particularly the politics surrounding relationships between Irish and Swiss management.

Even though flexibility has been highlighted as a core capability, there are also areas of the company where some historical inflexibilities are in evidence. This relates to marketing — even though selling EMC testers is different from selling automatic test equipment, some practices have not yet changed. There is a lot that the sales staff must learn about the new markets and the EMC products. This rigidity is one of the reasons why the P-MUX product failed.

The Pizza project helped the company to develop new technical skills and knowledge in the area of pulse-generator design. It was specifically to develop these skills that management in Ireland was eager to undertake the project. Schaffner/Intepro has also used software projects to develop skills needed to enter particular market niches.

Guiding Vision

While the Schaffner Corporation may be lacking in a clear vision, the Schaffner/Intepro division is not. Its guiding vision — to become a "Centre of Excellence in Project Development and Manufacturing for the Corporation" — originated with management in Ireland, and all Irish employees have been informed of it through internal documents, meetings, and directly by management.

There were also project guiding visions for the Pizza and the P-MUX projects. The Pizza project was to be a modular, computer-controlled, cost-effective solution to ISO 7637, the automotive EMC standard. The P-MUX project was intended to be the first modular interface for EMC test systems requiring only one point of contact. Both of these visions were clearly understood by management and by the project team-members.

Both projects also had well-defined project concepts with detailed specifications. New product specifications at Schaffner/Intepro are written by a Control of Product Marketing (CPM) group. The technical director is the chairman of this group and has a formal sign-off on all new product specifications. The product specifications of both NPD projects were adhered to.

Managing Performance Envelopes

The product-performance envelope for the Pizza project was close to state-of-the-art, though the envelope for the P-MUX project was very far behind. The process-performance envelope at Schaffner/Intepro is ahead of its competition, but the internal capabilities of the company are only average. Neither the Pizza nor the P-MUX project pushed either of these two performance envelopes forward.

The company is behind in its internal capabilities — its management systems — but it currently in the process of improving them. No dramatic improvements in the position of any of its performance envelopes have been made recently.

Schaffner/Intepro is very active in getting information about the state of technology. The company is also well informed about its customers' requirements, but it has only average access to the state of its competitors' technology.

Project Leadership and Organisation

The organisation of NPD at Schaffner/Intepro is quite traditional — both the Pizza and the P-MUX products were developed by functional teams — that is, by the R&D department. The engineers working on either project did not need to be specialist but needed to have a broad range of skills.

Project leaders from within the R&D department were appointed to look after each development project. Responsibility for the management of each project was focused on the project leader. These leaders had a strong influence on the project team, but only a weak influence on manufacturing and marketing. NPD teams were located together in both cases, and the link between the team-members and their functional groups was strong. This was to be expected, as they all operated within the R&D department.

The link between the Pizza project team and the market was strong, even though there was nobody with specific responsibility for ensuring that the project met customer needs. The fact that the project had such strong guiding visions at all levels, and that customer needs were incorporated into these visions, lessened the need for additional attention to be paid to the customer needs at lower levels. The P-MUX project did not, however, have a strong link to customers and the market. The problem lay in the fact that the original product idea was flawed. There had not been sufficient market awareness applied in developing the product vision and specification. Since the development team relied on this vision to be an accurate expression of customer needs, team members did not attempt to confirm that the product they were developing was in fact what the customers wanted.

Ownership and Commitment

Schaffner/Intepro does not give performance reviews based directly on the outcomes of NPD projects, but the link is very strong. Engineers who have helped to make development projects successful will do better at performance reviews. Being associated with successful projects will help an engineer's career progression within Schaffner/Intepro. The company gives an annual bonus to all employees, based on exceeding a pre-defined sales target.

Team members on both the Pizza and the P-MUX projects felt responsible for the projects. They felt that their individual effort could make a difference to the project outcome, and they were also aware of the consequences of project failure. There was some top-management support for both projects — an example of this is that the technical director strongly defended his engineers from criticism by the managing director. Management support was also demonstrated by the fact that a lot of management time was put into developing new-product specifications, and these specifications and the project goal were not changed for either project.

More effort was put into the Pizza project than into the P-MUX project. One reason for this was that the Pizza project was strongly linked by management with corporate success. It was seen as the first stage in the goal of becoming a "Centre of Excellence in Product Development and Manufacturing".

Ownership of, and commitment to, NPD projects is shared by all employees at Schaffner/Intepro in Limerick. This is illustrated by the fact that in neither the Pizza nor the P-MUX project were there any delays caused by lack of commitment on the part of other employees.

Prototyping: Rapid Learning and Early Testing

Prototypes are used extensively during all stages of NPD at Schaffner/Intepro. Models, mock-ups and computer simulations are frequently used at the very start of the development project. The first functional prototype is usually built less than 25 per cent of the way into the development process. Subsystem prototypes, engineering prototypes and production prototypes, or combinations of these, were used on both the Pizza and the P-MUX projects. At each prototyping stage, between one and three prototypes were built. It is common practice at Schaffner/Intepro to omit some features from prototypes — for example, aesthetic details and technically simple features would frequently be left out.

The manufacturing department was responsible for building the prototypes for both projects. The development group does not have any specific facilities. Even though prototypes were extensively used, there were some engineering changes late in the development of the Pizza project. The P-MUX project was never fully completed.

Integration within a Development Project

Integration of different functions within a development happens at an early stage in Schaffner/Intepro. Less dominant functions in the company, such as manufacturing, quality and purchasing, are involved in a project once it reaches the prototyping stage, and have the power to make changes. If conflict arises between functions, it is normally resolved through negotiation.

There are some problems with integration within development projects at Schaffner/Intepro. The NPD procedures require that the purchasing department is given three sources for any component that is to be used in a new product. This is not always practical and causes problems and delays for the development department. On the other hand, the development department has been known to specify components that are almost impossible to buy. Increased integration and co-operation of these two departments within development projects would help each department to see that the overall goal is to have a "manufacturable", quality product and not simply to stick rigidly to procedures.

Problems can also occur when components are required urgently for a project. It sometimes happens that progress on a project stops if components are not available. The purchasing department is motivated to buy components at the lowest price and to get the best deal. But this can take time and often the savings achieved through haggling are outweighed several times by the losses in the development schedule.

There is no clear hand-over of a new product from development to production. There is a point in the procedure when production is supposed to take responsibility. In reality, when any problems occur later, development engineers are called in to solve them.

VITALOGRAPH (IRELAND) LTD.

In 1991, Vitalograph, a UK-based company that designs and manufactures medical instruments, moved its R&D facility to Ennis, Co. Clare. The company's new R&D director, Ardawan Lalui, set up the operation. Initially, much of the engineering work was subcontracted outside the company and was managed by project managers directly employed by Vitalograph. None of the original R&D staff who had worked in the UK moved to Ireland, but some continued to do subcontract work for the company.

Vitalograph employs 90 people at its plant in Ennis. There are 13 engineers and 3 support staff (18 per cent) working in the R&D department. In 1994, the company had a turnover of £3.4 million and spent £500,000 (15 per cent) on R&D. On average it takes the company 18 months to two years to develop a new product, but it hopes to reduce this to one year. Vitalograph releases an average of four new products every year. New products are always formally launched.

Vitalograph has never had an NPD failure, so this case study addresses only one new product — an electronic Peak Flow Meter. Previous peak flow meters, used to measure lung capacity, were mechanical. The electronic peak flow meter developed by Vitalograph can store and analyse data and can also transmit data to a computer for future analysis. The new peak flow meter met its schedule and exceeded the company's expectations in the market-place and in meeting its business and technical objectives.

Core Capabilities and Core Rigidities
Co-operation and unity are judged to be the most valuable core capabilities at Vitalograph. The management systems in the company encourage team-work. These capabilities, which relate to the values and management systems within the company, were critical to the

success of the peak flow meter project.

The technical skills available within the company, or those that could be easily sourced externally in subcontractors, were also essential for the project success. Knowledge of the flow meter market was important too. The physical systems within Vitalograph that contributed to the success of this project were:

- The quality system ISO 9001, which includes product development

- The CE mark (a European conformance mark) that has been awarded to Vitalograph's products

- Well-organised management of the project.

The core capabilities mentioned above have contributed to the success of all of Vitalograph's new projects. Vitalograph has never undertaken an NPD product in order to develop a core capability.

There were several core rigidities at Vitalograph that hampered the progress of the peak flow meter project. The company is not very open to new ideas and sometimes has trouble in looking at alternative technologies. The production process at Vitalograph is not as up-to-date as it needs to be. The peak flow meter project required a knowledge of SMT (Surface Mount Technology) and ATE (Automatic Test Equipment). Some of this knowledge was available in-house, but a lack of sufficient skills in these areas caused delays in the project schedule.

The success of the project was also limited by cultural differences between departments in the company. For example, different departments tended to look after their own interests. Instead of looking at the complete project and being concerned with its overall success, they were only interested in making their own jobs easier. This "self-interest" is still apparent in Vitalograph, but management is attempting to rectify the situation.

Guiding Vision

The guiding vision at Vitalograph is encapsulated in a one-page mission statement:

> To bring safe, effective, ethical, innovative products to the market, to develop a partnership between customers, employees, suppliers and shareholders, and to create an environment in which the financial objectives of the company can be met.

The mission statement originated with the managing director and the shareholders. The company is a family-owned business and the managing director is one of the principal share-holders. All employees at Vitalograph are aware of the mission statement but do not often refer to it. The R&D staff were made aware of the statement through talks given by the R&D director.

The peak flow meter project also had a guiding vision — the company saw a gap in the market and intended to develop a new product to fit it. The forces that drove the company to develop this product were a combination of technology, marketing and cost. The guiding vision for the product was documented in a market brief, written by a steering committee consisting of senior managers. This market brief was given to the project team as part of a well-defined NPD procedure.

The product guiding vision was well understood by everyone working on the project. The project team was made up of staff from all over the company — for example, the store manager was on the team. This helped the vision of the new product to be spread throughout the company. There was also a well-defined product concept and product specification for the peak flow meter. The specification was written and signed off by the steering committee. It was reviewed on a regular basis and was updated when necessary.

Managing Company Performance

The peak flow meter was a new-to-the-world product — it was the first such electronic medical instrument developed. Therefore, the company's product performance envelope was ahead of that of its competition. Vitalograph's process and internal capabilities envelopes were not, however, ahead of the competition, and could only be rated as average. The peak flow meter project did move some of the company's process performance envelopes forward. The project required the company to introduce new technologies (SMT and ATE) into its production process.

There are very many different levels of internal capabilities in Vitalograph. The R&D director pointed out that the R&D staff are highly qualified and young and that the capabilities within that group were very good. While management at Vitalograph has not recently made any major improvements to any of its performance envelopes, internal capabilities are being developed.

Vitalograph is very active in getting information on new technology and considers itself up-to-date in most areas of technology. The company is also reasonably good at getting information about the state of its competitors' technology, but this is not critical to the company as it is not interested in following competitors. The development department in Ireland is not as good at getting information about its customers' requirements. The main reason for this is that marketing is all handled through the UK.

Project Leadership and Organisation

The organisation of NPD at Vitalograph is similar to the light-weight development team structure. Project teams are made up of people from different functions within the company. The leader of a project team, who is not a senior manager, is appointed by the steering committee. The steering committee keeps a close eye on the progress of NPD projects.

Responsibility for the management of an NPD project is centred in the project leader. Management at Vitalograph encourages project leaders, who are given a lot of responsibility. Project leaders have a medium to strong influence on the project team, which is expected to work through co-operation The project leaders also have quite a strong influence on marketing and manufacturing. R&D engineers at Vitalograph do not need to be specialists — if experts are needed, external consultants are used. Members of a project team are normally located in the Ennis facility but do not all work in the one area. If external consultants are used, the project team can become more dispersed. The link between project team-members and their functional departments is usually strong, but this can vary depending on the project leader and the team-member.

The link between the project team and the market is usually strong, but no one person on an NPD project team is given specific responsibility for ensuring that the new product meets customers needs. All team members are expected to put themselves in the customer's shoes. The marketing and quality representatives of an NPD team are particularly aware of customer needs.

Ownership and Commitment

R&D engineers at Vitalograph are given reviews based on their contribution to projects and project teams, rather than on the outcome of a project. Rewards for successful projects include training courses or being given responsibility for additional projects. Salaries are based on general performance and on industry norms.

Members of project teams are responsible for the outcome of projects and feel that they can make a difference to this outcome. They are also aware of the consequences of project failure and take responsibility for this. There are normally many different projects running in the R&D department at any one time, and it is not generally known who is working on which project until the new product is introduced onto the production line.

The team working on the peak flow meter put a lot of additional effort into the project. Team members regularly worked 50–60-hour weeks without overtime pay, in order to complete the project. Management supported this effort and provided additional keys to the factory so that team members could work over weekends. Top management linked corporate success with the success of this project, and team-members were aware of this link.

Vitalograph has a very well-organised NPD procedure — project progress is reviewed on a regular basis by the steering committee. Close to the end of a development project, it is very difficult to change a product specification, so this did not happen in the peak flow meter project. There were some delays on the project but these were caused by technical difficulties in achieving accurate flow measurements and calibration.

Prototyping: Rapid Learning and Early Testing

Prototypes are an integral part of the NPD process at Vitalograph. On the peak flow meter project, five different types of prototypes were used. These were:

- Cardboard models (one)

- Computer simulations (one version of the computer interface for the product)

- Mechanical prototypes (two/three, including engineering, built using a rapid prototyping process)

- Engineering prototypes

- Production prototypes (40-50 built for use in field trials).

The prototypes built were all complete models of the final product. There were not many engineering changes late in the project.

The manufacturing department at Vitalograph is responsible, whenever possible, for building prototypes. There is always a pre-production run before a product is released. But the R&D department does have some very powerful prototyping tools. The company has an electronic lung simulator, which was the first of its type in Europe. Some of the company's competitors have been allowed to test their products on this simulator, as management at Vitalograph felt that this would help the development of standards within the industry. The R&D group also has a machine shop at its disposal.

Integration within a Development Project

All functions at Vitalograph, with the exception of field service staff in the UK, were involved at a very early stage of the peak flow meter project. The project manager is responsible for a new product from concept to production, but production is involved and has an input at all stages of the project. After the pre-production run of a new product, there is a sign-off, handing over responsibility from R&D to production.

Vitalograph is very good at using project teams that help to integrate many functional departments within development projects. This is helped by the cross-functional training that is part of the company's policy.

There were no major inter-functional problems on the peak flow meter project. There were rarely communication problems between members of the project team. If, for example, technical terms were used that were not understood by a team-member, that person could simply ask for an explanation — although there was a slight misunderstanding at the start of the project when Gantt charts were introduced, as people did not know which way around to view them!

Sources: Interviews with company personnel.

16

Finance and the Small Business: Three Case Studies

Briga Hynes

Introduction

Financing the small business is one of the most difficult tasks facing the Irish entrepreneur. The ongoing financial management of business is a problem of almost equal difficulty. One of the most common reasons cited for small business failure is poor capitalisation and a lack of expertise in financial management. The three cases which follow highlight some of the key problems involved.

G & M INDUSTRIAL CLEANING

Figure 16.1: Summary Information

Owner/Manager	Audrey Glynn
No. of Employees	14
No. of years in business	7 years (1988)
Exports	Small percentage (No exact % available)
Product	Industrial Cleaning Products

Access to Finance on Start-up

Apart from personal funds, the primary source of finance for G&M Industrial Cleaning was bank finance. Audrey Glynn finds it increasingly difficult to get funds for the business. Banks now require more collateral and are looking for personal guarantees for smaller items than heretofore. Audrey Glynn is never sure that she will receive bank finance when required, and has always had a shortage of funds.

When bank finance is required, she approaches the bank for what she thinks they will give her, rather than what the business requires. In recent times, it has been necessary to provide detailed figures about what the money was going to be used for and how she intends financing the repayments. Similar requirements are necessary for the IDA.

According to Audrey Glynn, two things are necessary when approaching a bank for money: initially, you have to sell yourself and then you have to sell your idea. Many people, she feels, forget to sell themselves.

She recently took over another small business, and required bank finance, which she got with great difficulty.

Accounting Systems

The business presently has a wages and purchases system, with a computerised sales ledger, using Take 5, a standard integrated accounts package. Audrey Glynn does the wages and purchases, with her receptionist operating the sales ledger.

For the first three to four years, the business had severe problems with accounting systems and bookkeeping. Specifically, she did not know what she required in terms of record-keeping. When she learned what was required, she didn't know how to achieve it.

It was never made clear to her what was needed or what books she should keep. Her accountant she generally found unhelpful. He would not show her how to do anything, for fear he gave away any of his "trade secrets". What was required was someone to say "This is what is required, and this is how you do it". It was only when she decided to put in a computerised system using Take 5 that she realised that the business's manual system was totally inadequate. She believed all her problems would be solved by the computer but she found that, for a computerised system to work, there must be an effective manual system in place. This resulted in the computer being left idle for almost a year, because:

- Nobody had sufficient experience with computers and they lacked adequate computer knowledge to operate it effectively

- The manual systems in place were not adequate for the firm to computerise.

The computer was seen as forcing the business into systematised reporting. The business found little advice available for helping with record-keeping and book-keeping. The IDA was very marketing-oriented, in that they helped sell the product and, while they were good in some areas, Audrey Glynn felt "they left you high and dry in others".

Since undertaking an MBA, Audrey Glynn has progressed very significantly. An effective book-keeping and record-keeping system is in place and she prepares monthly accounts. This success she entirely attributes to the MBA. A stock control system is still a problem for the business and the implementation of a stock control system was found to be difficult, due to a lack of qualified personnel.

Accounting Information

In early 1994 she began preparing monthly management accounts and sales forecasts. Prior to this, the books would be given to the accountant to see whether the business had made a profit.

Planning or forecasting was non-existent for production and finance. Audrey Glynn said she was unaware of the whole idea of contribution of products and allocating overheads to products, or how to cost the business's products. Since beginning an MBA she has started costing the products and now can identify the contribution that each product is making. Contribution on each product is calculated — where this is above its direct cost, the business keeps the product; if not, the product is dropped.

The business did not prepare any management accounts or budgets prior to Audrey Glynn starting the MBA. This was attributed to a lack of knowledge and understanding regarding accounting information. Audrey Glynn wants more control over the business and to influence what is happening before it happens. This took five years to achieve. She thus went from a situation of "not having a clue" to one of being able to know what is happening and being able to fix any problems.

Prior to this the business was practising "seat of the pants" and "fire brigade" management. Decision-making was totally intuitive and on a common sense basis rather than relying on accounting or financial information.

Audrey Glynn now prepares her own VAT returns. For her, the problem is not preparing the VAT returns but rather paying them. VAT returns are required every two months. This causes problems, as more than likely the business would not have received all the money for these sales, yet it is required to pay VAT on them. Furthermore, if sales are unexpectedly high in one month, in two months time when VAT is due to be paid, it is unlikely that the money will be received, putting severe strains on cash flow.

Cash Management and Credit

Cash-flow has been a serious problem for the business. Audrey Glynn estimates that she could have trebled her sales, had the business the cash to finance those sales. For her, cash is one of the most important factors of any business.

> When you have cash it is possible to say what you will do. When you have no cash, you cannot afford to do anything.

Due to overtrading, in 1992 the business hit severe periods of cash-flow difficulties.

> We were probably overtrading, we came out with a profit, we struggled throughout and God it was painful, but we did it.

Audrey Glynn did not prepare a cash-flow forecast until 1993. A "ball park" figure of how much comes in every month in cheques is known, with one large monthly cheque that the business relies on. Audrey Glynn feels that up to 1994 she had kept good control of her bank account, by reconciling it weekly.

The business gives its customers 30 days credit, but finds that anything between 60 and 120 days credit is taken. Audrey Glynn has identified this as costly, as it costs the business money due to its bank account being overdrawn.

Prior to 1994 Audrey Glynn identified large debtors as beneficial for the business, as they were seen as money that the business would eventually get. High debtors are now equated with reduced cash. In 1995 the business adopted a strict policy towards credit. Audrey Glynn's mother is employed part-time on credit control and, if the business has difficulty getting paid by a particular customer, they use a debt collection company.

The business usually takes two weeks more credit than it gives, thus helping cash-flow.

Inventory

The business holds large quantities of stocks in inventory, as the benefits of holding stocks outweigh the costs of not holding them. This is attributed to the fact that the business imports a large proportion of its raw materials and it is shipping costs that determine whether a large quantity will be held in stock or not. It works out cheaper in terms of unit costs for the business to import a 40-foot container of raw material than to import a 20-foot container. As long as the business has the space to store stocks, Audrey Glynn feels it is beneficial to hold large quantities of stock.

PRINTING WIRE SUPPLIES

Figure 16.2: Summary Information

Owner/Manager	Paul Stokes
No. of Employees	15
No. of Years in Business	6
Exports	80%
Product	Manufacture of stationery parts

Access to Finance on Start Up

The principal sources of finance used at start-up were personal funds, bank finance and grants from the IDA. The business used bank finance to finance any investments after start-up. Acquiring finance was generally a long, drawn-out process, requiring numerous personal guarantees along with the provision of the assets of the business as security. While the banks eventually provided finance, the business found the requirements of the bank particularly stringent and has had difficulty getting finance from the bank, each time it was required.

The grants received from the IDA prevented them leasing machines so they had to purchase all machines, increasing borrowings.

Accounting Systems of the Business

The business uses a computerised sales ledger system and a manual purchase system. The accountants deal with the wages. The business does not encounter any difficulties with record-keeping. This Paul Stokes attributes to his prior experience of working in business. His wife does the book-keeping part-time.

Stokes hopes to install an integrated accounts package in the near future, incorporating a stock control system. He identifies the computer system as being very helpful, once he got to terms with it. He points out however, that it is difficult to get someone to talk about computers without talking jargon. A major problem identified, is lack of a standardised accounting system for the computer. The sales ledger used in the computer is custom-designed. This will cause problems in the near future, as the business endeavours to install a standard integrated accounts package. Few customised ledger packages are compatible with standard integrated accounts packages, such as Take 5 or Sage.

The business is very production-oriented, and tends not to be concerned with whether it can get the products cheaper but rather whether it can get the products at all.

Accounting Information

The business's accountants prepare quarterly management accounts — the primary accounting information used by the business. There is no formal system for preparing forecasts, budgets or production plans in place. The business relies on three-year plans.

When the business started, processes were small and little was exported. However, with the increase in exports and the need to deal in different currencies, the business found it increasingly difficult to judge changes in customers' requirements, due to fluctuating currencies.

Paul Stokes believes that financial accounts are important because they provide summary information, but he seldom relies on them, as they provide this information too late.

Cash Management and Credit

The business has not experienced cash shortages to date but it has not been able to utilise effectively the excess cash in the business. According to Paul Stokes, the business has always been cash-rich. This can be explained as follows:

- The business operates a niche market, with no similar manufacturer in Ireland.

- The total number of customers for the business is between 50 and 60, with a number of large customers.

- Very effective credit management.

The business has been making a profit since its inception. It never accepted that a business has to lose money in the first year, because Paul Stokes believes the business would be forever trying to catch up to clear its losses.

In the six years in business, bad debts have been insignificant. The business does not have a problem getting paid on time. Most of the business's customers pay within the 30 days. For overseas customers, it give a longer credit period but counteracts this by adjusting the exchange rate in its own favour. The debtor-base of the business is relatively small, with about 50 key customers —mostly large printing industries. An aged debtors listing is downloaded off the computer system every month to identify which debtors are not paying.

The business takes only 30 days credit. This Stokes regards as a discipline, in that, if the business can pay its creditors within 30 days, and give 60–90 days to debtors, he never has to worry about insolvency.

Inventory

The business holds large quantities of stocks in inventory but the cost of holding such stocks is not seen as a problem. The cost of raw materials is small — therefore not having a significant impact on cashflow — and, by holding stocks, the business facilitates extra demand and provides a better level of service to customers.

Ideally, the business would look for forward orders to operate a JIT system, but finds it generally cannot get these and therefore always has a reserve of stocks.

COMPRESS DESIGN LTD.

Figure 16.3: Summary Information

Owner/Manager	Brian Bennett
No. of Employees	15
No. of Years in Business	7
Exports	60%
Products	Injection Moulding Products

Access to Finance

Brian Bennett had relatively few problems with initial start-up finance. From the very beginning, he had three sources of finance:

- Two equity investors who brought in not only money but also management and technical skills.

- Grants from the IDA — both capital and management development grants.

- Bank borrowings — despite having equity investors, Bennett found the bank looking for personal guarantees and assets for security.

With three sources of finance, the business was able to spread the risk. Brian Bennett feels that being overly dependent on a bank is very dangerous since they are not geared towards supporting small business and could withdraw funds at any time. After two years in operation, the business required extra finance for expansion. A large portion of this came from bank borrowings, which were difficult to secure.

Accounting Systems

The business has experienced few problems with book-keeping or keeping financial records. This the owner/manger attributed to his experiences gained from university. He recognises that it was not easy and took a long time to get the book-keeping system correct but, once he knew what was required, things became much simpler. For him, the key to good book-keeping and accounting systems is to put simple manual systems in place first and gradually build on this, making them more sophisticated and giving more accurate information. This, he emphasises, has to be gradual as, for him, accounting is the servant of everything else.

Computers are used extensively in the business, with Microsoft Excel and Pegasus as the main software. The business has an integrated accounts system in place. It is currently working on an inventory-control, sales and purchase-order processing system. The success of the computerised system is attributed to simple, effective manual systems in place prior to the installation of computers. Once the organisation knew what it wanted from the manual system, it was easier to decide what was required from the computer system.

Accounting Information

Presently, the business produces weekly performance reports that focus on sales output, labour and materials usage. All the information produced is manufacturing-oriented. The P&L account is viewed as a "waste of time" for the small business, as it shows relatively fixed costs, which don't vary very much. The make or break is in the prime costs — direct materials and direct labour.

> If you can get sales figures, control the prime costs and make your contribution margins, then you are well on the way to success.

The business views budgeting as being very important as a control. Presently the business prepares weekly budgets for materials usage, labour usage and production planning. It also produces performance reports, which it compares against budgets. Performance, measured in terms of output per employee, is compared also to a four-week average. Any differences are investigated immediately to establish the cause of the difference. The key to budgeting is to be able to translate the budgets into day-to-day issues on the factory floor.

Weekly performance reports also show the sales, shipment and output values in the three departments — forming, assembly and finishing. All these are compared against sales forecasts.

Brian Bennett identifies keeping stock records as being much more important than keeping invoices, because stock records determine how to value work-in-progress. Keeping records on stock usage and materials and labour usage are crucial for him, as they are seen as a means of validating the accounts when they are prepared.

Financial accounts take a long time to prepare, time which the small business cannot afford.

> You cannot wait four weeks to find out you had a bad month.
> You have to know on a week-by-week basis how you are doing.

He feels that the small business should focus away from the traditional P&L account, which is based on historical cost, to performance measurement so that people can understand day-by-day how their business is doing.

Finally, the company prepares its own VAT returns. In 1994, the business took on a full-time accountant to help deal with the accounting requirements of the business. Before this, it had been using part-time accountants, who did not have the same "feel" for the business.

Cash Management and Credit

Compress Design experiences considerable problems with cash. For the managing director the problem is that the business is sinking money into investments — marketing, management, training — that could take six to nine months to develop.

The business produces weekly cash-flow forecasts. This allows it to plan and predict what sales it will have and how to prepare for them. The cash-flow forecast helps achieve stability, by helping the business prepare for large cash outflows before they arise.

Compress Designs supplies a niche market in the industry. Given that it is the sole supplier of goods in this niche and that most of its customers are reasonably large, the business has little difficulty getting paid. Customers are offered 30 days but pay within 45–60 days. The business takes 60 to 90 days from its suppliers, thereby helping its cash-flow.

Inventory

Previously, the business held large quantities of stock in inventory. Now with the use of production planning and budgets, as little stocks as possible are held in inventory. Holding stocks was identified as an unnecessary cost and a severe constraint on cash-flow.

Sources: Interviews with company personnel.

PART 4

SMALL BUSINESS MATURITY
AND DECLINE

Overview

After a period of rapid growth, many ventures enter a stage of maturity or stability and may in some cases start to decline. This period of stability, when it happens, requires the emphasis of the owner/manager to be redirected from a growth focus to ensuring that the venture consolidates its position and looks strategically to the future. Kuratko and Hodgetts (1992) call this the "swing stage". It is here that the actions, or lack thereof, on the part of the entrepreneur or owners will either propel the venture onwards to a higher level of profitability or result in its decline and failure.

Augar (1990) claims that the reasons for failure in small ventures are just the same as in relatively large firms but magnified. He argues that all the symptoms of impending decline are visible. The following are the main warning signs:

- Is the chairperson also the chief executive or managing director? In the smaller venture the appropriate question is, does the boss have too many jobs?

- Is gearing more than 100 per cent? Debt far greater than equity is a fatal liability for the small venture. Many small ventures attempt to borrow their way out of trouble.

- Has a director departed in the recent past?

- Are short-term borrowings larger than long-term borrowings? Many small ventures fall into the trap of taking out short-term finance.

- Has turnover grown at more than 50 per cent per annum over the last five years? Rapid expansion can often lead to overtrading with the situation emerging where the venture does not have ready cash to pay bills even though the order book is full.

[215]

- Is the company in a cyclical industry? Many ventures may operate in an industry which is high risk or which suffers from seasonability.

The first case in this section, Blarney Woollen Mills, illustrates that the small venture may have many periods of growth and stability. The case also illustrates that the small family-run venture may reach a crisis point where a major director leaves and there is a difficult transition to be made. Blarney Woollen Mills successfully made that transition and its profitability was initially not affected.

The case of the Irish Credit Union movement is interesting because it illustrates that while it had steady growth for many years, in the last ten years it has experienced very significant growth. This growth has brought with it major problems, in particular the need to formulate strategic plans for what was previously seen as a voluntary sector. In order to deal with an increasingly competitive environment, it has had to take on board strategic issues such as national legislation, savings protection schemes and the development of new services and competition. The case study is also interesting because it focuses on a sector in which over 90 per cent of the individual business units employ less than 10 people and in which there is still a major voluntary contribution.

The Foxford Woollen Mills case demonstrates how a venture suffered decline primarily due to external competition and an inability to find alternative products. Foxford faces fierce competition both at home and abroad, and as a result its share of the market declined. Its decline prompted drastic actions which have resulted in a renaissance of sorts. It has transformed itself into a much smaller venture and has managed to become efficient by diversifying into a number of related areas.

Leadmore Ice Cream demonstrates how a successful venture can decline quickly in the face of extreme competition, and factors outside the control of the business — in this case, poor weather. The company's market became overwhelmed by multinational products and the domestic producer did not know how to respond. Consequently, the venture went into liquidation.

17

Blarney Woollen Mills

Barra Ó Cinnéide, Thomas N. Garavan
and Fergus Walsh

Background

"An Bhlarna" — The Plain (population 995)

Apart from providing several tourist features that have become world-renowned, the village of Blarney has been responsible for the addition of a new word to the English language. Two of its features are world famous — Blarney Castle and the magic Blarney Stone with its traditional power of conferring eloquence on all those who kiss it. Centuries ago, "Blarney" found a place in English dictionaries. The word is supposed to have originated in the dealings of Queen Elizabeth's government with the then Lord of Blarney, Cormac MacDermot MacCarthy. Repeatedly, he was asked by the Queen's Deputy, Carew, to come in "off his keeping" (to conform to established authority), to renounce the traditional system by which the clans elected their chief, and to take the tenure of his lands from the Crown. But, while seeming to agree to this proposal, he put off the fulfilment of his promise from day-to-day "with fair words and soft speech" until at last Carew became the laughing stock of Queen Elizabeth, and she declared, "This is all Blarney, what he says he never means". Thus, Blarney came to mean pleasant talk intended to deceive without offending.

Blarney Castle

Over the past century, Blarney has become an important destination on the itineraries of many visitors to Ireland. Blarney Castle consists, principally, of a massive square keep or tower with a battlemented parapet 83 feet above the ground. Originally a fortress of the Mac-Carthys of south Munster, it withstood several sieges from the fif-teenth to the seventeenth century. Among others, Cromwell, Ireton and Fairfax attacked Blarney, and the army of King William was the last to take the castle, after the Battle of the Boyne. Much of the interior of the old structure was then demolished but sufficient of the original building remains in place to provide visitors with a fascinating journey through an exciting time-warp of Irish history.

The view from the top of the castle over the wooded hills of Muskerry is panoramic. Within the grounds there is the little Blarney Lake of many folk-tales. Beside the castle is the pretty dell called the Rock Close. Incorporated in the castle are two caves — one beneath the outer wall of the keep, the other (which, artificially enlarged, may have been used as a dungeon) reached by a staircase within the castle.

The castle was built in two sections: the first, a tall and narrow tower containing a staircase and small rooms; the second — adjoining and overlapping the earlier work — a massive keep of oblong plan, remarkable for the graceful batter of its walls. The battlements crowning the keep are typically Irish in form.

Below the battlements, set in the wall, is the famous Blarney Stone. To kiss it — as is traditional — one has to lean over backwards (grasping an iron railing) from the parapet walk of the battlements. Such endeavours are well worth the effort since, by tradition, the "Stone" bestows the gift of "the Blarney" on intrepid visitors who perform the ritual.

Industrial Tradition

Long before its castle or "kissing the stone" became part of Ireland's tourist trail, the little village of Blarney, six miles from Cork City, was one of Ireland's major industrial sites. For two centuries, the battlements of the Blarney Woollen Mills have been an imposing feature of the village which has developed a whole new business dynamic in recent times.

In the middle of the eighteenth century, Timothy Mahony, a wealthy landowner in county Kerry, was faced with a problem. He was threatened with destitution and ultimate ruination due to confiscation of his property. Reluctantly, he bade farewell to his ancestral homestead and took the road, by a circuitous route, to the southern capital of Ireland, Cork, to start a new life.

In 1750, at Glanmire, near Cork city, he started a small woollen mill and, by dint of hard work and attention to detail, he established a successful family business. Increasing market demand led to significant expansion of the enterprise, and a major re-siting of the operation became necessary. At this particular point, Timothy's sons and grandsons, who were now managing the business, decided to purchase a site in the village of Blarney.

Founded in 1824, Martin Mahony's Woollen Mills was a model of industrial grace and beauty. Almost an industrial village in itself, the mill, built of red quarry stone, was laid out in courtyards through which the local river had been diverted to provide power. Across the road, the Mahonys built a church and, just inside the main gates, their own stately Victorian mansion. Once the first looms were set in motion, with great care and skill, a range of Blarney tweeds, worsteds, knitting wools and hosiery was developed. Over time, Blarney products became renowned throughout the world for their high standard and quality.

A century and a half later, disaster struck. The great mill, which at its height had employed nearly 700 workers, succumbed to intensive competitive pressure. The textile recession, brought about by international competition, especially from the Indian sub-continent and the Pacific Rim, eventually ground the mill wheels to a halt. In 1975 the mill and its long stone building fell silent. The machinery was sold or scrapped, the stately mansion was closed, and the fine panelled rooms emptied of all their furniture. It was the end of an era for the Mahony family and the village of Blarney.

Renaissance

In 1929, a local youth, Christy Kelleher, had gone to work in the Blarney mill. He began his apprenticeship in the twisting and winding department of the mill, which prepared raw material for making the worsted tweeds. For 20 years he worked his way through the organisation and became assistant supervisor. However, in 1951 he left "Mahonys" to join an insurance corporation.

As well as selling insurance, Christy Kelleher undertook a vegetable round at weekends and justified his passion for motor cars by acting as hackney driver to the local Gaelic Athletic Association (GAA) and harriers' club. He had ideas for selling something more tangible in a market with which he was familiar. Christy, out-going and talkative, seemed to fit the archetypal Blarney role model, for he was the epitome of the visitor's idea of the Irishman.

Christy Kelleher purchased the local cinema/dancehall. This was a dual-purpose investment as it functioned as a mid-week cinema and weekend dance-hall. The younger members of the family rotated from being ushers/usherettes to undertaking the many menial tasks associated with maintaining a busy public venue, such as brushing the floors. The older boys were responsible for humouring the ever-temperamental projector, which had a personality of its own and broke down at least twice a night. Changing over from cinema to dance hall was not easy and consumed a lot of the children's spare time. They had weekly chores for which they received weekly wages — not pocket money, but wages! Christy always encouraged his children by giving incentives to do better.

It is apparent that the Kellehers always tried to move with the times — to anticipate a fashion, whether it was entertainment, decor or clothing. Slowly, the enterprise grew with Christy at the helm and six of the seven children on the board. Maureen, his wife, remained in the background, but was a person with a strong personality. Each of the Kellehers began to find their niche and their father was careful to exploit and encourage their talents.

From the earliest days, the Kellehers worked as a family and were conscious of the firm's responsibilities to employees and other parties whose lives and prosperity depended on the success of the Blarney group of enterprises. It is interesting that Christy Kelleher believed in family empires — perhaps he had the success, over generations, of Levi Strauss' jeans dynasty or the Guinness brewery family in mind!

The Swinging Sixties and Stormy Seventies

In 1966, Christy Kelleher established Blarney Handcrafts Ltd. This venture was set up in a traditional Irish thatched cottage alongside Blarney Castle. With diligence and perseverance he built up a steady family business. Three years later, on a very small scale, he started his own factory in Blarney, manufacturing ladies and gents knitwear for the home and export markets. Through personal and family effort, Blarney Handcrafts began to achieve recognition for its range of knitwear products and, over time, the Kellehers developed a mail-order operation to cater for the increasing overseas demand for their products.

The sixties were an exciting, vibrant decade. Times were changing, and Christy Kelleher was ready to change with them. He recognised the quality of Irish woollens and the spending power of visitors. What is more, he realised the importance of fashion set by the Clancy Brothers and Tommy Makem, the Irish folk group who made Aran sweaters famous worldwide.

Christy Kelleher was deeply saddened by the closure of Mahony's mills in 1975. A year later, the Kellehers decided to acquire the mills with a view to developing their expanding Blarney Handcrafts enterprise. The Victorian mansion, once the home of the O'Mahony family, was renovated and operated as a hotel for a number of years until the lower mill section was tastefully developed into the present property now aptly known as "Christy's Hotel". Built within the mill, the hotel retained the old world charm of the original building, while modern facilities were added to provide the "creature comforts" demanded by international tourism.

The Kellehers then transferred their knitwear factory to the top floor of the mill. By 1981, 80 local people, plus 250 outworkers engaged in knitting the traditional Arans, were employed. They expanded the mail-order and packing departments, and opened a craft and gift shop on the ground floor. The mail-order service now deals with up to 500 customers per day.

What was once known as "the Combing Department" has now become one of Ireland's finest craft centres within the distinctive shopping facility now internationally promoted as "Blarney Woollen Mills". The large craft shop sells woollens and tweeds and co-ordinates under the "Blarney Woollen Mills" label, as well as glassware, crystal, porcelain and other goods — "95 per cent Irish", as Christy Kelleher was always proud to emphasise.

The Exciting Eighties

The 1980s period was an exciting (and exacting) time in the annals of the Blarney group. In the early part of the decade a small retailing base was established in Duke Street, Dublin. In 1986, a decision was taken to transfer the Dublin operation to a large, newly constructed retail premises in Nassau Street.

In May 1988, Blarney opened an exclusive menswear store in Grafton Street, under the new name of "Tricot Marine". Later in the summer, Tricot Marine opened a tourist shop in Windsor in the UK. In late 1988, the Blarney Woollen Mills Group acquired the Kilkenny Shop in Nassau Street, in Dublin. It was on the same street, though not beside, the Woollen Mills outlet. The cost of the acquisition by Blarney has not been disclosed.

In 1989, Blarney Woollen Mills officially launched Ireland's first UK high street retailing operation in Cambridge. The 3,000-square-foot store offers an exclusively Irish range of classic ladies fashion, knitwear, co-ordinated menswear, and giftwear, and competes with long-established shops such as Laura Ashley. It was believed that the store, in which the Nassau Street, Dublin, shop-frontage was exactly reproduced, would become a flagship in Britain for Irish merchandise. The newspaper reports indicated that, at this point, Blarney Woollen Mills employed 250 people and that more than 400 Irish firms supplied the group, including products promoted through the two million catalogues distributed annually.

"Blarney Castle Knitwear" Development

Throughout the 1970s, Blarney produced acrylic knitwear in large quantities for wholesalers under the "Blarney Castle Knitwear" label. In 1980 one of these customers started to source abroad. This wholesaler was responsible for 50 per cent of sales, and very quickly it was realised that wholesalers had excessive control of the Woollen Mills' destiny. Consequently, serious consideration was given to closing the operation. It was decided to give it one more try by trading up and introducing a brand that could become identified and accepted on both the international and domestic markets.

Thus "Blarney Castle Knitwear" got another chance. The product was upgraded by using natural fibres and designing marine style sweaters. It was agreed, also, to sell the range directly to retailers. The presentation and packaging were redesigned and prototypes produced. The market leaders had been identified and it was felt that the new products were highly competitive. It was decided to change the knitwear's brand name as "Blarney Castle" was not considered exclusive enough for customers — it didn't portray the right image. As a result, a new name, "Le Tricot Marine" was adopted. The press took an interest in why an Irish company was using a French name. This interest gave rise to media coverage, which in turn helped to build the superior image.

Blarney Mills Buys Donegal Knitwear Firm

In 1990, Blarney acquired Kilgar Knitwear based in Co. Donegal, which had produced hand-loomed sweaters before its closure. After acquisition, the Donegal plant re-employed 30 of the 50 original staff who had been made redundant when the mill closed. Freda Hayes, one of Christy's daughters, who oversaw the investment by the Kellehers, was confident Kilgar Knitwear could be turned around. She decided to exploit the up-market image and prestigious trade position that the newly acquired knitwear capability provided, with the Donegal cachet.

Kilgar specialises in very high class gents' country knitwear aimed at the US market, with garments selling at the top end of the range, for approximately $200, at most of the big department stores in the US.

The Blarney Gift Catalogue

Blarney Woollen Mills' business includes three shops in Blarney, one in Dublin and one in Cambridge, England; Christy's Hotel Blarney; Christy's Sports Complex, Blarney; knitwear factories in Blarney and Donegal; Kilkenny shops in Dublin and Killarney; Club Tricot shops in Dublin and Blarney; the Sweater Company in Killarney; and of course the Blarney Gift Catalogue.

The Blarney Gift Catalogue was set up out of necessity. American tourists who had shopped in one of the Irish shops would write to the company requesting more merchandise or to exchange the merchandise they bought. So effectively Blarney was operating a mail-order business of sorts, from its offices in Blarney to their American customers. This developed into the setting up of the catalogue company circa 1990.

Certain elements of the mail-order business are still based in Blarney — all credit card clearance, disputed billing investigating and some stock-holding is still handled there. Based in New Jersey in an office and a warehouse, the vast majority of catalogue merchandise is shipped in bulk from Blarney to New Jersey via UPS container or Federal Express. When an order is placed, the New Jersey stock is available to facilitate Blarney's seven-day guaranteed delivery time to customers. The office in New Jersey basically consists of a returns department and phone centre — both for ordering and customer service. When the office closes at 6.00 p.m., Blarney's answering service, ICT, based in Philadelphia, takes over the answering of the order lines. This allows for a 24-hour ordering service which is important in the US due to different time zones (the west coast being 5 hours behind New Jersey on the east coast), and for the convenience of busy working people, especially shift workers.

Staff in New Jersey varies from 20 during off-peak times to as many as 40 in the peak Christmas period. Staff in Blarney are also allocated to the mail-order business and include office staff, as well as warehouse staff who pack the regular shipments that are received in New Jersey. The Blarney Catalogue actually pays more wages in the Irish office than it does in New Jersey.

Blarney based in New Jersey after examining the results of its and independent market research. The location had to be convenient for shipping — Fairfield, in New Jersey is a half hour away from both JFK Airport, New York and Newark Airport, and New Jersey and is relatively near the ports of entry (in Vermont). The location is in a business campus (industrial estate) on a major highway, approximately a half hour from New York city. There are no parking or trucking problems. As the business is not open to the public there was no need for a store front in a high traffic area, so the campus was ideal. The company has a turnover of £4.5m. The Catalogue is in its fifth year of existence and is beginning to show profit, having made a loss in the first three years.

Family Differences

Freda Hayes had been the chief executive of Blarney Woollen Mills for 14 years before her departure from the company in 1993. During that period she had expanded the company's business significantly — to a turnover figure of £30 million, and employment of over 350 people.

After leaving school at the age of 14, she worked with her father in a "thatched cottage" on wheels in the town of Blarney, selling souvenirs to foreign visitors. This "cottage industry" soon blossomed and her father, Christy Kelleher, bought the Mahony Mills in the town of Blarney in 1975 and used it as the basis for a knitwear factory (see earlier). Freda was the middle of seven children and assumed the mantle of chief executive of the firm on the retirement of her father from the day-to-day activities of the company. At this stage four other members of the family worked in the business.

After the death of her father in 1991, Freda Hayes was increasingly of the view that the company needed to expand existing markets but more importantly saw the need to move into new markets outside Ireland. She also held the opinion that the company required an influx of professional managers so as to ensure the continued growth and survival of the company. Freda Hayes had always recognised the importance of the loyalty and shared work ethic of the family firm, but did however recognise the need for professionalism and saw that there was no room for sentimentality in the modern business world. This was a departure from the company's traditional business strategy and was met with opposition from the family members who wished to expand existing markets while keeping control of the business within the immediate family.

In early May 1993, matters came to a head when the other family members refused to take on board her ideas for the future of the company. At this point she attempted to buy out the others but with little success. Over the following three weeks her brothers and sisters put together a deal to buy out Freda Hayes and her 20 per cent shareholding for a figure of £1.73 million.

To many commentators' surprise she accepted the offer and ceased all connections with the company she had been involved with for the previous 24 years. Following her departure, her sister Marion O'Gorman assumed the position of chief executive.

In 1993 Freda Hayes set about re-entering the industry she had worked in for the better part of her lifetime. Between May and November that year she acquired the "House of James" retail chain from Dublin businessman Jim Canning for an undisclosed sum and attracted many of the top executives from Blarney Woollen Mills, including the group's financial controller.

The House of James chain has shops in Galway, Naas and Cork and had a turnover in 1992 of £3 million. Freda Hayes bought the goodwill and stock of the stores but leased the premises. The product lines include artware, pottery, table and fashionwear which is strikingly similar to the lines provided by the Blarney operation. Freda Hayes came into direct competition with her family's business, particularly in the Cork region.

Freda Hayes controls the majority shareholding in the House of James and holds the position of chief executive and chairperson. Other shareholders include some of those executives who joined the firm from Blarney Woollen Mills.

Blarney Woollen Mills did not insert a restrictive clause into Freda Hayes' contract which would have prevented her from directly enter-

ing into competition with the family business. Many at the time believed this to be a significant oversight by Blarney Woollen Mills
given Freda Hayes' proven track record in the retail industry.

Since Freda Hayes' departure, Blarney Woollen Mills has continued to be profitable in its business activities. In 1994 it increased its
profit before tax from £536,303 to £688,453, while sales grew from
£19.3 million to £22.5 million. The breakdown of sales shows that
£19.7 million was generated in the retail side of the business while
£2.8 million was recorded in the hotel and catering side. Dividends of
£240,000 were paid in 1994 compared with nil in the previous year,
while shareholders' funds show a figure of £3.4 million and company
reserves have been built up to £2.4 million. By the end of 1994 the
company employed 355 people with over half of these employed in the
retail area.

The impact of Freda Hayes' departure does not appear to have had
an immediate effect on the profitability of Blarney Woollen Mills.
However, it remains to be seen whether the company will suffer in
the long-term as a result of the departure of one of the company's key
assets.

Sources: Interviews with company personnel.

18

The Irish Credit Union Movement

Thomas N. Garavan and Mary Garavan

Development of the Credit Union Movement in Ireland

In 1958 the first two credit unions opened their doors to the public. They were situated at Donore Avenue and Dun Laoghaire, Dublin, and were the result of great effort on the part of Nora Herlihy. Nora, a Cork-born teacher, was committed to the co-operative philosophy and strongly believed in the need for adult education, voluntary service to the community and a fresh approach to finance in Ireland. She saw the credit union movement, developed in Germany by Friedrich Wilhelm Raiffeisen in 1884, as a perfect way of achieving these needs.

The development of the credit union movement in Ireland has been remarkable. In less than three decades, from 1958 to 1995, the total membership has increased from just 94 to over 1.8 million members throughout Ireland. The number of credit unions in that period has risen from two to over 500 and the savings have jumped from just £311 to an estimated £2 billion.

Industrial and Provident Societies 1893–1936

At the initial stage of the growth of the credit union movement there was no legal standing for their existence. The Industrial and Provident Societies Act 1893 legislated in some way for the development of the movement in Ireland. The provisions of this Act facilitated co-op principles — for example, by requiring "one member, one vote" on special resolutions for specific purposes under Section 51. This legislation was far from ideal as it was not specific enough for the credit union movement to grow and prosper in Ireland.

After prolonged negotiations, Nora Herlihy and other pioneers succeeded in getting the specific legislation that the movement required. The Credit Union Act 1966 was vital for the growth of the Irish credit union movement. The Act provided for the registration of each credit union with the Registrar of Friendly Societies, who controls and regulates the operation of the individual credit unions. Loans are also restricted; the maximum repayment period for any loan is five years; the maximum interest to be charged is limited to 1 per cent per month and no loan may exceed 10 per cent of the total assets held by the credit union. The Act specified that the maximum number of shares to be held by any member was to be restricted to 6,000; anything above this is considered a deposit and interest, not dividends, is paid on this excess amount. No shares can be withdrawn from the credit union unless the amount of the loan repayment outstanding is less than the amount of shares the member held.

The objectives of a credit union as defined by the 1966 Act are:

- To promote thrift among members by accumulating their savings.

- To create sources of credit for the benefit of its members at a fair and reasonable rate of interest.

- To use members' savings for the mutual benefit of members.

It is also necessary for each individual credit union to have at least one of the "common bonds" as set out in the Credit Union Act 1966. The common bond is defined in the Act as the "relationship which each member of the credit union has to all the other members". The bond must be one of the following:

- *Association* other than for the purpose of forming a credit union

- *Occupation*

- *Residence* or *employment* within a given locality

- *Employment by a common employer*

- *Membership* of a bona fide organisation

- *At the discretion of the Registrar* where the common bond is not covered under the Act.

Credit Union Membership and Reasons for Joining

The existing membership consists of 1.8 million spread over 529 credit unions in 25 chapters. Figure 18.1 provides a profile of current credit union membership.

In terms of the reasons for joining, members most often cite the desire to open a savings account, followed by the need to get a loan. Other less important reasons include the location of the credit union, the credit union philosophy and on the recommendation of existing members.

Figure 18.1: Current (1995) Credit Union Membership

Figures in ( ) relate to total population

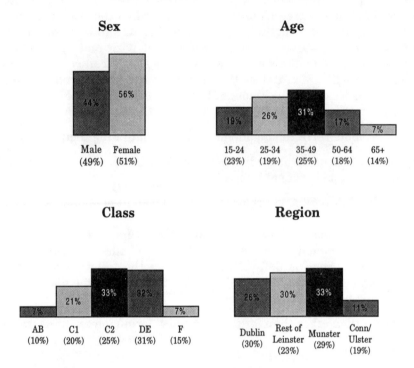

Sex

Male   Female
(49%)   (51%)

Age

15-24   25-34   35-49   50-64   65+
(23%)   (19%)   (25%)   (18%)   (14%)

Class

AB   C1   C2   DE   F
(10%)   (20%)   (25%)   (31%)   (15%)

Region

Dublin   Rest of   Munster   Conn/
(30%)   Leinster (29%)   Ulster
         (23%)   (19%)

Source: Irish League of Credit Unions, Annual Report 1995

Figure 18.2 presents a summary of the perceived performance of credit unions by credit union members and the adult population in Ireland.

The Structure of the Credit Union Movement

The organisational structure of Irish credit unions has developed over the last 30 years and can be divided into three components: Credit Unions; Chapters; the Irish League of Credit Unions.

Credit Unions

The Credit Union is the primary element of the organisation. It comprises all the individual credit unions throughout Ireland. Each paid up member is a part-owner of the credit union. The members control the credit union at the Annual General Meeting, based on a "one member, one vote" principle. Policy issues, future developments, election of directors and supervisory committee members are all matters that the credit union members decide.

Figure 18.2: Perceived Performance of Credit Unions

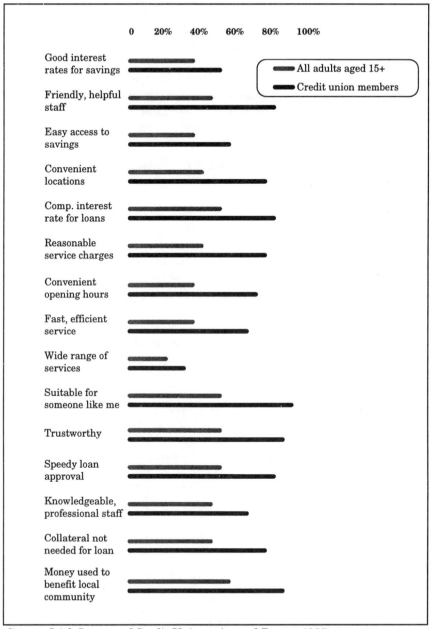

Source: Irish League of Credit Unions, Annual Report 1995

The Board of Directors' responsibilities are clearly defined in the Credit Union Act. They are responsible for determining loan interest rates, fixing maximum limits on shares and deposits in accordance with law and making investment decisions. The board is entitled to appoint committees to ensure the smooth running of the credit union. All operations of the Board are closely scrutinised by Supervisory Committees. The supervisory committee is required by law to safeguard the interests of credit union members.

The Credit Union management is selected by the Board of Directors to carry out the day-to-day running of the credit union. Both staff and voluntary employees are under the control of the Board.

Chapters

In 1964 Irish credit unions, following the example of American counterparts, were formed into chapters. Chapters relate to the grouping of individual credit unions on a geographical basis. Each chapter has chapter officers who represent the credit unions within their group. The chapter officers act as co-ordinators, and are fundamental for communication purposes with the Irish League of Credit Unions. Currently there are 25 chapters in Ireland and their officers meet regularly to discuss the development of the movement.

Irish League of Credit Unions

The Irish League of Credit Unions was formed in 1960 with a membership of only four credit unions. This membership has expanded with over 500 credit unions affiliated with the League in 1996. The League, much like an individual credit union, is controlled by its members who elect a board of 16 directors. These directors work under a supervisory committee of three people. Full-time staff are responsible for the running of the League and report to a General Secretary.

The function of the Irish League of Credit Unions is to ensure that credit unions operate within the law and on behalf of their members. The League provides an extensive range of services including:

- Central financial services
- Granting emergency loans to credit unions that are in financial difficulty
- The operation of a Savings Protection Scheme
- Protecting the savings of members
- Providing a means for credit unions to invest surplus funds
- Negotiating on behalf of credit unions for introduction of legislation.

The Weaknesses in the Credit Union Movement

A report published in 1993 by the Registrar of Friendly Societies identified a number of weaknesses relating to the management of some individual credit unions. The study involved 14 credit unions over a period of three years. The weaknesses cited most often included:

- Inadequate performance of statutory duties by Supervisory Committees

- Inadequate procedures relating to loan approvals and therefore imprudent loan approvals

- Inadequate knowledge of the principles of book-keeping

- Inadequate or even non-existent financial planning

- Poor board structures and lack of board expertise.

At present credit unions operate under two separate pieces of legislation, which has proven to be very restrictive. Many commentators point to the need for a new Act to consolidate the existing legislation. Ruairi Quinn TD, Minister for Finance, expressed concern at the ". . . obsolete and inadequate legislative base of the credit union movement" and said it was ". . . unacceptable that credit unions continue to have legislation rooted in the Victorian era of 1893".

The new legislation is expected to lift some of the restrictive regulations that prevent credit unions from offering new services — in particular, the statutory requirement that limits members' access to their savings. At present members may have cash at their disposal in the credit union but they cannot make use of it unless they enter the credit union office. It is hoped that this situation will be alleviated in the new legislation by allowing the movement the right to develop an Automatic Teller Machine system, allow members to hold cheque books and, possibly, introduce credit cards. Another issue to be addressed is the inter-credit union system, whereby in future it will be possible for members of a Limerick credit union, for example, to carry out transactions in Cork.

New Developments

Negotiations between the Irish League of Credit Unions and the government on the introduction of new legislation have taken place over the last seven years. In 1988 a credit union working group on legislation recommended that free-standing legislation was required. It was hoped this legislation would recognise the credit unions' role in the financial sector and give the movement a sound but flexible legal basis on which to operate. The Credit Union movement is of the firm belief that this new legislation is required in order for the credit union movement to grow successfully.

The ability of credit unions to provide a full range of financial services to all credit union members is seen by most as extremely important. Restrictions under current legislation curtail the Irish credit union movement from doing so. Ruairi Quinn TD, then Minister for Enterprise and Employment, in his address to the Irish League of Credit Unions' Annual Conference in 1994 expressed this view, stating that he wished to ". . . remove some of the shackles which at present limit the introduction of new services".

The Planning Committee set up to investigate the operations of the movement also found that not enough effort was directed at providing the services that members require. While assets, loans and membership have multiplied over the years, the credit unions are basically offering the same services as they did when the movement was first founded. An Irish Marketing Survey report published in 1990 found that a majority of credit union members held, and made regular use of, accounts in other financial institutions. Therefore, while membership is high and the benefits of membership are recognised, the local credit union is not satisfying all the needs of its members.

Under current legislation it is necessary for each credit union to have a common bond. If a member moves outside the common bond they are still entitled to maintain membership but are only allowed loans which are equal to their share value. There are numerous ways that a member can lose their common bond. It is hoped that new legislation will entitle members who have moved outside their common bond to retain their full rights, including voting rights, continued savings and loans equal to that of ordinary members. The only limitation on this is that the number of members of any one credit union outside the common bond is unlikely to be allowed to exceed a certain percentage of the membership of the credit union. This is to protect one of the features that makes credit unions unique — the fact that members have a common bond. The limit is expected to be around 10 per cent of the total membership of the credit union.

The Government has expressed concern at the amount of property and land that credit unions hold, believing that credit unions should hold land and buildings solely for the purpose of carrying out their business. New legislation is likely to prevent the credit union from speculative investment in property and to curtail their freedom of investment in order to protect the savings of the members.

Many, but not all, credit unions pool their funds through the Irish League of Credit Unions' Central Agency Agreement (CAA) — a common fund that invests on behalf of the credit unions. Only DIRT-free investments are used and the agreement is governed by the

Authorised Trustee Investment Act, 1957. It is probable, in an effort to ensure safe and secure investments by all credit unions, that the CAA will be used as the only investment option.

The current limit on shares per member is considered very restrictive. It is believed that no deposits will be acceptable until the member concerned holds at least £5,000 in shares. The total savings of individual credit unions will also come under legislative restrictions and at no time will a credit union be allowed debts in excess of 50 per cent of its aggregate liabilities for shares.

Minister Ruairi Quinn, at the Irish League of Credit Union Annual Conference 1994, expressed the intention of giving the Registrar the power to put additional limits on shares, deposits, interest charged and the size and period of loans. He felt this was necessary to avoid a situation where a "small group of members, in terms of their savings or indebtedness get into a position where they can exercise undue influence over the affairs of the credit union".

The new legislation is expected to set the number of directors to a minimum of seven and a maximum of 15. The term that a director will serve will be set at three years though they will be entitled to stand for re-election. The paid employees of a credit union will no longer be entitled to become members of the Board of Directors.

The supervisory committees which are in existence and are currently a legal requirement will remain but directors will be prohibited from sitting on such committees. It is also expected that directors, ordinary members and employees will be curtailed from entering discussions that would affect their own pecuniary interests.

Currently credit unions are restricted to a loan repayment period of five years. This has posed problems for many credit unions. Sizeable loans, where funds are available and members would be able to make the repayments, are not an option, where the repayment of such loans would not be possible within the five year period. The new repayment period is expected to be somewhere in the region of 10 years. This would provide an opportunity for credit unions to enter into medium-term loans — including mortgage lending and house building finance.

As it presently stands credit unions are obliged under the rules of the Irish League of Credit Unions to be members of the League's Savings Protection Scheme, which protects and insures the savings of credit union members up to a limit of approximately £10,000 per member. It is expected that this scheme will be written into legislation as a legal requirement.

The Minister for Employment and Enterprise surprised many credit union officials at the 1994 Annual Conference when he announced that credit unions were going to be allowed to give funding for local enterprise and employment projects. These loans will complement the County Enterprise Boards who assist in developing many localities to combat the problem of unemployment. This is very much in line with the whole ideology of the credit union whose purpose is to provide loans for a provident or productive purpose.

Many within the credit union movement are concerned that the co-operative ethos is relevant. The voluntary nature of many of its staff, the unifying link of the common bond and the non-profit making orientation are what they believe makes the credit unions distinct from the commercial banks.

The Future

The Irish credit union movement has reached a significant point in its development. A survey carried out by the Irish League of Credit Unions in 1994 came up with five important conclusions:

- The penetration of credit union membership in the Republic of Ireland stands at over one-third of the population. This has shown steady growth since 1989. Northern Ireland has a membership percentage of one-tenth of the population, which has remained static in the last seven years.

- The overall view of the credit union market is that it is widely spread with no distinctive concentration in any particular age category, economic sector or geographical area.

- The members' perceptions of credit unions is very positive, but simple. It is focused on only two products — savings and loans — and there is little awareness of, or consequent demand for, other products.

- Member and non-member awareness of the unique features of credit union products is extremely low. This suggests that these products cannot be viewed as factors that add value to the core product.

- Non-members' awareness of credit unions is extremely low.

The credit union movement is on the threshold of an era of new service development but its progress very much depends upon the enactment of new legislation. This has not yet happened despite many promises. There is a considerable degree of debate about the introduction of new services. Issues like the electronic transmission of money and other technology-based services have generated much discussion and concern in terms of their implications for the status of credit unions.

The development of an ATM system is particularly controversial. The League president, Tony Callinan, has cautioned that it would be premature to consider developing a dependent ATM system — one that is owned, controlled and priced to the movement by an outside organisation whose interests might not coincide with those of the movement. The 1995 annual report also points out that only two per cent of members and non-members view ATMs as a significant factor in encouraging them to join a credit union.

The movement is also aware of the need to develop an effective marketing strategy, which will be aimed at facilitating greater awareness of credit unions. Tony Callinan believes that this can be achieved through the sponsorship of youth-related activities and the provision of a cost-effective, friendly, efficient and relevant service. He also pointed to the need for a strategic plan that will take the movement into the next millennium.

The new legislation which Minister Pat Rabbitte introduced to the Dáil in early 1997 proposes significant changes in loan limits, board structures and the types of services which credit unions can offer their members.

Sources: Annual reports and interviews with individual credit unions.

19

Foxford Woollen Mills

Barra Ó Cinnéide and Fergus Walsh

Introduction

The brainchild of an enterprising nun, Mother Arsenius, Foxford Woollen Mills was established in 1891 in Mayo to provide employment in an area that had been badly affected by the Famine in 1847. John Charles Smith, a staunch Presbyterian from Tyrone, who owned Caledon Woollen Mills, agreed to help Mother Arsenius and the Sisters of Charity in establishing the mill. The Congested District Board provided £7,000 to build the mill on the banks of the Moy. It soon transformed Foxford and the factory steadily grew. By the mid-1980s there were over 220 people employed at the mill.

Traditionally, Foxford concentrated on the domestic market, making bed blankets, travel rugs, báinín and flannels. During its long history, it earned a reputation as a high quality manufacturer of sought-after products.

Production Process

From its inception Foxford was a vertical mill, in that it takes in wool as raw material and produces a finished product.

Its wool-scouring plant initially washes and dries all the wool, before passing on the raw wool to a blending unit. Wool can be processed in white and the subsequent cloth dyed, or the raw wool itself can be dyed, producing coloured yarns from which patterned cloths with mixtures of coloured yarns can be made.

After blending, the wool is carded, and then spun into yarn, from where it goes forward for preparatory processes of winding and warfing for weaving. The weaving plant has SOMET rapier looms which are up-to-date, fast running looms.

After weaving, the cloth is "mended" to rectify any faults or remove any knots in the yarn. The cloth is then passed through a wet finished process, where again, a scouring takes place. The wet finishing process is called "milling", and avails of a characteristic of the wool fibre that, under conditions of heat and a certain pH, it will swell and thicken. This produces a felted material for blankets and rugs. The fabric goes on for pressing and the blankets and rugs go on for "raising" (a process that gives blankets a fluffy rather than a smooth finish). Sometimes, upholstery fabric, depending on the customer's requirement, may have to get additional treatments for flame-proofing and moth-proofing.

The equipment in the mills' wet processing area is modern, and the dry finishing machinery for tweeds and upholstery fabrics is also up-to-date. About 50 per cent of the plant and equipment in the carding and spinning section is up-to-date. There are very few differences between the newer and older machines although, on the carding equipment in particular, there are safety refinements on the newer machines. Otherwise the "spinning mule" and carding machines are much as they were originally invented.

Blankets are made by the firm on a continuous basis and orders supplied from stock. An exception to this would be government contracts for blankets different from the normal commercial size. Hotels may also require a large quantity of blankets, all the same colour, but blankets are not usually produced in batches — instead, they are made continuously. Apparel and upholstery fabrics are usually made for special orders. The mills carry stock in the upholstery range to ensure quick delivery of orders. In the apparel fabric, when, as is common, a customer orders less than the company's Economic Order Quantity (EOQ), the mill processes an EOQ, supplies the customer and puts the balance in stock for sale in its retail outlets.

Quality Control

Because Foxford produces a top quality product, the firm views quality control as important enough to engage an executive in charge of this area. What is made imperfectly is disposed of among the staff and locally. In fact, some traders are often piqued that they never get an offer of seconds in any quantity from Foxford, to which Foxford's reply is "We don't make seconds".

Design

The firm believes it is preferable to employ trained designers rather than "grow our own timber". In its long history, Foxford has had only a handful of designers. As well as design, styling is very important for the survival of the firm. Consultant stylists have been employed by the firm in the past, to advise on trends. The firm looks to them for a forecast of what styles and colouring will be in fashion in a period 18 months to two years ahead. While designs for rugs and blankets change slowly, changes in styles and colouring for clothing may change seasonally. As far as upholstery fabrics are concerned, change is also a factor, but not to the same extent as in apparel fabrics.

Finance

In the early 1980s heavy investment, particularly in updating machinery, was needed. This was done through a combination of bank and ICC (Industrial Credit Company) loans. The firm also qualified for a 45 per cent grant from the IDA, while the Sisters of Charity made available a loan to the factory from their own resources. The firm had been to a large extent self-financing until the mid-1980s.

Personnel

In 1996, 28 people were employed by the mill. However, in the past this figure has reached 200 — this was at the stage when it took one weaver to operate one loom. Now one weaver can operate four looms. The installation of other machinery has also reduced staff numbers. Most of the staff are from the Foxford area. Labour relations in the mill have always been good. Such differences as did arise could be compared to those that occur in any large family.

Marketing

At the time of writing there is no executive solely in charge of marketing. The General Manager has taken upon himself this responsibility. Foxford believes that because it is small, it cannot offer the same remuneration to a good applicant that can be offered by larger firms. The General Manager claims:

> If you have a good person, they get great exposure by being present at all exhibitions, etc. and your competitors get to know if the person is good, and they can come along and make an offer that can't be refused. In our opinion, for textiles of our quality, a deep knowledge of the product technology is required and someone who is trained in designing and producing textiles is necessary. It's not the same as marketing a product like cigarettes or razor blades — a marketing person can do that — and that's what gives us the problem of getting a suitable marketing person.

Products

The products now produced by the firm have changed from those that were originally made. Though they are still essentially woollen fabrics, their end use is different. The main product range now made by the firm includes rugs and blankets, apparel fabrics, and upholstery fabrics.

In the upholstery trade, not many orders are placed directly with the firm. Most of the upholstery fabric is sold through a firm in Dublin who have been supplied with shade cards of a stock range which they distribute to potential users. The number of shade cards carried varies from time to time. "I can only say that we always carry too many," was the Managing Director's comment. There are basically one dozen cloths and in each of these cloths there might be 10 separate designs or colourings.

It is about 10 years since Foxford first moved into upholstery fabrics, and since then they have been learning about this trade. Initial success in upholstery fabrics came from New York. The firm hopes to see upholstery cloth becoming more popular in the future and that this will help to make up for the decline in the rugs and blanket trade.

Tweed, and the demand for it varies. It becomes fashionable, and then the fashion business moves to smoother worsted cloths, then comes back to tweeds again, so one can never say that one will always have a steady demand for tweeds. The tweed and the apparel industry are strongly influenced not only by fashions, but also by the state of the economy. "During a depression, people have to eat, but they can do with last year's clothes", as one person has put it.

Stagnation in domestic sales, and particularly the decline of the tourist trade, have affected product policy in the mill. The diversification into upholstery fabrics, and the seeking of markets abroad, have forced a wider range of products on the firm. Products sold in France or Italy have not often got the colourings that are sold in the more northern latitudes — for example, Ireland and Britain. Hopefully when this recession is over, the product ranges will settle down and the firm can be selective about the products it will carry in the future. But at the moment, all options have to be kept open.

Distribution

For the distribution of tweed and apparel fabrics, the country is covered by three salesmen. One salesman has an office in Dublin, one covers the west and northwest, while a third covers the south. A fourth salesman covers Northern Ireland, where he mainly sells rugs and blankets. These salesmen are paid on a combination of commission and other arrangements, but the commission is the major element of remuneration. They deal with wholesalers, retailers and clothing manufacturers, and are constantly looking for new business. In fact, the firm looks on its salesmen as the eyes and ears of the firm.

> They are out in the market place, they know of new places set-
> ting up, and good sales people are invaluable for the information
> that they can bring back.

The firm holds monthly sales meetings at Foxford between salesmen
and executives. These meetings ensure that everyone is kept in the
picture, and allow salesmen to explain what customers are saying
and the production people to explain some of the problems in dealing
with their orders.

Orders are sent back by the salesmen to Foxford, from where customers are supplied directly.

Buyers of the apparel fabrics can be one of two kinds: Factory purchasers who make garments from the cloth or retail shops where the
fabric is sold across the counter. Blankets and rugs are mainly sold
through retail outlets. There are very few woollen wholesalers left
now in Ireland. Most retailers have grouped themselves into buying
organisations that buy directly, so that the trade is really to retailers
and to manufacturers of garments.

Of the three salesmen in the Republic, two of them worked in the
warehouse in Foxford for a number of years. They got the opportunity
to move into selling, when vacancies occurred on the sales side. The
sales representative in Dublin is the third generation in his family to
be engaged in sales for the company. He trained in Leeds in the design and manufacture of textiles and, in fact, has experience of
working in a woollen mill. Salesmen for the firm are very much tex-
tile-trained with an extensive background in the trade.

For the distribution of upholstery fabric, the firm has an agreement with a Dublin distributor which specialises in upholstery fabrics. This distributor, while selling Foxford — an all-wool fabric —
also distributes other forms of fabric such as draylons and leather-
ettes.

The firm leans heavily on CIE (Coras Iompair Éireann, the State
transport system) for distribution. The company owns a van, but this
is used only in cases of emergency. There are occasions when customers will insist that they can't wait for CIE and that they must have it,
and so the van is called to use.

Due to the increased number of people coming to visit the factory,
the company decided to set up a tourist shop. Visitors wished to buy
something from the firm and this was taking place in the warehouse.
As this impeded dispatch work, it was decided to open a factory shop.
This is a development which is now widespread here and in Britain
— even to the extent that mills in Britain that have closed continue
to operate a mill shop.

Exporting

About 30 per cent of the turnover is exported. North America is the main export market for both upholstery fabrics and apparel fabrics. Separate agents are employed to handle the two fabric lines, working on a commission basis, and carrying products from other firms along with Foxford's products. France is a good market for apparel fabrics, especially in fabrics for women's wear, and tweeds are always fashionable there. Some exporting takes place to the UK and again, separate agents have been appointed in London to sell upholstery and apparel fabrics. In the past, rugs were a big export business, but this is not the case at the moment, although some rugs are still exported to the US.

Advertising and Promotion

On the home market the firm is engaged in both advertising and promotions. Abroad it takes part in some exhibitions. Under the umbrella of An Bord Tráchtála (Irish Export Board) the company takes part in the Frankfurt Fair, which is the main exhibition for woollen products. Though a costly event, the firm believes it is worthwhile. On the home market, some advertising is done, but in-store promotions are preferred. Generally, the firm aids these promotions with support, in the form of posters, literature, displays, etc. Along with in-store promotions, some newspaper advertising is undertaken. This is found to be an effective method of promoting the company.

For years, the best method of promotion used by the company was a stand at the Royal Dublin Society's Spring Show and Horse Show, but this became very expensive and difficult, and the results did not warrant the effort. However, Foxford did have a stand at the World Show Jumping Championship at the RDS in 1982.

Competition

Competition within the woollen industry is very keen. Within Ireland, traditional handloom companies — Magee's of Donegal, Gaeltarra Éireann, McNutt's of Donegal — project a "hand-made" image, even though much of their cloth is now produced by modern automatic looms. The main sources of competition for Foxford come from Hills of Lucan, Dripsey, Handley of Ballyartulla, Gaeltarra Éireann, Convoy of Donegal, Magee of Donegal, McNutt of Donegal and Eadie of Beaufort, Co. Kerry.

Foxford also faces fierce competition from Scotland and Yorkshire. The main European competition comes from France and Italy, where woollen industries have been well developed for centuries.

Pricing

While the company claims that it is not directly in competition with synthetic fabrics, it does admit that these do influence its price structure. Woollen products cannot be "widely" different in price from similar synthetic products. The company claims that, because it has decided to remain a 100 per cent woollen mill, other wool products are seen as its competition rather than other fabric manufacturers.

Market Research

The importance of having good market information cannot be overstressed. Because the company operates within an industry that changes seasonally, the need for good, accurate market information is essential for the survival of the firm. The choice of designer is very important, as are their abilities to work on available information, and produce what the customer will require in a period of 18 months to two years. For Foxford, a lot of information comes from its designer. He travels abroad to the various exhibitions and also visits particular customers abroad. These customers also have their sources of information about the marketplace, and so the information gets back to Foxford.

As stated previously, Foxford relies on its sales force and specialist consultants to relay customers' needs and style trends, respectively, back to management.

There are pros and cons in being a vertical operation like Foxford. So far the advantages have outweighed the disadvantages. The advantages being that, as the firm is using mostly Irish wool, it is in a position to buy it fairly economically. The company also feels that this verticality helps it meet its own delivery requirements. In a word, the firm believes that it has control over their total operations, and this is important to it.

Renaissance

In 1987, the Sisters of Charity requested that the company be put into receivership and, in August, the ICC appointed local accountant Rory Quinn as receiver. Mr. Quinn ran the business as a going concern for over 12 months. Although many individuals and institutions, including a Kenyan blanket manufacturer, expressed an interest, it was not until October 1988 that buyers were found. They were a local consortium of businessmen and previous employees of the firm. One of the accountants who worked with the receiver, Joe Queenan, and Foxford's production designer, Ivars Zauers, set up a BES company, which also included among its shareholders Jim Conway and Tim Mahony of Emblem Weavers in Wexford and Brian McCarthy, who was Foxford's representative in Dublin. This company, Belasa Weavers, made the receiver an offer for the firm's plant and equipment, paying £105,000 for all of the assets. The new owners also received assistance from the IDA.

It was imperative that a buyer be found during this period. If none were found the mill would have closed as the Autumn tweed sales season for that year would have been lost. If the company had not received the major injection of cash it would not have been able to exhibit its clothes at international trade shows and therefore orders from fashion houses for the 1989 Autumn Season would have been lost.

The first six months for Foxford's new owners were difficult. Employees had to be recruited, suppliers and agents advised, new designs produced and machines decommissioned. In addition to this, they also had to try to win back overseas customers. The company got a major boost when it won the contract to supply blankets to the Conrad Hilton and Doyle Group of hotels. In addition, major department stores such as Switzers and Brown Thomas were once again stocking Foxford products.

Since the successful rescue of the firm, Foxford went on in 1990 to purchase Castleisland Fabrics of Portadown, which supplies furnishing fabrics to large companies at home and abroad. That year also saw profits rise from £28,000 to £352,000. In 1992 a Heritage Centre was opened with the aid of large injections of capital, particularly from the EU in the form of rural development funds. It provides a historical tour of the centre which retells the story of the influence of the Sisters of Charity in setting up the mills. It also gives demonstrations in wool-spinning. The marketing strategy for the centre was devised by University College Dublin's marketing development programme and has won many awards. The centre attracted 25,000 people in its first year, 58,000 in 1993 and 64,000 in 1994. The centre employs 28 people in the high season.

Since Foxford ran into difficulties in the later part of the 1980s, it has emerged like a phoenix from the flames. The new owners, Joe Queenan and Ivars Zauers, have transformed the business and regained the strong position which the company held prior to going into receivership. Although employment and profit figures are not quite at the level they were prior to receivership, the organisation has become very efficient and has successfully diversified into related areas.

Source: Interviews with company personnel.

20

Leadmore Ice Cream

Thomas N. Garavan and Mary Garavan

Introduction

Through the years the Irish ice cream industry was characterised by innovation. It developed from small dairy producers finding a novel way of disposing milk surpluses. All has changed however. They have now become the distributors of innovative products, but not their own brand. This has led to a demise of market share. International competition has resulted in many smaller producers going out of business or suffering major declines in their market share. In the case of Leadmore Ice Cream it led to its demise.

The Irish Market for Ice Cream

The Irish market for ice cream can be segmented into two broad categories. The first, the take-home sector, includes all ice cream purchased for use in the home including standard blocks, multipacks, premium ice cream and deserts. The second sector consists of products purchased for immediate consumption and includes soft and scooping ice cream and wrapped bars.

Total consumption of ice cream in Western Europe is fairly static although Ireland has the second highest consumption per capita, with the average person consuming 8.5 litres in 1995. The total ice cream market in Ireland is valued at approximately £60 million with 30 million litres of ice cream consumed per annum.

Significant changes have taken place in the ice cream market. Before 1980, the traditional ice cream market consisted mainly of impulse sales. However, by the mid 1980s a significant shift had occurred with an average of 60 per cent of total ice cream sales now been taken home. This shift occurred primarily due to a declining birth rate in a number of European countries which threatened to restrict volume growth of impulse buys by children who historically had dominated the market. Furthermore, the rapid growth in home freezer ownership resulted in consumers demanding take-home ice cream. Ireland has not, however, followed this trend as quickly as other European countries, primarily due to its younger population. Take-home products account for approximately 40 per cent of sales.

A shift has also occurred from child-oriented to adult-oriented products. Under-15s traditionally eat more than 50 per cent of all ice cream produced. However, manufacturers in the late 1970s began developing and targeting products specifically at adults. Since the 1980s the majority of new ice cream products have been adult premium lines. By launching high-quality adult-oriented products Irish and European manufacturers have expanded their consumer base and product added value items to compete successfully with other forms of desert. In Ireland, the children's sector is still the primary focus for most manufacturers. However, the last five years have witnessed a greater emphasis on adult purchases.

Consumption of ice cream in Ireland is universal and consumers are perfectly representative of the total population. Ice cream is consumed by most adults, and children consume approximately four times as much impulse ice cream per head than adults. Ice cream purchasing on a regular basis is weighted towards C_2 households and those with children aged 6–15.

Premium lines represent the main growth area. Demand has grown for sophisticated, indulgent and adult-oriented products, in both take-home and impulse sectors. Growth has also occurred at the health end of the market. However, the Irish response to "slim and light" ice cream has been modest. Take-home ice cream is under considerable threat from soft frozen yoghurt which has already captured 40 per cent of the ice cream market in the US. In Ireland this sector is already worth £14 million annually and is growing.

Recent years have witnessed a significant increase in both the number and range of outlets selling ice cream. The larger players dominate impulse purchase sales, but independents and multiples are increasing their share with the growth of multipacks. Take-home sales are dominated by the multiples. Other outlets include small grocers and delicatessens. A major issue relates to cabinet exclusivity. While shop exclusivity agreements are effectively valid until December 1997, the courts have ruled in favour of freezer exclusivity agreements at shops which sell impulse ice cream. These shops tend to be small and have room for only one freezer. Cabinet exclusivity is a major entry barrier.

Competition in the Irish Market

The ice cream market is dominated by HB (a wholly owned subsidiary of Unilever since 1973) which has a 60 per cent share of the market. Valley Ice Cream claims a 17 per cent share but this includes the Mars range which the company distributes. Leadmore Ice Cream has a 10 per cent market share but concentrates mainly on the Munster region. Dale Farm, Northern Ireland's largest producers claims a market share of 8 per cent and concentrates mainly in the Munster area. Own label brands account for 43 per cent of take-home blocks. The soft ice cream sector is dominated by Prichell Foods. There are many producers such as Silver Pail, McCambridges Fine Foods and Kerry Foods which have a small market share.

In terms of ownership the idea of a domestically owned production facility is disappearing fast. The main players are constituted as follows:

- **HB**: The largest supplier within Ireland. The company is owned by the multinational conglomerate, Unilever, and controlled by Van de Berg foods. Their product lines are internationally recognisable: whether you buy a "Cornetto" in France (Miko), the UK (Walls) or the US (Good Humor), the product is instantly recognisable.

- **Valley Ice Cream**: A relatively large supplier holding about 10 per cent of the average cabinet space for its own products. This company is also the franchise holder for the distribution of Mars Ice Cream products in Ireland. Valley are domestically owned.

- **Dale Farm**: Much of this company is owned by the Bachelors Corporation. The company is based in Eastern Ulster, but also holds a good percentage of the Leinster cabinet. Penetration in Connaught and Munster is very low, but it is slowly increasing. Product lines vary from premium to economy and low-fat product.

- **Mars**: Mars accounts for approximately 7 per cent share in the national ice cream stakes. This is very significant, as the product is positioned primarily as an impulse one, with a certain level of multipack sales at retail multiples.

- **Silver Pail**: Although commanding less than 5 per cent of the domestic market, this Fermoy-based company has one strategic advantage which is quite important to the ice cream industry, that is, the company is export-oriented. It supplies the British and French multiples, as well as the Irish retail multiples with bulk ice-bricks, litre tubs and multi-packs.

- **Haagen Dazs**: This is another new player in the Irish market, but the unmistakable American-style stand-up freezer cabinet has penetrated the market successfully, and is in many of the major retail multiples.

Premium ice cream is a rapidly expanding segment; in Ireland there are presently three premium take-home brands. Carte D'Or is manufactured by HB and comes in eight varieties. It was launched in 1989 and while it is the market leader in Ireland (approximately 55 per cent market share) it has faired poorly in Europe. Haagen-Dazs Ice Cream is produced by Grand Metropolitan and sells eight varieties in Ireland. It is classed as a super-premium ice cream and was launched in December 1992 in Ireland. It has 25 per cent of the premium take-home market in Ireland and claims a 61 per cent share of the US market. The third premium ice cream is McCambridges Real Irish Ice Cream which comes in six varieties. It was launched in 1974 and has a market share of 20 per cent. It was only launched nationwide in December 1992.

The Rise and Fall of Leadmore Ice Cream

Back in the 1940s, operating from his farm at Leadmore, Kilrush, George Glynn was looking towards the future. He was selling his farm's produce from a downtown outlet. Innovative by nature, he believed that anything he did, he should do properly. The farm had two acres of land under glass for vegetable production and a separate glasshouse for mushrooms and tomatoes. This glasshouse was heated by an engine he had constructed himself.

George also supplied milk to the townspeople. Even at a time of little emphasis on quality control, he carried out a regular bacteria count. Leadmore farm provided West Clare with its first taste of homogenised bottled milk. During a glass shortage, he provided a service, whereby the customer could take milk from the churn with their own containers, as he ventured door to door. George saw how this could lead to health risks, so he imported cartons from Sweden, becoming one of the first distributors of pasteurised milk in cartons in this country.

By 1946, the company, now called Leadmore Dairies, faced a surplus of milk, but George viewed this as an opportunity to realise a life-long ambition to commercially produce ice cream. He had already researched the idea, but now with the possibility of realising the ambition, he began to tour ice cream plants in Ireland and the UK. Once he was satisfied that he had the know-how, he began production of ice cream at the farm, and brought it to his downtown produce shop, where the bulk ice cream was packed in steel containers and frozen in a freezer plant which he built himself. Due to his refrigeration expertise, George was area representative for L.E. Sterne and Co., Electrolux Ltd. and Bosch Ltd.

George put much emphasis on experimentation and quality control. On numerous occasions throughout the 50s, 60s and 70s, Leadmore Dairies won awards for excellence in competitions held by the Ice Cream Alliance (a self regulatory body based in the UK, which sets down industry guidelines).

By the 1960s Leadmore Ice Cream was distributed throughout the Clare–Limerick region. George had a marketing-oriented approach towards his business and developed the market for his ice cream in the area. A logo of two Eskimos was developed and much point of sale material was distributed — posters, stickers, badges and flags. All delivery trucks were painted with the logo. Within company resources, a significant marketing effort was carried out until the early 1980s.

In 1969 demand for Leadmore had far outgrown supply, so a new ultra-modern plant was constructed, with sufficient production and storage capacity to facilitate nation-wide coverage. This was operational by 1971. During the 1970s Leadmore acquired depots in Cork, Galway, Tullamore, Kerry, Wexford and Waterford with agents throughout the Republic of Ireland and Northern Ireland.

With this expansion, the farm could no longer support the dairy requirements of the company. The milk distribution activity was phased out primarily because of the risks of potential infection of on-site food production. The company altered its name to Leadmore Ice Cream Ltd. and changed its logo to a penguin.

The 1980s began on a high note. With Peter Glynn in full control of his father's company, a new brand image and some significant interest within the United Kingdom, the company was gaining much penetration within stores. In-store refrigeration was constantly updated, with state-of-the-art freezers coming from the Gram Corporation of Denmark. A succession of two poor seasons, due to bad weather conditions, caused the company to rely more on agents and to reduce much of their own distributor network. They held on to Cork and Waterford until the mid-1980s. During the busier seasons, however, the smaller the distribution network they had to control themselves, the less costly it was for the firm. Agents seemed to be performing to a capacity which production could barely meet. The factory was manufacturing for the peak months over six days a week, 24 hours a day, to meet demand. In 1989, a heat wave in early August was a godsend for the company.

After this successful season huge investment was channelled into refrigeration, in order to maintain the quality of the ice cream. A major reconstruction of their enormous cold storage facility was undertaken, with state-of-the-art design, to maximise wind-chill factors and minimise temperatures. New freezer compressors were purchased and the company invested in new delivery trucks which, together with the freezer technology, ensured a maximum quality product for the cabinets.

Disaster struck with a run of five bad seasons, due primarily to poor weather. Some emergency management decisions were made such as changing the company name, this time from Leadmore Ice

Cream to Leadmore Farm and more investment in quality, in particular the introduction of foil wrapping, creamier recipes and changing the 1 pint brick wrap to the same colour scheme as HB's Hazelbrook Farm range.

In 1993, due to the increasing poor health of his mother, Peter stepped back from the day-to-day running of the company, and engaged marketing consultants to do an overall review of the company's strategy. The study was carried out by James Hoblyn and Peter O'Hara of Grant Thornton Consulting Ltd. James Hoblyn proposed himself as the person who could implement a turnaround strategy. In October 1993 he took up the position of managing director of Leadmore.

In addition to appointing Hoblyn as Managing Director, fresh equity of £75,000 was introduced into the company by family members. The board faced 1994 with confidence in the new management and the potential for an upturn in fortunes.

Midway through the summer of 1994, it became apparent that targets were not being reached and that a serious cash-flow problem had developed. The company was left with two options: either to secure outside investment or else sell the company in its entirety. Creditors were demanding payment. Little progress was made, and on 9 December 1994, protective notice was served to employees.

Leadmore Ice Cream came to an end in 1995 with the liquidation of the company. This left a near 10 per cent gap in the market which was quickly filled by competitors.

Bibliography

Atkinson, J. and Meager, N. (1994), "Running to Stand Still: The Small Firm in the Labour Market", in Atkinson, J. and Storey, D. J. (eds.), *Employment, The Small Firm and the Labour Market*, London: Routledge.

Augar, P. (1990), cited in C. Barrow, *The Essence of Small Business*, Englewood Cliffs, NJ: Prentice Hall, 1996.

Burns, P. and J. Dewhurst, (eds.) (1991), *Small Business and Entrepreneurship*, London: Macmillan.

Cross, M. (1983), "The United Kingdom", in Storey, D. (ed.) *The Small Firm — An International Review*, London: Croom Helm.

Denning, B.W., Hussey, D.E. and Newman P.G. (1978), *Management Development: What to Look For,* London: Harbridge House.

Dodge, H.R. and Poblins J.E. (1992), "An Empirical Investigation of the Organisational Life Cycle Model for Small Business Development and Survival", *Journal of Small Business Management,* January, Vol. 30, No. 1, pp. 27–37.

Duratko, D.F. and Hodgetts, R.M. (1992), *Entrepreneurship: A Contemporary Approach,* Fort Worth, Texas: The Dryden Press.

Hofer, C.W. and Mahon, J.F. (1980), "From Entrepreneurial to Professional Management: A Set of Guidelines", *Journal of Small Business Management,* Vol. 18, No. 1.

Jones, J.E. and Woodcock, M. (1983), *Manual of Management Development Strategy, Design and Instruments for Programme Improvement,* Aldershot: Gower.

Kuratko, D.F. & Hodgetts, R.M. (1992), *Entrepreneurship A Contemporary Approach*, Fort Worth, Texas: The Dryden Press.

Storey, D.J. (ed.) (1983), *The Small Firm: An International Survey,* London: Croom Helm.

Storey, D.J. (ed.) (1987), *Small Firms in Regional Economic Development,* Cambridge: Cambridge University Press.

Storey, D.J. (1991), "The Birth of New Firms — Does Unemployment Matter? A Review of the Evidence", *Small Business Economics*, Vol. 3, No. 3, pp. 167–178.

Storey, D.J. (1994), *Understanding the Small Business Sector,* London: Routledge.

Storey, D. J. and Johnson, S. (1987), *Are Small Firms the Answer to Unemployment?,* London: Employment Institute.

Task Force on Small Business (1994), Dublin: Government Stationery Office.

Wynerczyk, P., Watson, R., Storey, D.J., Short, H. and Keasy, K. (1993), *The Managerial Labour Market in Small and Medium Sized Enterprises,* London: Routledge.